by Robert Pinsky

POETRY

The Figured Wheel

The Want Bone

History of My Heart

An Explanation of America

Sadness and Happiness

Dante's Inferno (translation)

PROSE

Landor's Poetry

The Situation of Poetry

Poetry and the World

The Sounds of Poetry

The poetry of this book is composed in 10/13 Fairfield LH Light
with the display set in Minion Condensed and Bold Condensed
Composition by PennSet, Inc.
Manufacturing by Haddon Craftsmen
Book design by Margaret M. Wagner

Library of Congress Cataloging-in-Publication Data
Americans' favorite poems : The Favorite Poem Project anthology /
edited by Robert Pinsky and Maggie Dietz

p.   cm.

Includes index.

ISBN 0-393-04820-9

1. Poetry.   I. Pinsky, Robert.   II. Dietz, Maggie.   III. Favorite Poem Project (U.S.)

PN6101.A46 1999

808.81—dc21   99-31979

CIP

W. W. Norton & Company, Inc., 500 Fifth Avenue, New York, N.Y. 10110
www.wwnorton.com

W. W. Norton & Company Ltd., 10 Coptic Street, London WC1A 1PU

3 4 5 6 7 8 9 0

AMERICANS'

FAVORITE POEMS

THE FAVORITE POEM PROJECT ANTHOLOGY

edited by Robert Pinsky

and Maggie Dietz

W · W · Norton & Company   New York   London

AMERICANS'

FAVORITE POEMS

ACKNOWLEDGMENTS

By its nature, involving the participation of many people, the Favorite Poem Project has entailed many debts of gratitude. This book, as an outgrowth of the Project, shares that debt.

The editors are grateful to many organizations and individuals for their contributions and dedication to the Favorite Poem Project. Schools, libraries, bookstores, and other organizations organized Favorite Poem Readings across the United States, and helped solicit letters from thousands of volunteers.

We are also pleased to thank our organizational partners: the New England Foundation for the Arts, where Sam Miller, Doug DeNatale, and Anita Lauricella have provided wise guidance; also the Library of Congress for the encouragement and support of Librarian of Congress James H. Billington, John Cole of the Center for the Book, and Prosser Gifford and Jennifer Rutland of the Office of Scholarly Programs; Boston University, where Jon Westling and John Silber have been reliable friends of our work, and where Richard Mendez and Susan Mix helped create the Favorite Poem website; and our newest partner, the Academy of American Poets, with special thanks to Jonathan Galassi, Bill Wadsworth, Kelleen Zubick, and Jennifer O'Neal. Ellen Lovell of the White House Milliennium Council helped start the project's public presence with a memorable reading at the White House. Juanita Anderson and Louis Massiah have given invaluable guidance in the production aspects of the project.

For support of the project thus far thanks also to the National Endowment for the Arts and Cliff Becker, director of the NEA's literature program, the William and Flora Hewlett Foundation, and the John S. and James L. Knight Foundation.

We owe a special debt (and praise) to Christine Bauch, Jill Kneerim, Jill McDonough, and Laura Mikols for their hard work and enthusiasm.

Above all, we thank over 17,000 people who wrote to us about poems. We are grateful to them for enabling us to assemble this book and for confirming its principles.

M.D., R.P.

CONTENTS

Introduction   3

ANNA AKHMATOVA (1889–1966)   5
   The Sentence

A. R. AMMONS (B. 1926)   6
   Mansion

ARCHILOCHOS (SEVENTH CENTURY B.C.E.)   8
   Will, lost in a sea of trouble

MATTHEW ARNOLD (1822–1888)   9
   Dover Beach

JOHN ASHBERY (B. 1927)   11
   The Improvement

MARGARET ATWOOD (B. 1939)   12
   Variation on the Word *Sleep*

W. H. AUDEN (1907–1973)   14
   In Memory of W. B. Yeats
   Refugee Blues

AMIRI BARAKA (LeRoi Jones) (B. 1934)   18
   Preface to a Twenty Volume Suicide Note

ELIZABETH BISHOP (1911–1979)   19
   One Art
   At the Fishhouses

BLACK ELK (1863–1950)   23
   Everything the Power of the World does is done in a circle

WILLIAM BLAKE (1757–1827)   24
    Eternity
    The Ecchoing Green
    The Little Black Boy

EAVAN BOLAND (B. 1944)   27
    The Emigrant Irish

ANNE BRADSTREET (1612–1672)   28
    Before the Birth of one of her Children
    To my Dear and loving Husband

RUPERT BROOKE (1886–1915)   30
    The Soldier

GWENDOLYN BROOKS (B. 1917)   31
    We Real Cool
    The Bean Eaters

ELIZABETH BARRETT BROWNING (1806–1861)   33
    Sonnet 43 (How do I love thee? Let me count the ways.)

ROBERT BROWNING (1812–1889)   34
    My Last Duchess

JULIA DE BURGOS (1914–1953)   36
    Ay, Ay, Ay of the Kinky-Haired Negress

ROBERT BURNS (1759–1796)   38
    Address to a Haggis

GEORGE GORDON, LORD BYRON (1788–1824)   40
    She Walks in Beauty
    from Manfred

LEWIS CARROLL (1832–1898)   44
    Jabberwocky

WILLA CATHER (1876–1947)   46
    Grandmither, Think Not I Forget

CATULLUS (84–54 B.C.E.)   48
    31

C. P. CAVAFY (1863–1933)   49
    The City

PAUL CELAN (1920–1970)   50
    from Zeitgehoft

GEOFFREY CHAUCER (CA. 1342–1400)   51
  from The General Prologue to The Canterbury Tales

SANDRA CISNEROS (B. 1954)   52
  You Called Me *Corazón*

LUCILLE CLIFTON (B. 1936)   53
  The Lost Baby Poem

SAMUEL TAYLOR COLERIDGE (1772–1834)   54
  from The Rime of the Ancient Mariner

HART CRANE (1899–1933)   58
  Proem: To Brooklyn Bridge
  Voyages (III)

ROBERT CREELEY (B. 1926)   61
  The Rain
  I Know a Man

COUNTEE CULLEN (1903–1946)   63
  Yet Do I Marvel

E. E. CUMMINGS (1894–1962)   64
  i sing of Olaf glad and big

ROBERT DESNOS (1900–1945)   66
  Last Poem

JAMES DICKEY (1923–1997)   67
  The Bee

EMILY DICKINSON (1830–1886)   70
  I'm Nobody! Who are you? (288)
  I never saw a Moor—(1052)
  A little Madness in the Spring (1333)
' "Hope" is the thing with Feathers—(254)
  A Bird came down the Walk—(328)

JOHN DONNE (1572–1631)   74
  The Flea
  A Valediction: Forbidding Mourning

MARK DOTY (B. 1953)   77
  The Embrace

RITA DOVE (B. 1952)   78
  Daystar

MICHAEL DRAYTON (1563–1631)   80
   Since ther's no helpe, Come let us kisse and part (10)

ALAN DUGAN (B. 1923)   81
   Love Song: I And Thou

PAUL LAWRENCE DUNBAR (1872–1906)   82
   We Wear the Mask

HUSSEIN ELHAMI (TWENTIETH CENTURY)   83
   A Lyric in Exile

T. S. ELIOT (1888–1965)   84
   The Love Song of J. Alfred Prufrock
   Dry Salvages (II)

RALPH WALDO EMERSON (1803–1882)   91
   The Rhodora

ROBERT FROST (1874–1963)   92
   The Road Not Taken
   Acquainted with the Night
   Immigrants
   Birches
   A Hillside Thaw
   "Out, Out—"

ALLEN GINSBERG (1926–1997)   99
   The Terms in Which I Think of Reality

LOUISE GLÜCK (B. 1943)   101
   The Queen of Carthage

THOM GUNN (B. 1929)   102
   Baby Song

DONALD HALL (B. 1928)   103
   Names of Horses

THOMAS HARDY (1840–1928)   105
   The Darkling Thrush

ROBERT HASS (B. 1941)   107
   Meditation at Lagunitas

ROBERT HAYDEN (1913–1980)   109
   Those Winter Sundays
   Monet's "Waterlilies"

SEAMUS HEANEY (B. 1939)   *112*
Mid-Term Break

WILLIAM ERNEST HENLEY (1849–1903)   *114*
Invictus

GEORGE HERBERT (1593–1633)   *116*
Church-musick
Vertue

ZBIGNIEW HERBERT (B. 1924)   *118*
The pebble

NAZIM HIKMET (1902–1963)   *119*
Things I Didn't Know I Loved

HUGO VON HOFMANNSTHAL (1874–1929)   *123*
Do you see the town?

HOMER (MID NINTH CENTURY B.C.E)   *124*
from the Iliad (*Book Six, lines 439–79*)

GERARD MANLEY HOPKINS (1844–1889)   *126*
God's Grandeur
Pied Beauty
The Windhover

A. E. HOUSMAN (1859–1936)   *129*
Diffugere Nives

LANGSTON HUGHES (1902–1967)   *131*
Minstrel Man
Merry-Go-Round
Mother to Son

RICHARD HUGO (1923–1982)   *134*
Driving Montana

RANDALL JARRELL (1914–1965)   *136*
Next Day
Losses

ROBINSON JEFFERS (1887–1962)   *140*
The Purse-Seine

JAMES WELDON JOHNSON (1871–1938)   *142*
The Creation

BEN JONSON (1573–1637)   *146*
    Song To Celia
    On My First Son

JAMES JOYCE (1882–1941)   *148*
    Ecce Puer

JOHN KEATS (1795–1821)   *149*
    Ode to a Nightingale
    Sonnet VII (O Solitude! if I must with thee dwell)
    This Living Hand

JANE KENYON (1947–1995)   *153*
    Otherwise

GALWAY KINNELL (B. 1927)   *154*
    St. Francis and the Sow

YUSEF KOMUNYAKAA (B. 1947)   *156*
    Facing It

STANLEY KUNITZ (B. 1905)   *157*
    Hornworm: Autumn Lamentation

LAO TZU (CA. FOURTH TO THIRD CENTURIES B.C.E)   *159*
    from Tao te Ching

D. H. LAWRENCE (1885–1930)   *160*
    Snake

EMMA LAZARUS (1849–1887)   *163*
    The New Colossus

DENISE LEVERTOV (1923–1997)   *164*
    Come into Animal Presence

PHILIP LEVINE (B. 1928)   *166*
    You Can Have It

HENRY WADSWORTH LONGFELLOW (1807–1882)   *168*
    A Psalm of Life

FEDERICO GARCIA LORCA (1898–1936)   *171*
    The Moon Sails Out
    Song of the Barren Orange Tree

AMY LOWELL (1874–1925)   *173*
    Patterns

JAMES RUSSELL LOWELL (1819–1891)   *177*
   The First Snow-Fall

ROBERT LOWELL (1917–1977)   *179*
   Waking in the Blue

HAKI R. MADHUBUTI (B. 1942)   *181*
   Big Momma

ANDREW MARVELL (1621–1678)   *183*
   To His Coy Mistress

HERMAN MELVILLE (1819–1891)   *185*
   Art

W. S. MERWIN (B. 1927)   *186*
   Strawberries

EDNA ST. VINCENT MILLAY (1892–1950)   *187*
   Sonnet XXIV (When you, that at this moment are to me)
   Dirge Without Music

A. A. MILNE (1882–1956)   *189*
   Happiness

CZESLAW MILOSZ (B. 1911)   *190*
   On Pilgrimage

JOHN MILTON (1608–1674)   *191*
   Lycidas

WILLIAM VAUGHN MOODY (1869–1910)   *196*
   Harmonics

MARIANNE MOORE (1887–1972)   *197*
   Poetry
   I May, I Might, I Must

THOMAS MOORE (1779–1852)   *199*
   The Time I've Lost in Wooing

PABLO NERUDA (1904–1973)   *200*
   Ode to My Socks

JACOB NIBENEGENASÁBE (1900–1977)   *203*
   Quiet Until the Thaw

FRANK O'HARA (1926–1966)   *204*
   A True Account of Talking to the Sun at Fire Island

MARY OLIVER (B. 1953)   207
The Summer Day

WILFRED OWEN (1893–1918)   208
Dulce et Decorum Est

PHAM TIEN DUAT (B. 1941)   210
To Return to the Urges Unconscious of Their Beginnings

CARL PHILLIPS (B. 1959)   211
Luncheon on the Grass

SYLVIA PLATH (1932–1963)   213
The Night Dances
Lady Lazarus
Polly's Tree

HYAM PLUTZIK (1911–1962)   219
Cancer and Nova

ALEXANDER POPE (1688–1744)   220
from Epistle to Dr. Arbuthnot

EZRA POUND (1885–1972)   222
The River-Merchant's Wife: A Letter

ALEXANDER PUSHKIN (1799–1837)   224
I loved you

FRANCISCO DE QUEVEDO (1580–1645)   225
Love Constant Beyond Death

SIR WALTER RALEIGH (1552–1618)   226
The Nymph's Reply to the Shepherd

HENRY REED (1914–1986)   227
Naming of Parts

ADRIENNE RICH (B. 1929)   229
To the Days
Prospective Immigrants Please Note

RAINER MARIA RILKE (1875–1926)   231
Entrance

ARTHUR RIMBAUD (1854–1891)   232
Romance

YANNIS RITSOS (1909–1990)   234
    Our Land

EDWIN ARLINGTON ROBINSON (1869–1935)   235
    Eros Turannos
    Mr. Flood's Party

THEODORE ROETHKE (1908–1963)   239
    My Papa's Waltz
    Night Journey
    The Waking

JALAL AL-DIN RUMI (1207–1273)   243
    Who Says Words with My Mouth

CARL SANDBURG (1878–1967)   244
    Chicago

SAPPHO (612 B.C.E.)   246
    Equal to the gods

GEORGE SEFERIS (1900–1971)   247
    An Old Man on the River Bank

WILLIAM SHAKESPEARE (1564–1616)   249
    Sonnet 18 (Shall I compare thee to a summer's day?)
    Sonnet 29 (When, in disgrace with fortune and men's eyes)
    Sonnet 138 (When my love swears that she is made of truth)

STEVIE SMITH (1902–1971)   252
    Not Waving But Drowning

WILLIAM STAFFORD (B. 1914)   253
    Scars

WALLACE STEVENS (1879–1955)   254
    The Idea of Order at Key West
    The Snow Man
    Tea at the Palaz of Hoon
    Girl in a Nightgown

ROBERT LOUIS STEVENSON (1850–1894)   259
    Block City
    Home No More Home to Me, Whither Must I Wander?

MARK STRAND (B. 1934)   261
    Pot Roast

WISLAWA SZYMBORSKA (B. 1923)   263
Notes from a Nonexistent Himalayan Expedition

RABINDRANATH TAGORE (1861–1941)   265
Gift

ALFRED, LORD TENNYSON (1809–1892)   267
Ulysses

ERNEST LAWRENCE THAYER (1863–1940)   270
Casey at the Bat

DYLAN THOMAS (1914–1953)   273
Do Not Go Gentle into That Good Night
In My Craft or Sullen Art
Fern Hill

CHIDIOCK TICHBORNE (CA. 1558–1586)   277
Tichborne's Elegy

DEREK WALCOTT (B. 1930)   278
A Far Cry from Africa

ROBERT PENN WARREN (1905–1989)   280
Arizona Midnight

WALT WHITMAN (1819–1892)   281
An Old Man's Thought of School
from Song of the Open Road
    (1, 4, & 8)
To a Certain Cantatrice
from Song of Myself
    (46 & 52)

RICHARD WILBUR (B. 1921)   287
Love Calls Us to the Things of This World

C. K. WILLIAMS (B. 1936)   289
My Fly

WILLIAM CARLOS WILLIAMS (1883–1963)   291
To Elsie
Danse Russe

WILLIAM WORDSWORTH (1770–1850)   295
from The Prelude (*Book IV, lines 354–70*)
Lines (Tintern Abbey)

SIR HENRY WOTTON (1568–1639)   *301*
  On a Bank As I Sat Fishing

JAMES WRIGHT (1927–1980)   *302*
  A Blessing

THOMAS WYATT (1503–1542)   *303*
  Forget Not Yet

WILLIAM BUTLER YEATS (1865–1939)   *304*
  Politics
  When You Are Old
  Sailing to Byzatium

SONE NO YOSHITADA (LATE TENTH CENTURY)   *307*
  The lower leaves of the trees

ADAM ZAGAJEWSKI (B. 1945)   *308*
  To Go to Lvov

ZAWGEE (1907–1990)   *311*
  The Way of the Water-Hyacinth

Permissions   *313*

Index   *321*

AMERICANS'

FAVORITE POEMS

INTRODUCTION

THE people whose words are quoted along with the poems in this book, in their diverse tastes, origins, and viewpoints, reflect the almost chaotically various nature of American culture: its many sources, its ongoing immigration, its polylglot, sometimes unruly quirks and improvisations. The quotations that accompany the poems were selected from thousands of letters from every state in the Union, written by volunteers of many different ages, occupations, kinds of education, ethnicities, and circumstances. Each person responded to a national call for volunteers willing to say a treasured poem aloud, and to comment on the poem's personal significance, for a national video and audio archive: the Favorite Poem Project.

Maggie Dietz and I have tried in this book to represent the variety and interest of the letters received by the Favorite Poem Project while also making an anthology of literary interest. We also hope that the two kinds of interest illuminate one another: that the diversity of readers may give some insight into the poems, and that the sometimes surprising selections of particular poems, breaking stereotypes, may enrich the perception of Americans.

In a fluid culture, with a thriving mass art based on the blendings or collisions of its many sources, poetry cannot have the relatively stable place that it might among Bengalis or Persians or Russians. Like many other elements of national life, poetry has a shifting, ambiguous status, a role that is sometimes improvised—a fluctuating, sometimes invisible yet vigorous life that some have mistaken for neglect. In one stereotype, Americans are too pragmatic, or too undereducated, or too distracted by mass culture, to cherish this ancient art.

The vigorous response to the Favorite Poem Project contradicts that conventional notion. In addition to many thousands of letters and visitors to the web site (at www.favoritepoem.org), that public response has included hundreds of readings in communities around the country. Mayors and state governors have joined school children, homeless Americans, police officers, workers, and business people in reading poems written not only in English but in languages including Thai, Polish, Yiddish, Navajo, Italian, Russian, and Chinese. Often the readings reflected their communities; sometimes, they were occasions for disparate elements of a town or city to join together.

In Provincetown, Massachusetts, a Portuguese-American woman read a love poem by Camoens in Portuguese, and her son read the poem in his English translation; they were followed by the drag star Musty Chiffon; other readers that evening included a tree surgeon who read D. H. Lawrence. In Atlanta, Nancy Nersessian read an excerpt from Anna Akhmatova's poem "The Sentence" (p. 5, below), relating it to her brother's traumatic experience of combat in Vietnam. She was preceded by a postal worker who read a fiery poem by Amiri Baraka, and followed by an eleven-year-old boy who read "Casey at the Bat." At the White House, the president read Emerson's "Concord Hymn," the First Lady read Howard Nemerov's "The Makers," a Washington public school student read Langston Hughes's "Life is Fine," and a disabled war veteran read Robert Frost's "Stopping by Woods on a Snowy Evening," pronouncing the repeated final line "And miles to go before I sleep" with empathic determination.

At such events, in the letters from volunteers, and in the archive itself, the American context of the Favorite Poem Project has emphasized certain aspects of the art of poetry, notably the art's double nature as inward and outward. Poetry is intimate and on an individual, human scale by nature of its medium, which is any reader's voice. Yet the art is made of the communal and public materials of language, the arrangements of words people exchange all day like coins. In a different country—say, one where the great national poets were shared as part of patriotic feeling, or where there was social prestige in having lines by heart—this duality of poetic feeling might be less poignantly distinct, or at any rate take a different form. Simply by asking that each person express a personal attachment to a poem, the Project has dramatized a relation between individual feeling and the communal setting.

When the video and audio recordings are completed, they will present something like a snapshot of the United States at the turn of the millenium year, through the lens of poetry. We hope that this book anticipates that national portrait a little, while providing the interest of poetry, of human personality, and of the interaction between them.

R.P.
Truro, Massachusetts
May 1999

ANNA AKHMATOVA

RUSSIA • 1889–1966

This poem is very meaningful to me because when I first read it in the late 1970's it struck me very forcefully as capturing the struggle that my brother faced with all the other traumatized Vietnam vets. In 1969, my brother David was commissioned at the age of 19 as an officer in the Green Beret in Fort Benning, Georgia. He was the youngest commissioned officer that they had ever had. He was smart. He was funny. He was full of promise. He had planned a military career. He volunteered for Vietnam. In that year, before going, he married his childhood sweetheart and they had a son. He shipped out for Vietnam in January 1970 and after a year in continuous combat he returned home a highly decorated war hero and a broken man of 21. By the time I read this poem I realized, the realization had sunk in, that this was my brother's life. My brother was never going to learn to live again because the struggle was too hard.

—Nancy Nersessian, 51, Professor of Cognitive Science, Atlanta, Georgia

The Sentence

And the stone word fell
On my still-living breast.
Never mind, I was ready.
I will manage somehow.

Today I have so much to do:
I must kill memory once and for all,
I must turn my soul to stone,
I must learn to live again—

Unless . . . Summer's ardent rustling
Is like a festival outside my window.
For a long time I've foreseen this
Brilliant day, deserted house.

Translated from the Russian by Judith Hemschemeyer

A. R. AMMONS

UNITED STATES • B. 1926

*Each time I read it I thrill to its tenderness, artistic perfection, quiet (even joyous) accep-
tance of death and its stunning beauty. Ammons has a deep relationship with wind—simi-
lar to what I feel about water, both marine and fresh. I respond to that. Others have similar
relationships with the land, or with mountains. With this poem as one's touchstone, how
can one fear dissolution?*

—Norma Feinberg, 66, Ichthyologist, Leonia, New Jersey

Mansion

So it came time
    for me to cede myself
and I chose
the wind
    to be delivered to

The wind was glad
    and said it needed all
the body
it could get
    to show its motions with

and wanted to know
    willingly as I hoped it would
if it could do
something in return
    to show its gratitude

When the tree of my bones
    rises from the skin I said
come and whirlwinding
stroll my dust
    around the plain

so I can see
    how the ocotillo does
and how saguaro-wren is
and when you fall
    with evening

fall with me here
    where we can watch
the closing up of day
and think how morning breaks

ARCHILOCHOS

GREECE • *Seventh Century* B.C.E.

For the last twenty-two years I have lived in an inner city neighborhood working through the church for social and economic justice and racial reconciliation. As a young woman, I admired this poem. Only now that I am older do I realize what really good advice it is, in addition to the beauty of its music.

—Maryann Whitty, 55, Social Worker, Detroit, Michigan

Will, lost in a sea of trouble

Will, lost in a sea of trouble,
Rise, save yourself from the whirlpool
Of the enemies of willing.
Courage exposes ambushes.
Steadfastness destroys enemies.
Keep your victories hidden.
Do not sulk over defeat.
Accept good. Bend before evil.
Learn the rhythm which binds all men.

Translated from the Greek by Kenneth Rexroth

MATTHEW ARNOLD

ENGLAND • *1822–1888*

The poem itself speaks the tragedy that tears at the gut of any thinking person.

—Diana Daniels, 45, Librarian, Hidden Valley, Pennsylvania

The soothing cadence of this poem was a comfort to me long before I ever even understood the scope of the ideas it offers. As a teen, I imagined the intimate setting shared by lovers as one draws the other to the window and speaks of the sea and moon, tides and eternity. As a girl whose mother maintained strength at home while my father fought mysterious wars in distant lands, I feared that war might someday carry into my own marriage. Would I be able to carry on with the same stamina my mother showed? The final stanza pleads for the security I hope will prevail amidst life's confusing mixture of hope and dread. Throughout my adult life, I have returned to this piece as a reminder that the strength I need comes from a loving relationship—and I have that in my marriage of twenty-six years.

—Barbara Williams, 46, Teacher, Clarksville, Tennessee

The sound of the sea is in it. It makes me sigh—and hope.

—Julie Suarez, 48, Teacher, Oneanta, New York

Dover Beach

The sea is calm tonight.
The tide is full, the moon lies fair
Upon the straits; on the French coast the light
Gleams and is gone; the cliffs of England stand,
Glimmering and vast, out in the tranquil bay.
Come to the window, sweet is the night-air!
Only, from the long line of spray
Where the sea meets the moon-blanched land,
Listen! you hear the grating roar
Of pebbles which the waves draw back, and fling,
At their return, up the high strand,
Begin, and cease, and then again begin,
With tremulous cadence slow, and bring
The eternal note of sadness in.

Sophocles long ago
Heard it on the Aegean, and it brought
Into his mind the turbid ebb and flow

Of human misery; we
Find also in the sound a thought,
Hearing it by this distant northern sea.

The Sea of Faith
Was once, too, at the full, and round earth's shore
Lay like the folds of a bright girdle furled.
But now I only hear
Its melancholy, long, withdrawing roar,
Retreating, to the breath
Of the night-wind, down the vast edges drear
And naked shingles of the world.

Ah, love, let us be true
To one another! for the world, which seems
To lie before us like a land of dreams,
So various, so beautiful, so new,
Hath really neither joy, nor love, nor light,
Nor certitude, nor peace, nor help for pain;
And we are here as on a darkling plain
Swept with confused alarms of struggle and flight,
Where ignorant armies clash by night.

JOHN ASHBERY

UNITED STATES • B. 1927

I read this poem and say, "Yes, John, your poem, my rooms and years, all gathered here in quiet happenstance, awake or asleep, then, now, forever, your poem is my life re-created. How did you write it without ever having met me?"

—Roger Smith, 60, Salesman, Holland Patent, New York

The Improvement

Is that where it happens?
Only yesterday when I came back, I had this
diaphanous disaffection for this room, for spaces,
for the whole sky and whatever lies beyond.
I felt the eggplant, then the rhubarb.
Nothing seems strong enough for
this life to manage, that sees beyond
into particles forming some kind of entity—
so we get dressed kindly, crazy at the moment.
A life of afterwords begins.

We never live long enough in our lives
to know what today is like.
Shards, smiling beaches,
abandon us somehow even as we converse with them.
And the leopard is transparent, like iced tea.

I wake up, my face pressed
in the dewy mess of a dream. It mattered,
because of the dream, and because dreams are by nature sad
even when there's a lot of exclaiming and beating
as there was in this one. I want the openness
of the dream turned inside out, exploded
into pieces of meaning by its own unasked questions,
beyond the calculations of heaven. Then the larkspur
would don its own disproportionate weight,
and trees return to the starting gate.
See, our lips bend.

MARGARET ATWOOD

CANADA * B. 1939

This is the most beautiful love poem I have ever read.

—Patricia Burn, 46, School Librarian, Queens, New York

I need to have poetry read aloud to me in order to experience it viscerally. This poem was one of the first I read to myself and had that experience—I feel it through every pore and cell.

—Marietta Phillips, 35, Clinical Social Worker, Anchorage, Alaska

Variation on the Word *Sleep*

I would like to watch you sleeping,
which may not happen.
I would like to watch you,
sleeping. I would like to sleep
with you, to enter
your sleep as its smooth dark wave
slides over my head

and walk with you through that lucent
wavering forest of bluegreen leaves
with its watery sun & three moons
towards the cave where you must descend,
towards your worst fear

I would like to give you the silver
branch, the small white flower, the one
word that will protect you
from the grief at the center
of your dream, from the grief
at the center. I would like to follow
you up the long stairway
again & become
the boat that would row you back
carefully, a flame
in two cupped hands
to where your body lies

beside me, and you enter
it as easily as breathing in

I would like to be the air
that inhabits you for a moment
only. I would like to be that unnoticed
& that necessary.

W. H. AUDEN

ENGLAND • *1907–1973*

This has been for years and still is a favorite poem. Reasons: Because it puts first time's worship of language—what makes a poem a poem and not just a good statement; because it recognizes that language isn't everything, that the masters of language can and do say powerfully things that may do harm and require pardon; and because it calls on the poet to do something beyond language: fully to face tragedy (it was written on the eve of the Second World War) and still persuades us to affirm life, even to praise it.

—Clara Park, 75, Williamstown, Massachusetts

In Memory of W. B. Yeats

(*d. Jan. 1939*)

I

He disappeared in the dead of winter:
The brooks were frozen, the airports almost deserted,
And snow disfigured the public statues;
The mercury sank in the mouth of the dying day.
What instruments we have agree
The day of his death was a dark cold day.

Far from his illness
The wolves ran on through the evergreen forests,
The peasant river was untempted by the fashionable quays;
By mourning tongues
The death of the poet was kept from his poems.

But for him it was his last afternoon as himself,
An afternoon of nurses and rumours;
The provinces of his body revolted,
The squares of his mind were empty,
Silence invaded the suburbs,
The current of his feeling failed; he became his admirers.

Now he is scattered among a hundred cities
And wholly given over to unfamiliar affections,
To find his happiness in another kind of wood
And be punished under a foreign code of conscience.

The words of a dead man
Are modified in the guts of the living.

But in the importance and noise of to-morrow
When the brokers are roaring like beasts on the floor of the Bourse,
And the poor have the sufferings to which they are fairly accustomed,
And each in the cell of himself is almost convinced of his freedom,
A few thousand will think of this day
As one thinks of a day when one did something slightly unusual.
What instruments we have agree
The day of his death was a dark cold day.

2

You were silly like us; your gift survived it all:
The parish of rich women, physical decay,
Yourself. Mad Ireland hurt you into poetry.
Now Ireland has her madness and her weather still,
For poetry makes nothing happen: it survives
In the valley of its making where executives
Would never want to tamper, flows on south
From ranches of isolation and the busy griefs,
Raw towns that we believe and die in; it survives,
A way of happening, a mouth.

3

Earth, receive an honoured guest:
William Yeats is laid to rest.
Let the Irish vessel lie
Emptied of its poetry.

In the nightmare of the dark
All the dogs of Europe bark,
And the living nations wait,
Each sequestered in its hate;

Intellectual disgrace
Stares from every human face,
And the seas of pity lie
Locked and frozen in each eye.

Follow, poet, follow right
To the bottom of the night,
With your unconstraining voice
Still persuade us to rejoice;

With the farming of a verse
Make a vineyard of the curse,
Sing of human unsuccess
In a rapture of distress;

In the deserts of the heart
Let the healing fountain start,
In the prison of his days
Teach the free man how to praise.

I grew up in U.K. during World War II. Refugees all over. I immigrated to U.S.A., married a Jewish man. Now I'm visiting a Congolese man detained by I.N.S. for a long time. Another refugee. He writes poetry. Auden's compassion for innocent suffering is an echo in my own heart.

—Roberta Nobleman, 57, Actor, Durmont, New Jersey

Refugee Blues

Say this city has ten million souls,
Some are living in mansions, some are living in holes:
Yet there's no place for us, my dear, yet there's no place for us.

Once we had a country and we thought it fair,
Look in the atlas and you'll find it there:
We cannot go there now, my dear, we cannot go there now.

In the village churchyard there grows an old yew,
Every spring it blossoms anew;
Old passports can't do that, my dear, old passports can't do that.

The consul banged the table and said,
"If you've got no passport you're officially dead":
But we are still alive, my dear, but we are still alive;

Went to a committee; they offered me a chair;
Asked me politely to return next year:
But where shall we go to-day, my dear, but where shall we go to-day?

Came to a public meeting; the speaker got up and said;
"If we let them in, they will steal our daily bread":
He was talking of you and me, my dear, he was talking of you and me.

Thought I heard the thunder rumbling in the sky;
It was Hitler over Europe, saying, "They must die":
O we were in his mind, my dear, O we were in his mind.

Saw a poodle in a jacket fastened with a pin,
Saw a door opened and a cat let in:
But they weren't German Jews, my dear, but they weren't German Jews.

Went down the harbour and stood upon the quay,
Saw the fish swimming as if they were free:
Only ten feet away, my dear, only ten feet away.

Walked through a wood, saw the birds in the trees;
They had no politicians and sang at their ease:
They weren't the human race, my dear, they weren't the human race.

Dreamed I saw a building with a thousand floors,
A thousand windows and a thousand doors:
Not one of them was ours, my dear, not one of them was ours.

Stood on a great plain in the falling snow;
Ten thousand soldiers marched to and fro:
Looking for you and me, my dear, looking for you and me.

AMIRI BARAKA (LeRoi Jones)

UNITED STATES • B. 1934

I first read this poem thirty years ago in a book titled An Anthology of American Negro Poetry. *I was eleven years old, in seventh grade—and was stunned. It set me on fire. I realized that poems could have meaning and value, and could save your life as well.*

—Peter Liotta, 42, Military Officer, Newport, Rhode Island

Preface to a Twenty Volume Suicide Note

(For Kellie Jones, born 16 May 1959)

Lately, I've become accustomed to the way
The ground opens up and envelops me
Each time I go out to walk the dog.
Or the broad edged silly music the wind
Makes when I run for a bus . . .

Things have come to that.

And now, each night I count the stars.
And each night I get the same number.
And when they will not come to be counted,
I count the holes they leave.

Nobody sings anymore.

And then last night, I tiptoed up
To my daughter's room and heard her
Talking to someone, and when I opened
The door, there was no one there . . .
Only she on her knees, peeking into

Her own clasped hands.

ELIZABETH BISHOP

UNITED STATES • 1911–1979

When I woke up to the realization that coping with golden years is no bowl of cherries, I was fortunate to remember this poem. I have heeded and practiced over the years Bishop's incantation, "The art of losing isn't hard to master." First there's the loss of the small stuff, which is a dress rehearsal for coping with the big ones: body loss that diminishes the pleasures of the senses and the grief of having to do without loved ones. Gone is the 20/20 vision, my step falters (and I'm not imbibing). My ears can only catch the low tones. I confuse b's with p's. Alone—I'm the last of my family generation. But the art of losing isn't hard to master. Even mastering grief—that's a big one. Thank you, Elizabeth Bishop. I am a retired radio writer, mail-order enterpreneur, creative advertising director. Currently holding back the hand of time by conducting journal-writing workshops for my peers in Chicagoland.

—Eleanor Perry, 84, Retired, Chicago, Illinois

One Art

The art of losing isn't hard to master;
so many things seem filled with the intent
to be lost that their loss is no disaster.

Lose something every day. Accept the fluster
of lost door keys, the hour badly spent.
The art of losing isn't hard to master.

Then practice losing farther, losing faster:
places, and names, and where it was you meant
to travel. None of these will bring disaster.

I lost my mother's watch. And look! my last, or
next-to-last, of three loved houses went.
The art of losing isn't hard to master.

I lost two cities, lovely ones. And, vaster,
some realms I owned, two rivers, a continent.
I miss them, but it wasn't a disaster.

—Even losing you (the joking voice, a gesture
I love) I shan't have lied. It's evident
the art of losing's not too hard to master
though it may look like (*Write* it!) like disaster.

Though about the Atlantic, and more particularly the Canadian coast (and thus perhaps not American), it expresses something free, dark, and very satisfying about the way I (and I think we) understand the world. I volunteer to read for the blind and dyslexic and think weekly about words that convey sense and sight. This poem comes as close as I know to telling the feel of vision and to replicating the bond between looking and understanding. I would read this to a blind person to explain sight.

—Alexander Scherr, 44, Law Professor, Athens, Georgia

At the Fishhouses

Although it is a cold evening,
down by one of the fishhouses
an old man sits netting,
his net, in the gloaming almost invisible,
a dark purple-brown,
and his shuttle worn and polished.
The air smells so strong of codfish
it makes one's nose run and one's eyes water.
The five fishhouses have steeply peaked roofs
and narrow, cleated gangplanks slant up
to storerooms in the gables
for the wheelbarrows to be pushed up and down on.
All is silver: the heavy surface of the sea,
swelling slowly as if considering spilling over,
is opaque, but the silver of the benches,
the lobster pots, and masts, scattered
among the wild jagged rocks,
is of an apparent translucence
like the small old buildings with an emerald moss
growing on their shoreward walls.
The big fish tubs are completely lined
with layers of beautiful herring scales
and the wheelbarrows are similarly plastered
with creamy iridescent coats of mail,
with small iridescent flies crawling on them.
Up on the little slope behind the houses,
set in the sparse bright sprinkle of grass,
is an ancient wooden capstan,
cracked, with two long bleached handles
and some melancholy stains, like dried blood,
where the ironwork has rusted.

The old man accepts a Lucky Strike.
He was a friend of my grandfather.
We talk of the decline in the population
and of codfish and herring
while he waits for a herring boat to come in.
There are sequins on his vest and on his thumb.
He has scraped the scales, the principal beauty,
from unnumbered fish with that black old knife,
the blade of which is almost worn away.

Down at the water's edge, at the place
where they haul up the boats, up the long ramp
descending into the water, thin silver
tree trunks are laid horizontally
across the gray stones, down and down
at intervals of four or five feet.

Cold dark deep and absolutely clear,
element bearable to no mortal,
to fish and to seals. . . One seal particularly
I have seen here evening after evening.
He was curious about me. He was interested in music;
like me a believer in total immersion,
so I used to sing him Baptist hymns.
I also sang "A Mighty Fortress Is Our God."
He stood up in the water and regarded me
steadily, moving his head a little.
Then he would disappear, then suddenly emerge
almost in the same spot, with a sort of shrug
as if it were against his better judgment.
Cold dark deep and absolutely clear,
the clear gray icy water . . . Back, behind us,
the dignified tall firs begin.
Bluish, associating with their shadows,
a million Christmas trees stand
waiting for Christmas. The water seems suspended
above the rounded gray and blue-gray stones.
I have seen it over and over, the same sea, the same,
slightly, indifferently swinging above the stones,
icily free above the stones,
above the stones and then the world.
If you should dip your hand in,

your wrist would ache immediately,
your bones would begin to ache and your hand would burn
as if the water were a transmutation of fire
that feeds on stones and burns with a dark gray flame.
If you tasted it, it would first taste bitter,
then briny, then surely burn your tongue.
It is like what we imagine knowledge to be:
dark, salt, clear, moving, utterly free,
drawn from the cold hard mouth
of the world, derived from the rocky breasts
forever, flowing and drawn, and since
our knowledge is historical, flowing, and flown.

BLACK ELK

UNITED STATES • 1863–1950

Four years ago I was paralyzed by a sudden stroke while feeding our horses. As I lay on the ground, two hawks came and circled above me. The thought came to me that there was a possible message to me in their motion. Many Native Americans see life and nature in a circular configuration—a view that is not strange to me, as I am part Cherokee. I saw the hawks' circles as a reminder that during our lives we encounter good times and bad times, and we continue coming out on the other side to live some more. It was a meaningful, encouraging, empowering thought. After partially recovering, I am now able to make Native American style drums. The log is a circle; the hide head of the drum is a circle; and playing and dancing is done in a sacred circle. This central theme in Native American philosophy is elegantly explored in Black Elk's words.

—Jerry Weaver, 66, Retired Architect and Artist, Lewis, Kansas

Everything the Power of the World does is done in a circle

Everything the Power of the World does
is done in a circle. The sky is round,
and I have heard that the earth is round
like a ball, and so are all the stars.
The wind, in its greatest power, whirls.

Birds make their nests in circles,
for theirs is the same religion as ours.

The sun comes forth and goes down again
in a circle. The moon does the same,
and both are round. Even the seasons
form a great circle in their changing,
and always come back again to where they were.

The life of man is a circle from childhood to childhood,
and so it is in everything where power moves.

From the Sioux, as told through John G. Neihardt

WILLIAM BLAKE

ENGLAND • *1757–1827*

I am a thirty-one-year-old locum tenens family physician—a traveling doctor. Born in Taiwan, having grown up in Argentina, and now living and working in different places in the United States, I am reminded time and again by this poem that Heaven is wherever I go.

—Cheng-Chieh Chuang, 31, Physician, Providence, Rhode Island

Eternity

He who bends to himself a joy
Does the winged life destroy;
But he who kisses the joy as it flies
Lives in eternity's sunrise.

It is my favorite poem because I live in South Dakota and it is mostly green in South Dakota. It describes certain things that can be found where I live. It describes the daily lives of people living here and what things happen, like kids playing sports from sunrise to sunset and old people watching the kids and thinking about their childhood. It reminds me of growing up and living in South Dakota because of the getting up and seeing the countryside and smelling the changing of seasons, as in the poem it changes to spring; and being able to tell the difference between the seasons, by weather and hearing and seeing the animals. Spring to me means that it is almost time for school to end, almost time for summer, and the beginning of a new birth.

—James Kezar, 18, Student, Vermillion, South Dakota

The Ecchoing Green

The Sun does arise,
And make happy the skies,
The merry bells ring
To welcome the Spring.
The sky-lark and thrush,
The birds of the bush,
Sing louder around,
To the bells' chearful sound.
While our sports shall be seen
On the Ecchoing Green.

Old John with white hair
Does laugh away care,
Sitting under the oak,
Among the old folk.
They laugh at our play,
And soon they all say:
"Such, such were the joys.
When we all, girls & boys,
In our youth-time were seen,
On the Ecchoing Green."

Till the little ones weary
No more can be merry
The sun does descend,
And our sports have an end:
Round the laps of their mothers,
Many sisters and brothers,
Like birds in their nest,
Are ready for rest;
And sport no more seen,
On the darkening Green.

While going round and round the hay fields doing custom hay baling in my farming days, I found comfort in the beauty of nature and in songs and poems. One I especially liked was William Blake's "The Little Black Boy." My cows have gone and the farms are quiet. Thank goodness I'm still on the farm—though at eighty-two years old, I don't bale as much hay.

—Nancy Wilsea, 82, Farmer, Kent, Connecticut

The Little Black Boy

My mother bore me in the southern wild,
And I am black, but O! my soul is white;
White as an angel is the English child:
But I am black as if bereav'd of light.

My mother taught me underneath a tree,
And sitting down before the heat of day,
She took me on her lap and kisséd me,
And pointing to the east, began to say:

"Look on the rising sun: there God does live,
And gives his light, and gives his heat away;
And flowers and trees and beasts and men receive
Comfort in morning, joy in the noon day.

"And we are put on earth a little space,
That we may learn to bear the beams of love,
And these black bodies and this sun-burnt face
Is but a cloud, and like a shady grove.

"For when our souls have learn'd the heat to bear,
The cloud will vanish; we shall hear his voice,
Saying: 'Come out from the grove, my love & care,
And round my golden tent like lambs rejoice.'"

Thus did my mother say, and kisséd me;
And thus I say to little English boy:
When I from black and he from white cloud free,
And round the tent of God like lambs we joy,

I'll shade him from the heat till he can bear
To lean in joy upon our father's knee;
And then I'll stand and stroke his silver hair,
And be like him, and he will then love me.

EAVAN BOLAND

IRELAND * B. 1944

I am not a poetry buff. I am a businessman, and I work in the finance department of a Boston ice-cream company. Most poetry escapes me as too complex or strange, but one poem helped me through the darkest times. A while back, my nephew became very sick. During his illness I came across this poem and I wept for what had escaped me before I found the poem. Subsequently my nephew died, but in my wallet I keep a copy of "The Emigrant Irish."

—Stephen Murphy, 33, Finance Manager, Somerville, Massachusetts

The Emigrant Irish

Like oil lamps, we put them out the back—

of our houses, of our minds. We had lights
better than, newer than and then

a time came, this time and now
we need them. Their dread, makeshift example:

they would have thrived on our necessities.
What they survived we could not even live.
By their lights now it is time to
imagine how they stood there, what they stood with,
that their possessions may become our power:

Cardboard. Iron. Their hardships parceled in them.
Patience. Fortitude. Long-suffering
in the bruise-colored dusk of the New World.

And all the old songs. And nothing to lose.

ANNE BRADSTREET

UNITED STATES • *1612–1672*

Anne Bradstreet is one of my favorite poets because of her intelligence, sensitivity, and un-usual education for a woman of her time. This poem is a prime example of her compassion-ate devotion to her family, her sturdy early American ethics, and the strength and sweetness of her character. As a mother of four fine children, I am able to empathize with this woman, her poem and her lifestyle.

—Anne Groben, 66, Adjunct Instructor/Registered Nurse, Stony Brook, New York

Before the Birth of one of her Children

All things within this fading world hath end,
Adversity doth still our joyes attend;
No tyes so strong, no friends so dear and sweet,
But with deaths parting blow is sure to meet.
The sentence past is most irrevocable,
A common thing, yet oh inevitable;
How soon, my Dear, death may my steps attend,
How soon't may be thy Lot to lose thy friend,
We both are ignorant, yet love bids me
These farewell lines to recommend to thee,
That when that knot's unty'd that made us one,
I may seem thine, who in effect am none.
And if I see not half my dayes that's due,
What nature would, God grant to yours and you;
The many faults that well you know I have,
Let be interr'd in my oblivious grave;
If any worth or virtue were in me,
Let that live freshly in thy memory
And when thou feel'st no grief, as I no harms,
Yet love thy dead, who long lay in thine arms:
And when thy loss shall be repaid with gains
Look to my little babes my dear remains.
And if thou love thy self, or loved'st me
These O protect from step Dames injury.
And if chance to thine eyes shall bring this verse,
With some sad sighs honour my absent Herse;
And kiss this paper for thy loves dear sake,
Who with salt tears this last Farewel did take.

I met my husband in December, 1944. He had just returned from overseas duty , as a pilot with the Eighth Air Force. We were introduced by his sister, with whom I shared an office. The rest is history. In 1946, we married. My husband enjoyed browsing through community yard sales. One day he returned with a rosy pink, hard-bound book in his hand. He hastily gave it to me—an anthology of poems titled How Do I Love Thee? *One poem above all seemed to speak to my heart. I can still remember the first day I read it, for I thought it perfectly described the deep love I felt for my husband. He was a kind man and tried to see good in the lives of those he touched. In 1992, my husband succumbed to skin cancer. If possible this poem has become even more meaningful to me. In my grief, I found comfort in reading it. The words were a reminder of my great love for him.*

—Betty Delanois, 72, Retired, Sarasota, Florida

To my Dear and loving Husband

If ever two were one, then surely we.
If ever man were lov'd by wife, then thee;
If ever wife was happy in man,
Compare with me ye women if you can.
I prize thy love more than whole Mines of gold,
Or all the riches that the East doth hold.
My love is such that Rivers cannot quench,
Nor ought but love from thee, give recompence.
Thy love is such I can no way repay,
The heavens reward thee manifold I pray.
Then while we live, in love lets so persever,
That when we live no more, we may live ever.

RUPERT BROOKE

ENGLAND • 1886–1915

I'm an immigrant. I have been in the U.S.A. for twenty-two years and after all this time I'm still homesick for England. And believe me, I'm not alone. Being an immigrant is not a onetime decision. It is a decision remade every day of one's life, my life. My husband is American, but all my "blood" family is 3½ thousand miles away, growing up, marrying, having children, dying. The homesickness never goes away. Yet I remain here, an American citizen. And I will die here, which brings me to Brooke's poem. Little did I know when I fell in love with the poem in school that the same fate would befall me, that I would be destined to one day enrich a corner of a foreign field. "The Soldier" sums up my feelings perfectly. I will never go home again. I'm not sure where home is anymore.

—Laura Sibley-Deml, 43, Nurse, Brooker, Florida

The Soldier

If I should die, think only this of me,
    That there's some corner of a foreign field
That is forever England. There shall be
    In that rich earth a richer dust concealed,
A dust whom England bore, shaped, made aware,
    Gave, once, her flowers to love, her ways to roam,
A body of England's, breathing English air,
    Washed by the rivers, blest by suns of home.

And think, this heart, all evil shed away,
    A pulse in the Eternal mind, no less
        Gives somewhere back the thoughts by England given,
Her sights and sounds; dreams happy as her day;
    And laughter, learnt of friends; and gentleness,
        In hearts at peace, under an English heaven.

GWENDOLYN BROOKS

UNITED STATES • B. 1917

My generation is living this poem. In 1997 we buried six kids under twenty because of the suicide plague that roams the streets of South Boston. Now a new plague has set in, the "heroin" plague. It has captured many of South Boston's youth who think they're real cool!

—John Ulrich, 20, Artist/Writer, South Boston, Massachusetts

Teenagers at times seem to have no sense of themselves because they are greatly influenced by modern society. Rap songs and all that other crap, talk about drugs, killing and harassing. Movies tend to play the same role in altering teenagers' minds. What exactly does this say to the teenage population? It makes them feel invincible. They think they can do whatever they want and not pay the consequences. This poem shows what happens if you think you are cool and act stupid. It shows that people are not invincible. We need poems like this to show us the right way. It is more down to earth than the Bible or old people or the news.

—David Solomon, 17, Student, Miami Beach, Florida

We Real Cool

THE POOL PLAYERS.
SEVEN AT THE GOLDEN SHOVEL.

We real cool. We
Left school. We

Lurk late. We
Strike straight. We

Sing sin. We
Thin gin. We

Jazz June. We
Die soon.

My family are bean eaters. My grandmothers have prepared many bean and cornbread dinners.

—Jennifer Higdon, 27, Teacher/Graduate Student, Denton, Texas

The Bean Eaters

They eat beans mostly, this old yellow pair.
Dinner is a casual affair.
Plain chipware on a plain and creaking wood,
Tin flatware.

Two who are Mostly Good.
Two who have lived their day,
But keep on putting on their clothes
And putting things away.

And remembering . . .
Remembering, with twinklings and twinges,
As they lean over the beans in their rented back room that
      is full of beads and receipts and dolls and cloths,
      tobacco crumbs, vases and fringes.

ELIZABETH BARRETT BROWNING

ENGLAND • 1806–1861

It makes me wonder if this kind of love really exists.
—Ngan Chan, 17, Student, Miami Lakes, Florida

I hope when couples marry, they feel this way.
—Katrina Beckley, 43, Nurse/Paralegal, Crandall, Indiana

In my youth—fifty years ago!—it was how I felt.
—Betty Levin, 77, Retired, Albuquerque, New Mexico

Sonnet 43

How do I love thee? Let me count the ways.
I love thee to the depth and breadth and height
My soul can reach, when feeling out of sight
For the ends of Being and ideal Grace.
I love thee to the level of everyday's
Most quiet need, by sun and candle-light.
I love thee freely, as men strive for Right;
I love thee purely, as they turn from Praise.
I love thee with the passion put to use
In my old griefs, and with my childhood's faith,
I love thee with a love I seemed to lose
With my lost saints—I love thee with the breath,
Smiles, tears, of all my life—and, if God choose,
I shall but love thee better after death.

ROBERT BROWNING

ENGLAND • 1812–1889

In high school, my English Teacher played a recording of Richard Burton reciting "My Last Duchess." Thirty years later, this haunting tale about the fate of the beautiful young Duchess remains my personal favorite. A clever mystery—it immediately brings me into the realm of fatal desire.

—Cuddy Murray, 50, Glen Head, New York

Until Browning's poem, I kept poetry at arm's length and felt unable to penetrate into the heart of any poem. I approached the poem as an actor would, searching for the Duke's objectives, for the source of his obsession. To me, through the language of the poem, the Duke is revealed subtly, frighteningly, as a man who is intelligent, articulate, and manipulative, but still powerless over his late wife. Although he seems satisfied to possess his wife as a portrait, the Duke's control over her remains a fantasy of which he is maddeningly aware.

—David Sullivan, 28, Teacher, Boston, Massachusetts

My Last Duchess

FERRARA

That's my last duchess painted on the wall,
Looking as if she were alive. I call
That piece a wonder, now: Frà Pandolf's hands
Worked busily a day, and there she stands.
Will't please you sit and look at her? I said
"Frà Pandolf" by design, for never read
Strangers like you that pictured countenance,
The depth and passion of its earnest glance,
But to myself they turned (since none puts by
The curtain I have drawn for you, but I)
And seemed as they would ask me, if they durst,
How such a glance came there; so, not the first
Are you to turn and ask thus. Sir, 'twas not
Her husband's presence only, called that spot
Of joy into the Duchess' cheek: perhaps
Frà Pandolf chanced to say "Her mantle laps
"Over my lady's wrist too much," or "Paint
"Must never hope to reproduce the faint
"Half-flush that dies along her throat": such stuff
Was courtesy, she thought, and cause enough

For calling up that spot of joy. She had
A heart—how shall I say?—too soon made glad,
Too easily impressed; she liked whate'er
She looked on, and her looks went everywhere.
Sir, 'twas all one! My favor at her breast,
The dropping of the daylight in the West,
The bough of cherries some officious fool
Broke in the orchard for her, the white mule
She rode with round the terrace—all and each
Would draw from her alike the approving speech,
Or blush, at least. She thanked men—good! but thanked
Somehow—I know not how—as if she ranked
My gift of a nine-hundred-years-old name
With anybody's gift. Who'd stoop to blame
This sort of trifling? Even had you skill
In speech—which I have not—to make your will
Quite clear to such an one, and say, "Just this
"Or that in you disgusts me; here you miss,
"Or there exceed the mark"—and if she let
Herself be lessoned so, nor plainly set
Her wits to yours, forsooth, and made excuse,
—E'en then would be some stooping; and I choose
Never to stoop. Oh sir, she smiled, no doubt,
Whene'er I passed her; but who passed without
Much the same smile? This grew; I gave commands;
Then all smiles stopped together. There she stands
As if alive. Will't please you rise? We'll meet
The company below, then. I repeat,
The Count your master's known munificence
Is ample warrant that no just pretense
Of mine for dowry will be disallowed;
Though his fair daughter's self, as I avowed
At starting, is my object. Nay, we'll go
Together down, sir. Notice Neptune, though,
Taming a sea-horse, thought a rarity,
Which Claus of Innsbruck cast in bronze for me!

JULIA DE BURGOS

PUERTO RICO • 1914–1953

It is a poem that represents the evolution of the slavery process in Puerto Rico. It's the pain and joy of being a new entity.

—Glaisma Perez-Silva, 41, Special Education Teacher, Hartford, Connecticut

Ay, Ay, Ay of the Kinky-Haired Negress

Ay, ay, ay, that am kinky-haired and pure black;
kinks in my hair, Kafir in my lips;
and my flat nose Mozambiques.

Black of pure tint, I cry and laugh
the vibration of being a black statue;
a chunk of night, in which my white
teeth are lightning;
and to be a black vine
which entwines in the black
and curves the black nest
in which the raven lies.
Black chunk of black in which I sculpt myself,
ay, ay, ay, my statue is all black.

They tell me that my grandfather was the slave
for whom the master paid thirty coins.
Ay, ay, ay, that the slave was my grandfather
is my sadness, is my sadness.
If he had been the master
it would be my shame:
that in men, as in nations,
if being the slave is having no rights
being the master is having no conscience.

Ay, ay, ay, wash the sins of the white King
in forgiveness black Queen.

Ay, ay, ay, the race escapes me
and buzzes and flies toward the white race,
to sink in its clear water;
or perhaps the white will be shadowed in the black.

Ay, ay, ay, my black race flees
and with the white runs to become bronzed;
to be one for the future,
fraternity of America!

Translated from the Spanish by Jack Agüeros

ROBERT BURNS

SCOTLAND • 1759–1796

My father's side of the family is Scottish, and, throughout my childhood, I attended many Scottish festivals and dinners. For example, we would go to Burns Nicht, which is a Scottish dinner celebrated annually around the world. I have heard this poem recited at every celebration. I like the poem because it seems to embody a sense of Scottish nationalism. Haggis, though vile to me, is a symbol of Scottish life and of my heritage.

—Mark Erskine, 18, Student, Memphis, Tennessee

Address to a Haggis

1

Fair fa' your honest, sonsie face,
Great chieftain o' the puddin-race!
Aboon them a' ye tak your place,
        Painch, tripe, or thairm:
Weel are ye wordy of a grace
        As lang's my arm.

2

The groaning trencher there ye fill,
Your hurdies like a distant hill,
Your pin wad help to mend a mill
        In time o' need,
While thro' your pores the dews distil
        Like amber bead.

3

His knife see rustic Labour dight,
An' cut ye up wi' ready slight,
Trenching your gushing entrails bright,
        Like onie ditch;
And then, O what a glorious sight,
        Warm-reekin, rich!

4

Then, horn for horn, they stretch an' strive:
Deil tak the hindmost, on they drive,

Till a' their weel-swall'd kytes belyve
                    Are bent like drums;
Then auld Guidman, maist like to rive,
                    "Bethankit!" hums.

    5

Is there that owre his French *ragout,*
Or *olio* that wad staw a sow,
Or *fricassee* wad mak her spew
                    Wi' perfect sconner,
Looks down wi' sneering, scornfu' view
                    On sic a dinner?

    6

Poor devil! see him owre his trash,
As feckless as a wither'd rash,
His spindle shank a guid whip-lash,
                    His nieve a nit;
Thro' bluidy flood or field to dash,
                    O how-unfit!

    7

But mark the Rustic, haggis-fed,
The trembling earth resounds his tread,
Clap in his walie nieve a blade,
                    He'll make it whissle;
An' legs, an' arms, an' heads will shed
                    Like taps o' thrissle.

    8

Ye Pow'rs, wha mak mankind your care,
And dish them out their bill o' fare,
Auld Scotland wants nae skinking ware,
                    That jaups in luggies;
But, if ye wish her gratefu' prayer,
                    Gie her a Haggis!

GEORGE GORDON, LORD BYRON

ENGLAND • 1788–1824

Every time I read this poem, it makes me think about how pretty my girlfriend is inside and out.

—Radhanes Veras, Student, Henrietta, New York

She Walks in Beauty

1

She walks in beauty, like the night
   Of cloudless climes and starry skies;
And all that's best of dark and bright
   Meet in her aspect and her eyes:
Thus mellowed to that tender light
   Which heaven to gaudy day denies.

2

One shade the more, one ray the less,
   Had half impaired the nameless grace
Which waves in every raven tress,
   Or softly lightens o'er her face;
Where thoughts serenely sweet express
   How pure, how dear their dwelling place.

3

And on that cheek, and o'er that brow,
   So soft, so calm, yet eloquent,
The smiles that win, the tints that glow,
   But tell of days in goodness spent,
A mind at peace with all below,
   A heart whose love is innocent!

I heard Robert Pinsky's request for favorite poems in a radio interview, while I was driving from my grandfather's funeral. This poem is the single work of poetry that I most commonly think of, though rarely quote from. The Faust tale has been told so many times, but the image of one man, one will, braving the world with his own uncompromising vision, is tremendously compelling. My grandfather grew up on the streets of Tulsa in the Dust Bowl, followed Patton across Europe, fought a lifelong battle against alcoholism and lived his en-

tire life on his own terms. He died on Easter Sunday. He taught me more about what it means to be a man (in both sex-specific and universal senses) than anyone else in my life. Manfred, for me, sings the Romantic/American vision of individualism in the most powerful way I have ever heard. I would love to read my two favorite passages from this poem in memory of my grandfather.

—Michael Graham, 36, Political Consultant/Columnist, Columbia, South Carolina

from Manfred

A DRAMATIC POEM

"There are more things in heaven and earth, Horatio,
*Than are dreamt of in your philosophy."**

ACT 2

SCENE 2. *A lower Valley in the Alps.—A Cataract.*

MANFRED [*alone*]. We are the fools of time and terror: Days
    Steal on us and steal from us; yet we live,
    Loathing our life, and dreading still to die.
    In all the days of this detested yoke—
    This vital weight upon the struggling heart,
    Which sinks with sorrow, or beats quick with pain,
    Or joy that ends in agony or faintness—
    In all the days of past and future, for
    In life there is no present, we can number
    How few—how less than few—wherein the soul
    Forbears to pant for death, and yet draws back
    As from a stream in winter, though the chill
    Be but a moment's. I have one resource
    Still in my science—I can call the dead,
    And ask them what it is we dread to be:
    The sternest answer can but be the Grave,
    And that is nothing—if they answer not—
    The buried Prophet answered to the Hag
    Of Endor; and the Spartan Monarch drew
    From the Byzantine maid's unsleeping spirit
    An answer and his destiny—he slew
    That which he loved, unknowing what he slew,

* William Shakespeare, *Hamlet* 1.5.166–67

And died unpardoned—though he called in aid
The Phyxian Jove, and in Phigalia roused
The Arcadian Evocators to compel
The indignant shadow to depose her wrath,
Or fix her term of vengeance—she replied
In words of dubious import, but fulfilled.
If I had never lived, that which I love
Had still been living; had I never loved,
That which I love would still be beautiful—
Happy and giving happiness. What is she?
What is she now?—a sufferer for my sins—
A thing I dare not think upon—or nothing.
Within few hours I shall not call in vain—
Yet in this hour I dread the thing I dare:
Until this hour I never shrunk to gaze
On spirit, good or evil—how I tremble,
And feel a strange cold thaw upon my heart.
But I can act even what I most abhor,
And champion human fears.—The night approaches.

ACT 3

SCENE 1. A Hall in the Castle of MANFRED. MANFRED and HERMAN.

I

MANFRED [alone]. The stars are forth, the moon above the tops
Of the snow-shining mountains.—Beautiful!
I linger yet with Nature, for the night
Hath been to me a more familiar face
Than that of man; and in her starry shade
Of dim and solitary loveliness,
I learned the language of another world.
I do remember me, that in my youth,
When I was wandering—upon such a night
I stood within the Coliseum's wall,
Midst the chief relics of almighty Rome.
The trees which grew along the broken arches
Waved dark in the blue midnight, and the stars
Shone through the rents of ruin; from afar
The watchdog bayed beyond the Tiber; and
More near from out the Caesars' palace came
The owl's long cry, and, interruptedly,

Of distant sentinels the fitful song
Begun and died upon the gentle wind.
Some cypresses beyond the timeworn breach
Appeared to skirt the horizon, yet they stood
Within a bowshot. Where the Caesars dwelt,
And dwell the tuneless birds of night, amidst
A grove which springs through leveled battlements
And twines its roots with the imperial hearths,
Ivy usurps the laurel's place of growth—
But the gladiators' bloody Circus stands,
A noble wreck in ruinous perfection!
While Caesar's chambers, and the Augustan halls,
Grovel on earth in indistinct decay.—
And thou didst shine, thou rolling moon, upon
All this, and cast a wide and tender light,
Which softened down the hoar austerity
Of rugged desolation, and filled up,
As 'twere anew, the gaps of centuries;
Leaving that beautiful which still was so,
And making that which was not, till the place
Became religion, and the heart ran o'er
With silent worship of the great of old—
The dead, but sceptered sovereigns, who still rule
Our spirits from their urns.—

                    'Twas such a night!
'Tis strange that I recall it at this time;
But I have found our thoughts take wildest flight
Even at the moment when they should array
Themselves in pensive order.

LEWIS CARROLL

ENGLAND • *1832–1898*

I love all the made-up words in it. Although I don't know the meaning to all the words I can still understand the story. Carroll might have thought it was going to be a flop, but he followed through and it turned out to be a wonderful poem. My grandfather read it to my father, and my father reads it to me, and I would love to read it to you and the rest of the world.

—Ben Copp, 12, Student, Providence, Rhode Island

Where else can you find a tale of danger, adventure, triumph, and jubilation—all so utterly wrapped in nonsense? It never fails to bring a smile.

—Judy Delawder, 41, Cashier, Roann, Indiana

I don't find this poem nonsense at all. I toil, as I think Harrison had said it, "in the plastic halls of TV where thieves run free and good men die like dogs." Also, some of this language kind of reminds me of our politicians.

—Lou Antonio, Television/Film Director, Burbank, California

Jabberwocky

'Twas brillig, and the slithy toves
   Did gyre and gimble in the wabe:
All mimsy were the borogoves,
   And the mome raths outgrabe.

"Beware the Jabberwock, my son!
   The jaws that bite, the claws that catch!
Beware the Jubjub bird, and shun
   The frumious Bandersnatch!"

He took his vorpal sword in hand:
   Long time the manxome foe he sought—
So rested he by the Tumtum tree,
   And stood awhile in thought.

And, as in uffish thought he stood,
   The Jabberwock, with eyes of flame,
Came whiffling through the tulgey wood,
   And burbled as it came!

One, two! One, two! And through and through
    The vorpal blade went snicker-snack!
He left it dead, and with its head
    He went galumphing back.

"And hast thou slain the Jabberwock?
    Come to my arms, my beamish boy!
O frabjous day! Callooh! Callay!"
    He chortled in his joy.

'Twas brillig, and the slithy toves
    Did gyre and gimble in the wabe:
All mimsy were the borogoves,
    And the mome raths outgrabe.

WILLA CATHER

UNITED STATES • 1876–1947

I love this poem not only because it speaks personally to my feelings about my own grand-mother and my feelings at losing a lover, but because Willa Cather is one of our nation's greatest writers. Her stories and poems speak so eloquently of our American history and of the great pioneers of the Midwest who sacrificed their lives to build this country. Her poetry sings. It delights in its eloquent simplicity. Her words challenge us to think and to feel. That's what all great poetry must do.

—Patricia Curren, 54, Purchasing Manager, Seattle, Washington

Grandmither, Think Not I Forget

Grandmither, think not I forget, when I come back to town,
An' wander the old ways again an' tread them up an' down.
I never smell the clover bloom, nor see the swallows pass,
Without I mind how good ye were unto a little lass.
I never hear the winter rain a-pelting all night through,
Without I think and mind me of how cold it falls on you.
And if I come not often to your bed beneath the thyme,
Mayhap 'tis that I'd change wi' ye, and gie my bed for thine,
　　　Would like to sleep in thine.

I never hear the summer winds among the roses blow,
Without I wonder why it was ye loved the lassie so.
Ye gave me cakes and lollipops and pretty toys a score,—
I never thought I should come back and ask ye now for more.
Grandmither, gie me your still, white hands, that lie upon your breast,
For mine do beat the dark all night and never find me rest;
They grope among the shadows an' they beat the cold black air,
They go seekin' in the darkness, an' they never find him there,
　　　An' they never find him there.

Grandmither, gie me your sightless eyes, that I may never see
His own a-burnin' full o' love that must not shine for me.
Grandmither, gie me your peaceful lips, white as the kirkyard snow,
For mine be red wi' burnin' thirst, an' he must never know.
Grandmither, gie me your clay-stopped ears, that I may never hear
My lad a'singin' in the night when I am sick wi' fear;
A-singin' when the moonlight over a' the land is white—
Aw God! I'll up an' go to him a-singin' in the night,
　　　A-callin' in the night.

Grandmither, gie me your clay-cold heart that has forgot to ache,
For mine be fire within my breast and yet it cannot break.
It beats an' throbs forever for the things that must not be,—
An' can ye not let me creep in an' rest awhile by ye?
A little lass afeard o' dark slept by ye years agone—
Ah, she has found what night can hold 'twixt sunset an' the dawn!
So when I plant the rose an' rue above your grave for ye,
Ye'll know it's under rue an' rose that I would like to be,
      That I would like to be.

CATULLUS

ROME • 84–54 B.C.E.

As a long-time scholar of Latin and the Classics, I find the language and style of Catullus fascinating. As a college student whose trips home are infrequent, I feel the personal attachment to home, just as Catullus felt and expressed it in this poem. Just as Bithynia was home to Catullus, my house and my home always find me safe and blissful. In the poem stands the intricacy of my—and human's—desire for home.

—Stephanie Ng, 19, Student, Cambridge, Massachusetts

31

Apple of islands, Sirmio, & bright peninsulas, set
in our soft-flowing lakes or in the folds of ocean,
with what delight delivered, safe & sound,

                           from Thynia
from Bithynia
        you flash incredibly upon the darling eye.
What happier thought
        than to dissolve
the mind of cares
        the limbs from sojourning,
and to accept the down of one's own bed
under one's own roof
        —held so long at heart . . .

and that one moment paying for all the rest.

So, Sirmio, with a woman's loveliness, gladly
echoing Garda's rippling lake-laughter,
and, laughing there, Catullus' house
                catching the brilliant echoes!

Translated from the Latin by Peter Whigam

C. P. CAVAFY

GREECE • 1863–1933

This is a poem for all emigrants, especially to America, who are trapped between nostalgia and regret and who do not realize that all cities—and all places—are one and the same everywhere.

—Steven Kassem, 22, Student, Bethesda, Maryland

The City

You said: "I'll go to another country, go to another shore,
find another city better than this one.
Whatever I try to do is fated to turn out wrong
and my heart lies buried like something dead.
How long can I let my mind moulder in this place?
Wherever I turn, wherever I look,
I see the black ruins of my life, here,
where I've spent so many years, wasted them, destroyed them totally."

You won't find a new country, won't find another shore.
This city will always pursue you.
You'll walk the same streets, grow old
in the same neighborhoods, turn gray in these same houses.
You'll always end up in this city. Don't hope for things elsewhere:
there's no ship for you, there's no road.
Now that you've wasted your life here, in this small corner,
you've destroyed it everywhere in the world.

Translated from the Greek by Edmund Keeley and Phillip Sherrard

PAUL CELAN

ROMANIA • 1920–1970

Celan can get the most meaning into the least number of words. It is tragic (for him) that he had to use German, the language of his ravagers, as the language he knew and loved best, the language of his murdered mother, for his work. But it is fortunate (for me) that German is the language I know most intimately. His poetry is like a space or a state or a brain in which thoughts and associations flash with subconscious speed to create a three-dimensional web, much richer than any written words on paper I have ever known. But these are not poems one can pick up and read for ease and comfort after a long day at work.

—Sonja Calabi, 71, Art Dealer, Newton Centre, Massachusetts

from Zeitgehoft

Not until
as a shade I touch you
will you believe
my mouth,

that clambers about
with late-minded things
up there
in time-courts,

you come to the host
of the seconds-utilizers among
the angels,

and a body that rages for silence
stars.

Translated from the German by Michael Hamburger

GEOFFREY CHAUCER

ENGLAND • CA. 1343–1400

Spring = the first lines of the Prologue.

—Fan Staunton Ogilvie, 54, Writer, Vineyard Haven, Massachusetts

Your mention of favorite poems awoke my love for the Prologue, which I met some forty years ago in school. I love the Middle English open vowels of "Whan that Aprill . . . " I'm not sure I remember it correctly, but nevertheless will recite it on occasion to evoke spring-like joy. I think something should be included in your project in appreciation of and homage to our distant, almost understandable, English-speaking relative. My wife and I live in a wooded area near Chapel Hill, North Carolina. I am fifty-nine and I work as a handyman, fixing all sorts of things. Part of this work is that I am a Zen teacher. I sometimes use the Prologue to demonstrate why I like to chant our Zen chants in an old language which is for the most part unknown, for the simple act of entering fully into the sound without the need for understanding; this, as an alternative to our educated proclivity to analyze everything to death.

—Sandy Stewart, 59, Handyman, Pittsboro, North Carolina

from The General Prologue to The Canterbury Tales

Whan that Aprill with his shoures sole
The droghte of Marche hath perced to the rote,
And bathed every veyne in swich licour,
Of which vertu engendred is the flour;
Whan Zephirus eek with his swete breeth
Inspired hath in every holt and heeth
The tendre croppes, and the yonge sonne
Hath in the Ram his halfe cours y-ronne;
And smale fowles maken melodye,
That slepen al the night with open yë—
So priketh hem Nature in hir corages—
Than longen folk to goon on pilgrimages,
And palmeres for to seken straunge strondes,
To ferne halwes, couthe in sondry londes;
And specially, from every shires ende
Of Engelond to Caunterbury they wende,
The holy blisful martir for to seke,
That hem hath holpen, whan that they were seke.

SANDRA CISNEROS

UNITED STATES • B. 1954

The poem displays such longing and that absolution you grant a lover who has done you wrong, because of a small word or gesture.

—Nicole Dunn, 29, Student, Chicago, Illinois

You Called Me *Corazón*

That was enough
for me to forgive you.
To spirit a tiger
from its cell.

Called me *corazón*
in that instant before
I let go the phone
back to its cradle.

Your voice small.
Heat of your eyes,
how I would've placed
my mouth on each.

Said *corazón*
and the word blazed
like a branch of *jacaranda*.

LUCILLE CLIFTON

UNITED STATES • B. 1936

I am a twenty-seven-year-old high school English teacher who is now married and planning on starting a family in the very near future. Lucille Clifton's poem was one of the things that got through to me during college when I lost my own baby. I still remember reading the line, "what did I know about waters rushing back" and thinking: I am not alone, someone else understands my loss.

—Virginia Graham, 27, Teacher, Danbury, Connecticut

The Lost Baby Poem

the time i dropped your almost body down
down to meet the waters under the city
and run one with the sewage to the sea
what did i know about waters rushing back
what did i know about drowning
or being drowned

you would have been born into winter
in the year of the disconnected gas
and no car   we would have made the thin
walk over Genesee hill into the Canada wind
to watch you slip like ice into strangers' hands
you would have fallen naked as snow into winter
if you were here i could tell you these
and some other things

if i am ever less than a mountain
for your definite brothers and sisters
let the rivers pour over my head
let the sea take me for a spiller
of seas   let black men call me stranger
always   for your never named sake

SAMUEL TAYLOR COLERIDGE

ENGLAND • 1772–1834

I was born in Egypt and came to the United States when I was one year old with my parents, because my father got a job in the United Nations. I started reading poetry when I was about eight or nine in the fourth grade. I never liked poetry; as a matter of fact, I hated poetry. In ninth grade, my English teacher, Mr. Appleman, gave me this long poem to read for homework. That poem was The Rime of the Ancient Mariner. I was mad. First of all, I didn't like poetry and, second, this poem was very long. But it had so much adventure, and the way it was written had a great effect on me. When I understood it, it just pulled me. Every time I read the poem I just get a special feeling in my gut and I just want to keep on reading it again and again.

—Mohamed Abdel-Fattah, 16, Student, Queens Village, New York

from The Rime of the Ancient Mariner

IN SEVEN PARTS

Facile credo, plures esse Naturas invisibiles quam visibiles in rerum universitate. Sed horum [sic] omnium familiam quis nobis enarrabit? et gradus si cognationes et discrimina et singulorum munera? Quid agunt? quae loca habitant? Harum rerum notitiam semper ambivit ingenium humanum, nunquam attigit. Juvat, interea, non diffiteor, quandoque in animo, in tabulâ, majoris et melioris mundi imaginem contemplari: ne mens assuefacta hodiernae vitae minutiis se contrahat nimis, et tota subsidat in pusillas cogitationes. Sed veritati interea invigilandum est, modusque servandus, ut certa ab incertis, diem a nocte, distinguamus. —T. BURNET*

PART I

An ancient Mariner meeteth three Gallants bidden to a wedding feast, and detaineth one.	It is an ancient Mariner And he stoppeth one of three. —"By thy long gray beard and glittering eye, Now wherefore stopp'st thou me?

*From Archaeologiae Philosophiae, p. 68. "I can easily believe that there are more invisible than visible beings in the universe. But of their families, degrees, connections, distinctions, and functions, who shall tell us? How do they act? Where are they found? About such matters the human mind has always circled without attaining knowledge. Yet I do not doubt that sometimes it is well for the soul to contemplate as in a picture the image of a larger and better world, lest the mind, habituated to the small concerns of daily life, limit itself too much and sink entirely into trivial thinking. But meanwhile we must be on watch for the truth, avoiding extremes, so that we may distinguish certain from uncertain, day from night." Burnet was a seventeenth-century English theologian.

The Bridegroom's doors are opened wide,
And I am next of kin;
The guests are met, the feast is set:
May'st hear the merry din."

He holds him with his skinny hand,
"There was a ship," quoth he.
"Hold off! unhand me, graybeard loon!"
Eftsoons his hand dropped he.

*The Wedding Guest is
spell-bound by the eye
of the old seafaring
man, and constrained
to hear his tale.*
He holds him with his glittering eye—
The Wedding Guest stood still,
And listens like a three years' child:
The Mariner hath his will.

The Wedding Guest sat on a stone:
He cannot choose but hear;
And thus spake on that ancient man,
The bright-eyed Mariner.

"The ship was cheered, the harbor cleared,
Merrily did we drop
Below the kirk, below the hill,
*The Mariner tells
how the ship sailed
southward with a good
wind and fair weather,
till it reached the line.*
Below the lighthouse top.

The Sun came up upon the left,
Out of the sea came he!
And he shone bright, and on the right
Went down into the sea.

Higher and higher every day,
Till over the mast at noon—"
The Wedding Guest here beat his breast,
For he heard the loud bassoon.

*The Wedding Guest
heareth the bridal
music; but the Mariner
continueth his tale.*
The bride hath paced into the hall,
Red as a rose is she;
Nodding their heads before her goes
The merry minstrelsy.

The Wedding Guest he beat his breast,
Yet he cannot choose but hear;

And thus spake on that ancient man,
The bright-eyed Mariner.

*The ship driven by a
storm toward the South
Pole.*

"And now the Storm-blast came, and he
Was tyrannous and strong;
He struck with his o'ertaking wings,
And chased us south along.

With sloping masts and dipping prow,
As who pursued with yell and blow
Still treads the shadow of his foe,
And forward bends his head,
The ship drove fast, loud roared the blast,
And southward aye we fled.

And now there came both mist and snow,
And it grew wondrous cold:
And ice, mast-high, came floating by,
As green as emerald.

*The land of ice, and of
fearful sounds where
no living thing was to
be seen.*

And through the drifts the snowy clifts
Did send a dismal sheen:
Nor shapes of men nor beasts we ken—
The ice was all between.

The ice was here, the ice was there,
The ice was all around:
It cracked and growled, and roared and howled,
Like noises in a swound!

*Till a great sea bird,
called the Albatross,
came through the
snow-fog, and was
received with great joy
and hospitality.*

At length did cross an Albatross,
Thorough the fog it came;
As if it had been a Christian soul,
We hailed it in God's name.

It ate the food it ne'er had eat,
And round and round it flew.
The ice did split with a thunder-fit;
The helmsman steered us through!

*And lo! the Albatross
proveth a bird of good
omen, and followeth
the ship as it returned
northward through fog
and floating ice.*
And a good south wind sprung up behind;
The Albatross did follow,
And every day, for food or play,
Came to the mariners' hollo!

In mist or cloud, on mast or shroud,
It perched for vespers nine;
Whiles all the night, through fog-smoke white,
Glimmered the white Moon-shine."

*The ancient Mariner
inhospitably killeth the
pious bird of good
omen.*
"God save thee, ancient Mariner!
From the fiends, that plague thee thus!—
Why look'st thou so?"—With my crossbow
I shot the Albatross.

HART CRANE

UNITED STATES • 1899–1933

The Brooklyn Bridge was built by men who were heroic and brave, including my great-grandfather, Ferdinardo Tanzi, who came to Brooklyn expressly to work on the bridge. He did not like New York and returned to Parma with money, in a time of great poverty in Italy. He did advise his sons that there was opportunity in America. This poem is full of bold and praising language. For me, poetry is about language and brave and hopeful people. Hart Crane is much ignored!

—Diane Tanzi, 65, Poet/Teacher/Gardener, Sarasota, Florida

Proem: To Brooklyn Bridge

How many dawns, chill from his rippling rest
The seagull's wings shall dip and pivot him,
Shedding white rings of tumult, building high
Over the chained bay waters Liberty—

Then, with inviolate curve, forsake our eyes
As apparitional as sails that cross
Some page of figures to be filed away;
—Till elevators drop us from our day . . .

I think of cinemas, panoramic sleights
With multitudes bent toward some flashing scene
Never disclosed, but hastened to again,
Foretold to other eyes on the same screen;

And Thee, across the harbor, silver-paced
As though the sun took step of thee, yet left
Some motion ever unspent in thy stride,—
Implicitly thy freedom staying thee!

Out of some subway scuttle, cell or loft
A bedlamite speeds to thy parapets,
Tilting there momently, shrill shirt ballooning,
A jest falls from the speechless caravan.

Down Wall, from girder into street noon leaks,
A rip-tooth of the sky's acetylene;
All afternoon the cloud-flown derricks turn . . .
Thy cables breathe the North Atlantic still.

And obscure as that heaven of the Jews,
Thy guerdon . . . Accolade thou dost bestow
Of anonymity time cannot raise;
Vibrant reprieve and pardon thou dost show.

O harp and altar, of the fury fused,
(How could mere toil align thy choiring strings!)
Terrific threshold of the prophet's pledge,
Prayer of pariah, and the lover's cry,—

Again the traffic lights that skim thy swift
Unfractioned idiom, immaculate sigh of stars,
Bending thy path—condense eternity:
And we have seen night lifted in thine arms.

Under thy shadow by the piers I waited;
Only in darkness is thy shadow clear.
The City's fiery parcels all undone,
Already snow submerges an iron year . . .

O Sleepless as the river under thee,
Vaulting the sea, the prairies' dreaming sod,
Unto us lowliest sometime sweep, descend
And of the curveship lend a myth to God.

To me this is one of the most intricate renderings of affection in verse. It is at once a cele-bration of the discovery of a love the speaker did not know could be spoken of and an im-passioned request for permission to give himself over to that love. Crane shows both what is gained and what is given up in this moment of clarity.

—Terry Kirts, 28, Lecturer, Indianapolis, Indiana

Voyages (III)

Infinite consanguinity it bears—
This tendered theme of you that light
Retrieves from sea plains where the sky
Resigns a breast that every wave enthrones;
While ribboned water lanes I wind

Are laved and scattered with no stroke
Wide from your side, where to this hour
The sea lifts, also, reliquary hands.

And so, admitted through black swollen gates
That must arrest all distance otherwise,—
Past whirling pillars and lithe pediments,
Light wrestling there incessantly with light,
Star kissing star through wave on wave unto
Your body rocking!
    and where death, if shed,
Presumes no carnage, but this single change,—
Upon the steep floor flung from dawn to dawn
The silken skilled transmemberment of song;

Permit me voyage, love, into your hands . . .

ROBERT CREELEY

UNITED STATES • B. 1926

It reminds me of what it is to be human. Stanzas two through four make me uneasy, but by five and six I feel content. In the poem I see myself, mankind, walking through the rain (the drops slowly falling between the words) thinking about relationships, the self, love. I feel that the poem is very earnest, so it reminds me to live life earnestly, to remember what humans can be for each other.

—Kimberly Williams, 29, Bookstore Manager, Lathrop Village, Michigan

The Rain

All night the sound had
come back again,
and again falls
this quiet, persistent rain.

What am I to myself
that must be remembered,
insisted upon
so often? Is it

that never the ease,
even the hardness,
of rain falling
will have for me

something other than this
something not so insistent—
am I to be locked in this
final uneasiness.

Love, if you love me,
lie next to me.
Be for me, like rain,
the getting out

of the tiredness, the fatuousness, the semi-
lust of intentional indifference.
Be wet
with a decent happiness.

As I am learning more about life and the way life can make you feel powerless, I begin to appreciate this poem.

—Caitlin McAuliffe, 14, Student, Tampa, Florida

I Know a Man

As I sd to my
friend, because I am
always talking,—John, I

sd, which was not his
name, the darkness sur-
rounds us, what

can we do against
it, or else, shall we &
why not, buy a goddamn big car,

drive, he sd, for
christ's sake, look
out where yr going.

COUNTEE CULLEN

UNITED STATES • 1903–1946

Cullen brazenly asked the questions before I had the courage to. Knowing that he was gay as well as black, I recognize some of his confusion and nurse an aching empathy. The pains of being the ultimate pariah, all in the eyes of my brothers and God, weigh on me everyday, pressing me nearly to death.

—Todd Hellems, 19, Student, Doraville, Georgia

Its classic message is still necessary to hear.

—Barbara Stevens, 62, Retired Postal Worker, Provincetown, Massachusetts

Yet Do I Marvel

I doubt not God is good, well-meaning, kind,
And did He stoop to quibble could tell why
The little buried mole continues blind,
Why flesh that mirrors Him must some day die,
Make plain the reason tortured Tantalus
Is baited by the fickle fruit, declare
If merely brute caprice dooms Sisyphus

To struggle up a never-ending stair.
Inscrutable His ways are, and immune
To catechism by a mind too strewn
With petty cares to slightly understand
What awful brain compels His awful hand.
Yet do I marvel at this curious thing:
To make a poet black, and bid him sing!

E. E. CUMMINGS

UNITED STATES • 1894–1962

(1) very American (2) very antiwar (3) very modern (4) very radical. This poem blew my mind in 1954 when I first read it. Gave me insight into the possibilities of poetry.

—Adina Kabaker, 60, Writer, Chicago, Illinois

i sing of Olaf glad and big

i sing of Olaf glad and big
whose warmest heart recoiled at war:
a conscientious object-or

his wellbelovéd colonel(trig
westpointer most succinctly bred)
took erring Olaf soon in hand;
but—though an host of overjoyed
noncoms(first knocking on the head
him)do through icy waters roll
that helplessness which others stroke
with brushes recently employed
anent this muddy toiletbowl,
while kindred intellects evoke
allegiance per blunt instruments—
Olaf(being to all intents
a corpse and wanting any rag
upon what God unto him gave)
responds,without getting annoyed
"I will not kiss your fucking flag"

straightway the silver bird looked grave
(departing hurriedly to shave)

but—though all kinds of officers
(a yearning nation's blueeyed pride)
their passive prey did kick and curse
until for wear their clarion
voices and boots were much the worse,
and egged the firstclassprivates on
his rectum wickedly to tease

by means of skilfully applied
bayonets roasted hot with heat—
Olaf(upon what were once knees)
does almost ceaselessly repeat
"there is some shit I will not eat"

our president,being of which
assertions duly notified
threw the yellowsonofabitch
into a dungeon,where he died

Christ(of His mercy infinite)
i pray to see;and Olaf,too

preponderatingly because
unless statistics lie he was
more brave than me:more blond than you.

ROBERT DESNOS

FRANCE • 1900–1945

I originally fell in love with this poem because of the use of shade vs. sun. When I learned that the poem had been written at Buchenwald, it became much more meaningful to me.

—Sandy Stout, 47, Homemaker, Richardson, Texas

Last Poem

I have so fiercely dreamed of you
And walked so far and spoken of you so,
Loved a shade of you so hard
That now I've no more left of you.
I'm left to be a shade among the shades
A hundred times more shade than shade
To be shade cast time and time again into your sun-transfigured life.

Translated from the French by X. J. Kennedy

JAMES DICKEY

UNITED STATES • 1923–1997

About twenty-five years ago, I was in college on a football scholarship. Poetry was one of the last things on my mind. I was assigned to read a number of poems in a Lit class and I half-heartedly read the first couple on the list. Then I started "The Bee." I was absorbed. I reread it several times. Here was a poet describing how he heard the ghost of his college football coach hollering at him as he rushed to save his young son from oncoming traffic. A poet who had played college football? I understood and felt everything he described. Now that I am middle-aged and have two sons of my own, this poem has become even richer to me. Most importantly, "The Bee" started my love of poetry. I might never have read Whitman, Rilke, Rimbaud, Eliot, Garcia Lorca, Heaney, or the other poets who are so important to me.

—Chip VanPelt, 43, Advertising Associate, Garland, Texas

The Bee

To the football coaches of Clemson College, 1942

One dot
Grainily shifting   we at roadside and
The smallest wings coming   along the rail fence out
Of the woods   one dot   of all that green. It now
Becomes flesh-crawling   then the quite still
Of stinging. I must live faster for my terrified
Small son   it is on him. Has come. Clings.

Old wingback, come
To life. If your knee action is high
Enough, the fat may fall in time   God damn
You, Dickey, *dig*   this is your last time to cut
And run   but you must give it everything you have
Left, for screaming near your screaming child is the sheer
Murder of California traffic: some bee hangs driving

Your child
Blindly onto the highway. Get there however
Is still possible. Long live what I badly did
At Clemson   and all of my clumsiest drives
For the ball   all of my trying to turn
The corner downfield   and my spindling explosions
Through the five-hole over tackle. O backfield

Coach Shag Norton,
Tell me as you never yet have told me
To get the lead out   scream whatever will get
The slow-motion of middle age off me   I cannot
Make it this way   I will have to leave
My feet   they are gone   I have him where
He lives   and down we go singing with screams into

The dirt,
Son-screams of fathers   screams of dead coaches turning
To approval   and from between us the bee rises screaming
With flight   grainily shifting   riding the rail fence
Back into the woods   traffic blasting past us
Unchanged, nothing heard through the air-
conditioning glass   we lying at roadside full

Of the forearm prints
Of roadrocks   strawberries on our elbows as from
Scrimmage with the varsity   now we can get
Up   stand   turn away from the highway   look straight
Into trees. See, there is nothing coming out   no
Smallest wing   no shift of a flight-grain   nothing
Nothing. Let us go in, son, and listen

For some tobacco-
mumbling voice in the branches   to say "That's
a little better,"   to our lives still hanging
By a hair. There is nothing to stop us   we can go
Deep   deeper   into elms, and listen to traffic die
Roaring, like a football crowd from which we have
Vanished. Dead coaches live in the air, son   live

In the ear
Like fathers, and *urge*   and *urge*. They want you better
Than you are. When needed, they rise and curse you   they scream
When something must be saved. Here, under this tree,
We can sit down. You can sleep, and I can try
To give back what I have earned by keeping us
Alive, and safe from bees: the smile of some kind

Of savior—
Of touchdowns, of fumbles, battles,

Lives. Let me sit here with you, son
As on the bench, while the first string takes back
Over, far away   and say with my silentest tongue, with the man-
creating bruises of my arms   with a live leaf a quick
Dead hand on my shoulder, "Coach Norton, I am your boy."

EMILY DICKINSON

UNITED STATES • 1830–1886

I'm fifteen years old. That makes me a teenager. I like hanging out, I like going to movies, I like going to all the normal stuff teenage girls do. But once in a while when life is going all great, you just want to stop, you know. You just want to sit down and be by yourself. You don't want anyone to bother you. Without your mom nagging about cleaning your room, or your friends talking about their boyfriends breaking up their hearts and stuff. That's why I like this poem. Because it tells me I can be by myself, and it's okay. I think everyone wants to be somebody, and everyone can be somebody. What is hard is to be a somebody with the humbleness of a nobody.

—Yina Liang, 15, Student, Atlanta, Georgia

I'm Nobody! Who are you? (288)

I'm Nobody! Who are you?
Are you—Nobody—Too?
Then there's a pair of us!
Don't tell! they'd advertise—you know!

How dreary—to be—Somebody!
How public—like a Frog—
To tell one's name—the livelong June—
To an admiring Bog!

It reminds me of my mother, who lived a very close life, yet accurately knew the workings of the world, and the hearts and minds of people she never met.

—Michael O'Hara, Ship Pilot

The poem expresses simply and elegantly the essence of faith—religious and otherwise. Faith, trust, and everyday wisdom regarding our world and life.

—Frances Boeckman, 77, Retired Librarian and Archivist, Jackson, Mississippi

I never saw a Moor—(1052)

I never saw a Moor—
I never saw the Sea—
Yet know I how the Heather looks
And what a Billow be.

I never spoke with God
Nor visited in Heaven—
Yet certain am I of the spot
As if the Checks were given—

_____

Because I am that clown.

—Elizabeth Stebbins, 83, Homemaker, Quincy, Illinois

A little Madness in the Spring (1333)

A little Madness in the Spring
Is wholesome even for the King,
But God be with the Clown—

Who ponders this tremendous scene—
This whole Experiment of Green—
As if it were his own!

_____

The poem seems to give off beautiful colors in every word. I'm only eleven but every word of this poem means a whole lot to me

 —Julia Stadum, 11, Student, Anchorage, Alaska

This poem gives me a feeling of warmth like the sun smiling upon me giving me hope when I am crouched in the corner. It reminds me that although bad things happen and I feel lonely and alone, hope is there protecting me.

—Aemy Chung, 16, Student, Beverly Hills, California

I'm a zookeeper at the Bronx Zoo. I've worked in the bird department for over eight years. I'm not a poet myself so it's not easy to describe this poem's meaning to me. But I do think that our capacity for hope is the most amazing thing about human beings. And it's not something that we control or consciously decide to have. It is like a small animal inside of us—or an animalistic part of us. And although it can die, it takes so ridiculously little to keep it alive. Even in the worst circumstances, when our conscious mind—our intellect— must conclude that the situation is wholly negative and likely to remain so, hope will pipe up. Like a bird's song, it's uncontrollable, unconscious, instinctive, and beautiful, thought- less and uplifting. Evolved instinct, maybe.

—Susan Gormaley, 32, Zookeeper, Valley Cottage, New York

"Hope" is the thing with Feathers—(254)

"Hope" is the thing with feathers—
That perches in the soul—
And sings the tune without the words—
And never stops—at all—

And sweetest—in the Gale—is heard—
And sore must be the storm—
That could abash the little Bird
That kept so many warm—

I've heard it in the chillest land—
And on the strangest Sea—
Yet, never, in Extremity,
It asked a crumb—of Me.

_____

I picked this poem because it has meaning in my life. Those bird creatures are my favorite animals. When I went to Mexico, my cousin saw a little one coming down this walk from her house and she gave the little bird to me because I love them so.

—Gladys Galvez, 10, Student, Phoenix, Arizona

A Bird came down the Walk—(328)

A Bird came down the Walk—
He did not know I saw—
He bit an Angleworm in halves
And ate the fellow, raw,

And then he drank a Dew
From a convenient Grass—
And then hopped sidewise to the Wall
To let a Beetle pass—

He glanced with rapid eyes
That hurried all around—
They looked like frightened Beads, I thought—
He stirred his Velvet Head

Like one in danger, Cautious,
I offered him a Crumb
And he unrolled his feathers
And rowed him softer home—

Than Oars divide the Ocean,
Too silver for a seam—
Or Butterflies, off Banks of Noon
Leap, plashless as they swim.

JOHN DONNE

ENGLAND • 1572–1631

I like this poem for many reasons. It was the first poem I read and understood without any-one explaining it to me. Also, it's the best argument for sex I've ever heard. Donne was the original smooth talker.

—Rachel Mackintosh, 17, Student, Conway, Arizona

The Flea

Mark but this flea, and mark in this,
How little that which thou deniest me is;
Me it sucked first, and now sucks thee,
And in this flea our two bloods mingled be;
Thou know'st that this cannot be said
A sin, or shame, or loss of maidenhead,
    Yet this enjoys before it woo,
    And pampered swells with one blood made of two,
    And this, alas, is more than we would do.

Oh stay, three lives in one flea spare,
Where we almost, nay more than married are.
This flea is you and I, and this
Our marriage bed and marriage temple is;
Though parents grudge, and you, we are met,
And cloistered in these living walls of jet.
    Though use make you apt to kill me
    Let not to that, self-murder added be,
    And sacrilege, three sins in killing three.

Cruel and sudden, hast thou since
Purpled thy nail in blood of innocence?
Wherein could this flea guilty be,
Except in that drop which it sucked from thee?
Yet thou triumph'st, and say'st that thou
Find'st not thy self nor me the weaker now;
    Tis true; then learn how false fears be:
    Just so much honor, when thou yield'st to me,
    Will waste, as this flea's death took life from thee.

My high school sweetheart, for whom I wrote many love poems, sent me this poem. After high school, we had been separated by our parents and went to different colleges. Writing to each other was all we had to dispel the loneliness of being apart. This poem tells of that loneliness and the desire to be together as one again. It does a far better job than any poem I wrote to her.

—Thomas Daley, 47, Attorney, Williamsville, New York

I have reached an age where every year now, people whom I have loved and who have loved me, are dying. The image of the compass, an ordinary tool I used in grade school to make perfect circles, is so familiar to my head and my eye and my memory that this poem comforts me and surprises me every time I read it.

—Jeanne Nichols, 74, Retired, Los Angeles, California

A Valediction: Forbidding Mourning

As virtuous men pass mildly away,
    And whisper to their souls to go,
Whilst some of their sad friends do say
    The breath goes now, and some say, No;

So let us melt, and make no noise,
    No tear-floods, nor sigh-tempests move,
'Twere profanation of our joys
    To tell the laity our love.

Moving of th' earth brings harms and fears,
    Men reckon what it did and meant;
But trepidation of the spheres,
    Though greater far, is innocent.

Dull sublunary lovers' love
    (Whose soul is sense) cannot admit
Absence, because it doth remove
    Those things which elemented it.

But we, by a love so much refined
    That our selves know not what it is,
Inter-assurèd of the mind,
    Care less, eyes, lips, and hands to miss.

Our two souls therefore, which are one,
    Though I must go, endure not yet

A breach, but an expansion,
　　Like gold to airy thinness beat.

If they be two, they are two so
　　As stiff twin compasses are two;
Thy soul, the fixed foot, makes no show
　　To move, but doth, if th' other do.

And though it in the center sit,
　　Yet when the other far doth roam,
It leans and hearkens after it,
　　And grows erect, as that comes home.

Such wilt thou be to me, who must
　　Like th' other foot, obliquely run;
Thy firmness makes my circle just,
　　And makes me end where I begun.

MARK DOTY

UNITED STATES • B. 1953

It recognizes two things that we all must learn in order to reconcile ourselves to this life:

1) there is sadness

2) there is mercy.

—Rebecca Marshall, 26, Clerk/Graduate Student, Provo, Utah

The Embrace

You weren't well or really ill yet either,
just a little tired, your handsomeness
tinged by grief or anticipation, which brought
to your face a thoughtful, deepening grace.

I didn't for a moment doubt you were dead.
I knew that to be true still, even in the dream.
You'd been out—at work maybe?—
having a good day, almost energetic.

We seemed to be moving from some old house
where we'd lived, boxes everywhere, things
in disarray: that was the *story* of my dream,
but even asleep I was shocked out of narrative

by your face, the physical fact of your face:
inches from mine, smooth-shaven, loving, alert.
Why so difficult, remembering the actual look
of you? Without a photograph, without strain?

So when I saw your unguarded, reliable face,
your unmistakable gaze opening all the warmth
and clarity of you—warm brown tea—we held
each other for the time the dream allowed.

Bless you. You came back, so I could see you
once more, plainly, so I could rest against you
without thinking this happiness lessened anything,
without thinking you were alive again.

RITA DOVE

UNITED STATES • B. 1952

This poem has haunted me ever since I read it the first time. As a mother of three children (ages 9, 5, and almost 3), and a pediatric intensive care nurse, I often feel like I spend all day giving myself to others and have nothing left that is just mine. What I search for is more than alone time. It is a period with an absence of sound, a time with absolutely no obligation to accomplish a task, no person needing, wanting, even loving me. This poem expresses my feelings better than I ever could.

—Sandra Nelson, 34, Registered Nurse, Zeeland, Michigan

It reminds me of the earliest days of my son's life. I, like the character in the poem, longed for a little place that could be my own. I wanted to be able to think about anything other than where I could get the best deal on diapers and formula. I wanted a place where, even if just for a few minutes, I could let my mind wander away from the worries of raising a child alone, and think about absolutely nothing if I so desired.

—Kristi Meccia, 30, Student/Receptionist/Youth Center Supervisor, Vermillion,
  South Dakota

Daystar

She wanted a little room for thinking:
but she saw diapers steaming on the line,
a doll slumped behind the door.

So she lugged a chair behind the garage
to sit out the children's naps.

Sometimes there were things to watch—
the pinched armor of a vanished cricket,
a floating maple leaf. Other days
she stared until she was assured
when she closed her eyes
she'd see only her own vivid blood.

She had an hour, at best, before Liza appeared
pouting from the top of the stairs.
And just *what* was mother doing
out back with the field mice? Why.

building a palace. Later
that night when Thomas rolled over and

lurched into her, she would open her eyes
and think of the place that was hers
for an hour—where
she was nothing,
pure nothing, in the middle of the day.

MICHAEL DRAYTON

ENGLAND • *1563–1631*

Over four hundred years ago, he expresses, with humor, thoughts my single friends have today.

—William Lynch, 50, Commodity Trader/Retired Aerospace Engineer, Boxborough,
   Massachusetts

Since ther's no helpe, Come let us kisse and part (10)

Since ther's no helpe, Come let us kisse and part,
Nay, I have done: You get no more of Me,
And I am glad, yea glad with all my heart,
That thus so cleanly, I my Selfe can free,
Shake hands for ever, Cancell all our Vowes,
And when We meet at any time againe,
Be it not seene in either of our Browes,
That We one jot of former Love reteyne;
Now at the last gaspe, of Loves latest Breath,
When his Pulse fayling, Passion speechlesse lies,
When Faith is kneeling by his bed of Death,
And Innocence is closing up his Eyes,
Now if thou would'st, when all have given him over,
From Death to Life, thou might'st him yet recover.

ALAN DUGAN

UNITED STATES • B. 1923

What I love most about the poem is the image of us constructing ourselves much as we would a house (with the attendant problems) and the admission of needing help.

—John Kaminsky, 50, Printer, Worthington, Massachusetts

Love Song: I And Thou

Nothing is plumb, level, or square:
   the studs are bowed, the joists
are shaky by nature, no piece fits
   any other piece without a gap
or pinch, and bent nails
   dance all over the surfacing
like maggots. By Christ
   I am no carpenter. I built
the roof for myself, the walls
   for myself, the floors
for myself, and got
   hung up in it myself. I
danced with a purple thumb
   at this house-warming, drunk
with my prime whiskey: rage.
   Oh I spat rage's nails
into the frame-up of my work:
   it held. It settled plumb,
level, solid, square and true
   for that great moment. Then
it screamed and went on through,
   skewing as wrong the other way.
God damned it. This is hell,
   but I planned it, I sawed it,
I nailed it, and I
   will live in it until it kills me.
I can nail my left palm
   to the left-hand crosspiece but
I can't do everything myself.
   I need a hand to nail the right,
a help, a love, a you, a wife.

PAUL LAWRENCE DUNBAR

UNITED STATES • 1872–1906

I first read this poem in high school and have never forgotten it. As a teenager, I always be-lieved that no one really understood me. This poem made me realize that we all feel that way at some time or another. Even though this poem has a dark mood, I think it is capable of opening up your eyes. Because only after you realize that you are wearing a mask are you able to take it off.

—Charlene Kerr, 26, Office Manager/Skydive Instructor, Galt, California

I feel this poem explains the African-American experience in America.

—Von Anderson, 21, Student, Jackson, Mississippi

I read this poem in ninth grade and immediately set about memorizing it. Through the years, it has gone from being a part of my thoughts to becoming a part of my soul. This poem transcends the African-American struggle in our society to emphasize everyone's strug-gle. There is not a person alive who has not struggled through life's occasional bitterness, hiding their real feelings behind a smile. This poem has helped me through many rough times. As strange as it may sound, it makes life easier knowing there are others out there also in pain but still "grinning and lying" to the world, along with me.

—M. Tarik Ajluni, 25, Law Student, Farmington Hills, Michigan

We Wear the Mask

We wear the mask that grins and lies,
It hides our cheeks and shades our eyes,—
This debt we pay to human guile;
With torn and bleeding hearts we smile,
And mouth with myriad subtleties.

Why should the world be overwise,
In counting all our tears and sighs?
Nay, let them only see us, while
    We wear the mask.

We smile, but, O great Christ, our cries
To thee from tortured souls arise.
We sing, but oh the clay is vile
Beneath our feet, and long the mile;
But let the world dream otherwise,
    We wear the mask!

HUSSEIN ELHAMI

IRAN • *Twentieth Century*

The poem describes the poet's yearnings for his motherland in a very sensitive way. At closing he humbles himself by not asking for too much, but seeds and an animal.

—Shmuel Shoshani, 72, Retired, Huntington, New York

A Lyric in Exile

If my feet will arrive again, at my home
    with sobs I'll kiss my land's soil.

If I'll be free from the pressures of this exile
    like a dove I'll travel to my nest.

In this foggy air and this alien twilight
    with tears I'll take my road to my habitat.

My heart, is pressed more than this rainy air,
I'll liberate it, perhaps with my weeping at night
    perhaps in my grieved chest I'll take refuge,
    as my heart has taken again its complaint.

I am a lonely tree which fell in wilderness' embrace,
    from which I separated my heart and its buds.

Where is the house of fate that I'll ask;
    did it have nothing but pain in its treasure?

A vain thought I inhibited to struggle with my fate,
    life made me surrender to its lashes.

All the universe to others I'll spare,
    I'll be satisfied with my seeds and animal.

Where is my town? that warm and dusty town?
    that I'll search again,
        my identity from its soil.

Translated from the Persian by Shmuel Shoshani

T. S. ELIOT

UNITED STATES • 1888–1965

While listening to my sophomore English teacher read this poem, I discovered that a poem can cause visions.

—Susan Corl, 38, Artist, Canton, Ohio

I've loved books from the time I teethed on them. I've been a student of comparative litera-ture and art history. I've lived in many countries, including Iceland, Philippines, Germany, Italy, and the United States. I have a daughter, who, as her father describes her, "reads books like a fish swims in water." I have a son who thinks in numbers. My husband thinks about the mechanics of thinking and cognition. These days I think mostly about why people need to have their questions about mortality all packaged in religion for them. Why is it hard for people to accept mortality and human life as it is? I'm not old; I'm not young. I'm neither fat nor thin. I'm healthy, but tired. The poem has so many compartments, so many facets to it—like the galleries in which "the women come and go talking of Michelangelo." I love the music of the poem and the weird imagery of a night spreading out "like a patient etherized upon a table." I wander from time to time into a thought and find myself contemplating an image that Eliot has painted for me. I want to catch up to those women and find out what they are whispering about. In this poem, I catch a meaning and then there's always some-thing else, some other idea there. It's endlessly fascinating to me.

—Julia Sutherland, 38, Database Programmer/Analyst, Bloomington, Indiana

The Love Song of J. Alfred Prufrock

> *S'io credesse che mia risposta fosse*
> *A persona che mai tornasse al mondo,*
> *Questa fiamma staria senza più scosse.*
> *Ma perciocche giammai di questo fondo*
> *Non tornò vivo alcun, s'i'odo il vero,*
> *Senza tema d'infamia ti rispondo.**

Let us go then, you and I,
When the evening is spread out against the sky
Like a patient etherized upon a table;
Let us go, through certain half-deserted streets,

---

*Dante, *Inferno*, XXVII. 61–66. These words are spoken by Gualdo da Montefeltro, whom Dante and Virgil have encountered in the Eighth Chasm, that of the False Counselors, where each spirit is concealed within a flame that moves as the spirit speaks: "If I thought my answer were given to anyone who would ever return to the world, this flame would stand still without moving any fur-ther. But since never from this abyss has anyone ever returned alive, if what I hear is true, without fear of infamy, I answer thee."

The muttering retreats
Of restless nights in one-night cheap hotels
And sawdust restaurants with oyster-shells:
Streets that follow like a tedious argument
Of insidious intent
To lead you to an overwhelming question. . .
Oh, do not ask, "What is it?"
Let us go and make our visit.

In the room the women come and go
Talking of Michelangelo.

The yellow fog that rubs its back upon the window-panes
The yellow smoke that rubs its muzzle on the window-panes
Licked its tongue into the corners of the evening,
Lingered upon the pools that stand in drains,
Let fall upon its back the soot that falls from chimneys,
Slipped by the terrace, made a sudden leap,
And seeing that it was a soft October night,
Curled once about the house, and fell asleep.

And indeed there will be time
For the yellow smoke that slides along the street,
Rubbing its back upon the window-panes;
There will be time, there will be time
To prepare a face to meet the faces that you meet;
There will be time to murder and create,
And time for all the works and days of hands
That lift and drop a question on your plate;
Time for you and time for me,
And time yet for a hundred indecisions,
And for a hundred visions and revisions,
Before the taking of a toast and tea.

In the room the women come and go
Talking of Michelangelo.

And indeed there will be time
To wonder, "Do I dare?" and, "Do I dare?"
Time to turn back and descend the stair,
With a bald spot in the middle of my hair—
[They will say: "How his hair is growing thin!"]

My morning coat, my collar mounting firmly to the chin,
My necktie rich and modest, but asserted by a simple pin—
[They will say: "But how his arms and legs are thin!"]
Do I dare
Disturb the universe?
In a minute there is time
For decisions and revisions which a minute will reverse.

For I have known them all already, known them all;
Have known the evenings, mornings, afternoons,
I have measured out my life with coffee spoons;
I know the voices dying with a dying fall
Beneath the music from a farther room.
　　So how should I presume?
And I have known the eyes already, known them all—
The eyes that fix you in a formulated phrase,
And when I am formulated, sprawling on a pin,
When I am pinned and wriggling on the wall,
Then how should I begin
To spit out all the butt-ends of my days and ways?
　　And how should I presume?

And I have known the arms already, known them all—
Arms that are braceleted and white and bare
[But in the lamplight, downed with light brown hair!]
Is it perfume from a dress
That makes me so digress?
Arms that lie along a table, or wrap about a shawl.
　　And should I then presume?
　　And how should I begin?
. . . . .
Shall I say, I have gone at dusk through narrow streets
And watched the smoke that rises from the pipes
Of lonely men in shirt-sleeves, leaning out of windows? . . .

I should have been a pair of ragged claws
Scuttling across the floors of silent seas.
. . . . .
And the afternoon, the evening, sleeps so peacefully!
Smoothed by long fingers,
Asleep . . . tired . . . or it malingers,
Stretched on the floor, here beside you and me.

Should I, after tea and cakes and ices,
Have the strength to force the moment to its crisis?
But though I have wept and fasted, wept and prayed,
Though I have seen my head [grown slightly bald] brought in upon a platter,
I am no prophet—and here's no great matter;
I have seen the moment of my greatness flicker,
And I have seen the eternal Footman hold my coat, and snicker,
And in short, I was afraid.

And would it have been worth it, after all,
After the cups, the marmalade, the tea,
Among the porcelain, among some talk of you and me,
Would it have been worth while,
To have bitten off the matter with a smile,
To have squeezed the universe into a ball
To roll it toward some overwhelming question,
To say: "I am Lazarus, come from the dead
Come back to tell you all, I shall tell you all"—
If one, settling a pillow by her head,
    Should say: "That is not what I meant at all.
    That is not it, at all."

And would it have been worth it, after all,
Would it have been worth while,
After the sunsets and the dooryards and the sprinkled streets,
After the novels, after the teacups, after the skirts that trail along the floor—
And this, and so much more?—
It is impossible to say just what I mean!
But as if a magic lantern threw the nerves in patterns on a screen:
Would it have been worth while
If one, settling a pillow or throwing off a shawl,
And turning toward the window, should say:
    "That is not it at all,
    That is not what I meant, at all."
. . . . .
No! I am not Prince Hamlet, nor was meant to be;
Am an attendant lord, one that will do
To swell a progress, start a scene or two,
Advise the prince; no doubt, an easy tool,
Deferential, glad to be of use,
Politic, cautious, and meticulous;
Full of high sentence, but a bit obtuse;

At times, indeed, almost ridiculous—
Almost, at times, the Fool.

I grow old . . . I grow old . . .
I shall wear the bottoms of my trousers rolled.

Shall I part my hair behind? Do I dare to eat a peach?
I shall wear white flannel trousers, and walk upon the beach.
I have heard the mermaids singing, each to each.

I do not think that they will sing to me.

I have seen them riding seaward on the waves
Combing the white hair of the waves blown back
When the wind blows the water white and black.

We have lingered in the chambers of the sea
By sea-girls wreathed with seaweed red and brown
Till human voices wake us, and we drown.

More than thirty-five years ago, I copied part II of Eliot's "Dry Salvages" onto paper which I filed away. It spoke to me then. In 1993, after thirty-six years of marriage, my husband left. In rereading the poem, I realized how it somehow foretold my life. "We had the experience but missed the meaning."

—Esther Clark, 63, Editorial Assistant, Chappaqua, New York

Dry Salvages (II)

Where is there an end of it, the soundless wailing,
The silent withering of autumn flowers
Dropping their petals and remaining motionless;
Where is there an end to the drifting wreckage,
The prayer of the bone on the beach, the unprayable
Prayer at the calamitous annunciation?

There is no end, but addition: the trailing
Consequence of further days and hours,
While emotion takes to itself the emotionless
Years of living among the breakage

Of what was believed in as the most reliable—
And therefore the fittest for renunciation.

There is the final addition, the failing
Pride or resentment at failing powers,
The unattached devotion which might pass for devotionless,
In a drifting boat with a slow leakage,
The silent listening to the undeniable
Clamor of the bell of the last annunciation.

Where is the end of them, the fishermen sailing
Into the wind's tail, where the fog cowers?
We cannot think of a time that is oceanless
Or of an ocean not littered with wastage
Or of a future that is not liable
Like the past, to have no destination.

We have to think of them as forever baling,
Setting and hauling, while the North East lowers
Over shallow banks unchanging and erosionless
Or drawing their money, drying sails at dockage;
Not as making a trip that will be unpayable
For a haul that will not bear examination.

There is no end of it, the voiceless wailing,
No end to the withering of withered flowers,
To the movement of pain that is painless and motionless,
To the drift of the sea and the drifting wreckage,
The bone's prayer to Death its God. Only the hardly, barely prayable
Prayer of the one Annunciation.

It seems, as one becomes older,
That the past has another pattern, and ceases to be a mere sequence—
Or even development: the latter a partial fallacy,
Encouraged by superficial notions of evolution,
Which becomes, in the popular mind, a means of disowning the past.
The moments of happiness—not the sense of well-being,
Fruition, fulfilment, security or affection,
Or even a very good dinner, but the sudden illumination—
We had the experience but missed the meaning,
And approach to the meaning restores the experience

In a different form, beyond any meaning
We can assign to happiness. I have said before
That the past experience revived in the meaning
Is not the experience of one life only
But of many generations—not forgetting
Something that is probably quite ineffable:
The backward look behind the assurance
Of recorded history, the backward half-look
Over the shoulder, towards the primitive terror.
Now, we come to discover that the moments of agony
(Whether, or not, due to misunderstanding,
Having hoped for the wrong things or dreaded the wrong things,
Is not in question) are likewise permanent
With such permanence as time has. We appreciate this better
In the agony of others, nearly experienced,
Involving ourselves, than in our own.
For our own past is covered by the currents of action,
But the torment of others remains an experience
Unqualified, unworn by subsequent attrition.
People change, and smile: but the agony abides.
Time the destroyer is time the preserver,
Like the river with its cargo of dead Negroes, cows and chicken coops,
The bitter apple and the bite in the apple.
And the ragged rock in the restless waters,
Waves wash over it, fogs conceal it;
On a halcyon day it is merely a monument,
In navigable weather it is always a seamark
To lay a course by; but in the somber season
Or the sudden fury, is what it always was.

RALPH WALDO EMERSON

UNITED STATES • 1803–1882

This poem reminds those of us who tend to be overly analytical—and who isn't these days—that sometimes things are just what they are.

—Barbara Juknialis, 52, Hospital Administrator, Cleveland, Ohio

As an artist, I find the poem visually satisfying. As an art teacher, I hope to impart the idea that any creative pursuit is worth the time and effort, that "Beauty is its own excuse for being."

—Sylvia Freeman Garrard, 56, Artist/Art Teacher, Durham, North Carolina

The Rhodora is my favorite flower; when I was little my family always had them in our yard. The flower resembles humans and their beauty.

—Svea Uellendahl, 18, Student, Miami Beach, California

The Rhodora

ON BEING ASKED, WHENCE IS THE FLOWER?

In May, when sea-winds pierced our solitudes,
I found the fresh Rhodora in the woods,
Spreading its leafless blooms in a damp nook,
To please the desert and the sluggish brook.
The purple petals, fallen in the pool,
Made the black water with their beauty gay;
Here might the red-bird come his plumes to cool,
And court the flower that cheapens his array.
Rhodora! if the sages ask thee why
This charm is wasted on the earth and sky,
Tell them, dear, that if eyes were made for seeing,
Then Beauty is its own excuse for being:
Why thou wert there, O rival of the rose!
I never thought to ask, I never knew;
But, in my simple ignorance, suppose
The self-same Power that brought me there brought you.

ROBERT FROST

UNITED STATES • 1874–1963

When I was in the eleventh grade, I went on a field trip to the University of Miami to hear a very aged Robert Frost read his poetry. After listening to his melodic recitation, I went up to meet him and noticed that his book was upside-down. He hadn't been reading at all. The last three lines of this poem illustrate my life as a mother and a teacher. I decided to have a child even though I was at an age when it was very risky. I was the "one in five" to conceive my first child at thirty-eight and then the "one in nine" to have an uncomplicated pregnancy and delivery. I have been blessed with a beautiful daughter, Hanni. As a teacher I took a risk to join the faculty at a school that was just in the early stages of developing a high school program. That was twenty years ago, and I have been an English teacher in love with my students, colleagues and my profession at Miami Country Day School ever since.

—Fredlyn Rosenfeld, 55, Teacher, Miami Beach, Florida

I am one of eight children from a small town in Idaho. I graduated from high school number two in my class in 1989. I accepted an NROTC scholarship to Loyola Marymount University having no idea what I was getting into—in the military or in the state of California—other than that I was not going to be just another person from my hometown who would end up going to Utah. I loaded up my '77 Celica and drove to LA by myself with a little over $700 in my pocket, tuition covered and no room and board. I have now been in the Navy for over 5½ years. I have been stationed in Georgia, Florida, Bahrain, and now Japan. I have visited over thirty countries throughout the world. This would never have been possible had I not taken this road.

—Cody Hodges, 28, Officer U.S. Navy, Preston, Idaho
   (currently stationed on the USS *Vandegrift*)

The older you become, the more you see "how way leads on to way."

—Fran Rall, 73, Homemaker, Madison, Wisconsin

The Road Not Taken

Two roads diverged in a yellow wood,
And sorry I could not travel both
And be one traveler, long I stood
And looked down one as far as I could
To where it bent in the undergrowth;

Then took the other, as just as fair,
And having perhaps the better claim,
Because it was grassy and wanted wear;

Though as for that, the passing there
Had worn them really about the same,

And both that morning equally lay
In leaves no step had trodden black.
Oh, I kept the first for another day!
Yet knowing how way leads on to way,
I doubted if I should ever come back.

I shall be telling this with a sigh
Somewhere ages and ages hence:
Two roads diverged in a wood, and I—
I took the one less traveled by,
And that has made all the difference.

It gives me a tranquil feeling. It melts away my angers.

—Dong-Eun Lee, 14, Student, Fairfax, Virginia

Acquainted with the Night

I have been one acquainted with the night.
I have walked out in rain—and back in rain.
I have outwalked the furthest city light.

I have looked down the saddest city lane.
I have passed by the watchman on his beat
And dropped my eyes, unwilling to explain.

I have stood still and stopped the sound of feet
When far away an interrupted cry
Came over houses from another street,

But not to call me back or say good-by;
And further still at an unearthly height,
One luminary clock against the sky

Proclaimed the time was neither wrong nor right.
I have been one acquainted with the night.

What I always dream about as I read or say this poem, is the following: My grandmother, Anna Golden, who came from Russia around 1903 or 1904, with my mother, then Golda (now Augusta) and my aunt Flo (then Faga), two and three years old, a feather bett, two Shabbos candle holders, and the samovar now in my dining room. Grandma is on the deck of this immigrant ship and the Mayflower *pulls alongside, and this big Pilgrim waves her the direction and calls out, "This way, Chantzi, this way; don't worry about a thing, Chantzi. Everything is going to be all right."*

—Laurence Berns, 70, Professor, Annapolis, Maryland

Immigrants

No ship of all that under sail or steam
Have gathered people to us more and more
But, Pilgrim-manned, the *Mayflower* in a dream
Has been her anxious convoy in to shore.

My dad was a steelworker and son of Slovakian immigrants in Bethlehem, Pennsylvania, where I grew up. At that time, it was assumed that girls would marry and raise families, so my dad struggled to put my two brothers through college so they wouldn't be stuck working for "The Steel" all their lives. (One is a doctor today and the other a lawyer). So, my education ended with a business course after high school. Because I spent two years in the U.S. Army, I earned G.I. Bill benefits, so when my benefits were about to expire, and when the youngest of our five children started kindergarten, I began college, and after many years and many moves, I graduated proudly. Here in Oklahoma, it was a two-hour drive each way to school, and I would play my Robert Frost tapes, which were narrated by the gruff-voiced poet himself, while I drove. At first, I just reveled in the beautiful language of the poems, but before long the poems took on meanings and shadings that became personal, until I felt like the poems were mine. In this poem, the lovely woodland images gave me a wonderful sense of peace, but, more than that, the poem made me feel like a "swinger of birches" who would some day be set down again, after the climb, to start anew. It gave me hope. Today I am sixty-five, and spend my time tutoring the children of a Vietnamese family.

—Evelyn Sharp, 65, Tulsa, Oklahoma

Birches

When I see birches bend to left and right
Across the lines of straighter darker trees,
I like to think some boy's been swinging them.
But swinging doesn't bend them down to stay
As ice storms do. Often you must have seen them

Loaded with ice a sunny winter morning
After a rain. They click upon themselves
As the breeze rises, and turn many-colored
As the stir cracks and crazes their enamel.
Soon the sun's warmth makes them shed crystal shells
Shattering and avalanching on the snow crust—
Such heaps of broken glass to sweep away
You'd think the inner dome of heaven had fallen.
They are dragged to the withered bracken by the load,
And they seem not to break; though once they are bowed
So low for long, they never right themselves:
You may see their trunks arching in the woods
Years afterwards, trailing their leaves on the ground
Like girls on hands and knees that throw their hair
Before them over their heads to dry in the sun.
But I was going to say when Truth broke in
With all her matter of fact about the ice storm,
I should prefer to have some boy bend them
As he went out and in to fetch the cows—
Some boy too far from town to learn baseball,
Whose only play was what he found himself,
Summer or winter, and could play alone.
One by one he subdued his father's trees
By riding them down over and over again
Until he took the stiffness out of them,
And not one but hung limp, not one was left
For him to conquer. He learned all there was
To learn about not launching out too soon
And so not carrying the tree away
Clear to the ground. He always kept his poise
To the top branches, climbing carefully
With the same pains you use to fill a cup
Up to the brim, and even above the brim.
Then he flung outward, feet first, with a swish,
Kicking his way down through the air to the ground.
So was I once myself a swinger of birches.
And so I dream of going back to be.
It's when I'm weary of considerations,
And life is too much like a pathless wood
Where your face burns and tickles with the cobwebs
Broken across it, and one eye is weeping
From a twig's having lashed across it open.

I'd like to get away from earth awhile
And then come back to it and begin over.
May no fate willfully misunderstand me
And half grant what I wish and snatch me away
Not to return. Earth's the right place for love:
I don't know where it's likely to go better.
I'd like to go by climbing a birch tree,
And climb black branches up a snow-white trunk
Toward heaven, till the tree could bear no more,
But dipped its top and set me down again.
That would be good both going and coming back.
One could do worse than be a swinger of birches.

_____

Frost brings to mind that nature is elusive. We have a need to understand and be part of nature. We are compelled to participate but cannot, except to observe and to revere. After all, are we not part of the wonder? I have seen in my childhood those small skiing fish in motion and remember them vividly. I see them clearly in Frost's words. I still want to put my foot on them while reading this poem. The preciseness and constancy of nature. The beauty. I am grounded, well grounded.

—Elizabeth Jacques, 67, Tour Guide/Teacher, Beverly, Massachusetts

A Hillside Thaw

To think to know the country and not know
The hillside on the day the sun lets go
Ten million silver lizards out of snow!
As often as I've seen it done before
I can't pretend to tell the way it's done.
It looks as if some magic of the sun
Lifted the rug that bred them on the floor
And the light breaking on them made them run.
But if I thought to stop the wet stampede,
And caught one silver lizard by the tail,
And put my foot on one without avail,
And threw myself wet-elbowed and wet-kneed
In front of twenty others' wriggling speed—
In the confusion of them all aglitter,
And birds that joined in the excited fun
By doubling and redoubling song and twitter—
I have no doubt I'd end by holding none.

It takes the moon for this. The sun's a wizard
By all I tell; but so's the moon a witch.
From the high west she makes a gentle cast
And suddenly, without a jerk or twitch,
She has her spell on every single lizard.
I fancied when I looked at six o'clock
The swarm still ran and scuttled just as fast.
The moon was waiting for her chill effect.
I looked at nine: the swarm was turned to rock
In every lifelike posture of the swarm,
Transfixed on mountain slopes almost erect.
Across each other and side by side they lay.
The spell that so could hold them as they were
Was wrought through trees without a breath of storm
To make a leaf, if there had been one, stir.
It was the moon's: she held them until day,
One lizard at the end of every ray.
The thought of my attempting such a stay!

Even just look at the title of the poem and consider its content. This boy's life is over. He is out—of—here. Why do I want to read this poem? Because I was transfixed by it from the start. The stage is set so well. I see clearly the boy, his sister, the busy mill. There is so much action in the poem's onset; then it is reduced to a weakening heartbeat and a few slow breaths. But it's the end line that I so often repeat to myself when I am reminded of the frequent apathy of a world calloused to the misfortunes of others. Life goes on. Supper is ready. . . . I'm happy to be on the planet. I've enjoyed writing this letter.

—Elizabeth Wojtusik, 37, Teaching Artist, New York, New York

"Out, Out—"

The buzz saw snarled and rattled in the yard
And made dust and dropped stove-length sticks of wood,
Sweet-scented stuff when the breeze drew across it.
And from there those that lifted eyes could count
Five mountain ranges one behind the other
Under the sunset far into Vermont.
And the saw snarled and rattled, snarled and rattled,
As it ran light, or had to bear a load.
And nothing happened: day was all but done.
Call it a day, I wish they might have said

To please the boy by giving him the half hour
That a boy counts so much when saved from work.
His sister stood beside them in her apron
To tell them "Supper." At the word, the saw,
As if to prove saws knew what supper meant,
Leaped out at the boy's hand, or seemed to leap—
He must have given the hand. However it was,
Neither refused the meeting. But the hand!
The boy's first outcry was a rueful laugh,
As he swung toward them holding up the hand,
Half in appeal, but half as if to keep
The life from spilling. Then the boy saw all—
Since he was old enough to know, big boy
Doing a man's work, though a child at heart—
He saw all spoiled. "Don't let him cut my hand off—
The doctor, when he comes. Don't let him, sister!"
So. But the hand was gone already.
The doctor put him in the dark of ether.
He lay and puffed his lips out with his breath.
And then—the watcher at his pulse took fright.
No one believed. They listened at his heart.
Little—less—nothing!—and that ended it.
No more to build on there. And they, since they
Were not the one dead, turned to their affairs.

ALLEN GINSBERG

UNITED STATES • 1926–1997

This poem relates to my thoughts on reality and how it can be difficult at times. It also makes me realize "how real the world is already."

—Tom Matragrano, 17, Student, Danville, Pennsylvania

The Terms in Which I Think of Reality

A.

Reality is a question
of realizing how real
the world is already.

Time is Eternity,
ultimate and immovable;
everyone's an angel.

It's Heaven's mystery
of changing perfection:
absolute Eternity

changes! Cars are always
going down the street,
lamps go off and on.

It's a great flat plain;
we can see everything
on top of a table.

Clams open on the table,
lambs are eaten by worms
on the plain. The motion

of change is beautiful,
as well as form called
in and out of being.

B.

Next: to distinguish process
in its particularity with
an eye to the initiation

of gratifying new changes
desired in the real world.
Here we're overwhelmed

with such unpleasant detail
we dream again of Heaven.
For the world is a mountain

of shit: if it's going to
be moved at all, it's got
to be taken by handfuls.

C.

Man lives like the unhappy
whore on River Street who
in her Eternity gets only

a couple of bucks and a lot
of snide remarks in return
for seeking physical love

the best way she knows how,
never really heard of a glad
job or joyous marriage or

a difference in the heart:
or thinks it isn't for her,
which is her worst misery.

LOUISE GLÜCK

UNITED STATES * B. 1943

I met and loved a brilliant man who, in his passion, said I was his Helen. I was moved beyond embarrassment to allow myself to think of myself like that. But he is a scientist and over time let me go, on behalf of the immediate and crushing demands of his practical life. I try to understand. This poem spoke to me of that relationship and of how to think about it and move on.

—Mary Ellen Bryan, Administrative Assistant, Kansas City, Missouri

The Queen of Carthage

Brutal to love,
more brutal to die.
And brutal beyond the reaches of justice
to die of love.

In the end, Dido
summoned her ladies in waiting
that they might see
the harsh destiny inscribed for her by the Fates.

She said, "Aeneas
came to me over the shimmering water;
I asked the Fates
to permit him to return my passion,
even for a short time. What difference
between that and a lifetime: in truth, in such moments,
they are the same, they are both eternity.

I was given a great gift
which I attempted to increase, to prolong.
Aeneas came to me over the water: the beginning
blinded me.

Now the Queen of Carthage
will accept suffering as she accepted favor:
to be noticed by the Fates
is some distinction after all.

Or should one say, to have honored hunger,
since the Fates go by that name also."

THOM GUNN

UNITED STATES • B. *1929*

I worked as an obstetrician in a small town in New Hampshire for my first ten years in practice. I would come home very late at night too wound up to sleep, feeling alone and drained. Poetry helped bring me back down and this poem became my favorite.

—Susan Tredwell, 47, Obstetrician, Boston, Massachussets

Baby Song

From the private ease of Mother's womb
I fall into the lighted room.

Why don't they simply put me back
Where it is warm and wet and black?

But one thing follows on another.
Things were different inside Mother.

Padded and jolly I would ride
The perfect comfort of her inside.

They tuck me in a rustling bed
—I lie there, raging, small, and red.

I may sleep soon, I may forget,
But I won't forget that I regret.

A rain of blood poured round her womb,
But all time roars outside this room.

DONALD HALL

UNITED STATES • B. 1928

I find this poem both incantatory and rooted, such that at every reading I feel that unnamable shiver of mortality which links us with all life on and beyond this earth.

—Susan Militzer Luther, 53, Writer/Teacher, Huntsville, Alabama

When someone asks me why I love poetry, I read "Names of Horses" to them, and they always say, "Oh, I didn't know poetry could be like that." And then they, too, say they love poetry.

—Mary Shannon, 48, Homemaker, Kagel Canyon, California

Names of Horses

All winter your brute shoulders strained against collars, padding
and steerhide over the ash hames, to haul
sledges of cordwood for drying through spring and summer,
for the Glenwood stove next winter, and for the simmering range.

In April you pulled cartloads of manure to spread on the fields,
dark manure of Holsteins, and knobs of your own clustered with oats.
All summer you mowed the grass in meadow and hayfield, the mowing machine
clacketing beside you, while the sun walked high in the morning;

and after noon's heat, you pulled a clawed rake through the same acres,
gathering stacks, and dragged the wagon from stack to stack,
and the built hayrack back, uphill to the chaffy barn,
three loads of hay a day, hanging wide from the hayrack.

Sundays you trotted the two miles to church with the light load
of a leather quartertop buggy, and grazed in the sound of hymns.
Generation on generation, your neck rubbed the window sill
of the stall, smoothing the wood as the sea smooths glass.

When you were old and lame, when your shoulders hurt bending to graze,
one October the man who fed you and kept you, and harnessed you every morning,
led you through corn stubble to sandy ground above Eagle Pond,
and dug a hole beside you where you stood shuddering in your skin,

and lay the shotgun's muzzle in the boneless hollow behind your ear,
and fired the slug into your brain, and felled you into your grave,

shoveling sand to cover you, setting goldenrod upright above you,
where by next summer a dent in the ground made your monument.

For a hundred and fifty years, in the pasture of dead horses,
roots of pine trees pushed through the pale curves of your ribs,
yellow blossoms flourished above you in autumn, and in winter
frost heaved your bones in the ground—old toilers, soil makers:

O Roger, Mackerel, Riley, Ned, Nellie, Chester, Lady Ghost.

THOMAS HARDY

ENGLAND • 1840–1928

Since so many Americans are now imprisoned, I thought that we should be represented as poetry lovers in the project. Thomas Hardy is my favorite poet. Interestingly, this poem was written on the eve of the turn of the century in 1900. It is a beautiful use of words that describes a scene and a mood, a sad end but a beginning as well.

—Richard Johnston, 42, State Prisoner, Norfolk Prison, Norfolk, Massachusetts

The Darkling Thrush

I leant upon a coppice gate
   When Frost was spectre-gray,
And Winter's dregs made desolate
   The weakening eye of day.
The tangled bine-stems scored the sky
   Like strings of broken lyres,
And all mankind that haunted nigh
   Had sought their household fires.

The land's sharp features seemed to be
   The Century's corpse outleant,
His crypt the cloudy canopy,
   The wind his death-lament.
The ancient pulse of germ and birth
   Was shrunken hard and dry,
And every spirit upon earth
   Seemed fervourless as I.

At once a voice arose among
   The bleak twigs overhead
In a full-hearted evensong
   Of joy illimited;
An aged thrush, frail, gaunt, and small,
   In blast-beruffled plume,
Had chosen thus to fling his soul
   Upon the growing gloom.

So little cause for carolings
   Of such ecstatic sound

Was written on terrestrial things
    Afar or nigh around,
That I could think there trembled through
    His happy good-night air
Some blessed Hope, whereof he knew
    And I was unaware.

DECEMBER 31, 1900

ROBERT HASS

UNITED STATES • B. *1941*

This poem was given to me by a coworker several years ago. When I first read the poem, it seemed to put the feelings and events of my life at the time into the words I could not seem to find. This poem speaks not only in my voice, but speaks of me through the eyes of my ex-fiancé, thinking the thoughts I constantly told him he was having. At this time, I was grieving the loss of my beloved mother to breast cancer. She left me alone to face my father's extreme disapproval. I then was pursuing a career as a modern dancer in New York City, much to my father's dismay. As a result of my mother's death, I called off my engagement to a man I had known over eight years and loved very much. I always told this man that his longing for me had nothing to do with me, but was just a reflection of his own need for affection. These exact thoughts, spoken in his voice, are written in the poem.

—Cheryl Swack, 40, Attorney, Coral Gables, Florida

I first came across this poem in college, the time of long nights discussing great things with friends over cigarettes and big bottles of cheap wine and lasagna. What first attracted me to this poem (and still does today), is how succinctly the poet reconciles the abstract world of thought to the material, the experiential, the real. It's that feeling of "violent wonder" at the world, what we have in it, as well as what we've lost. It is the voluptuousness of just saying the word blackberry, *like reading a poem aloud, that is one of the delights of life.*

—Jeff Ingram, 39, Library Clerk, Toledo, Oregon

I love this poem because it is about loss and grace, and it reminds me of California. It makes me cry.

—Lani Steele, 58, English Teacher, Phillipines

Meditation at Lagunitas

All the new thinking is about loss.
In this it resembles all the old thinking.
The idea, for example, that each particular erases
the luminous clarity of a general idea. That the clown-
faced woodpecker probing the dead sculpted trunk
of that black birch is, by his presence,
some tragic falling off from a first world
of undivided light. Or the other notion that,
because there is in this world no one thing
to which the bramble of *blackberry* corresponds,
a word is elegy to what it signifies.
We talked about it late last night and in the voice

of my friend, there was a thin wire of grief, a tone
almost querulous. After a while I understood that,
talking this way, everything dissolves: *justice,*
pine, hair, woman, you and *I.* There was a woman
I made love to and I remembered how, holding
her small shoulders in my hands sometimes,
I felt a violent wonder at her presence
like a thirst for salt, for my childhood river
with its island willows, silly music from the pleasure boat,
muddy places where we caught the little orange-silver fish
called *pumpkinseed.* It hardly had to do with her.
Longing, we say, because desire is full
of endless distances. I must have been the same to her.
But I remember so much, the way her hands dismantled bread,
the thing her father said that hurt her, what
she dreamed. There are moments when the body is as numinous
as words, days that are the good flesh continuing.
Such tenderness, those afternoons and evenings,
saying *blackberry, blackberry, blackberry.*

ROBERT HAYDEN

UNITED STATES • 1913–1980

I stoked the furnace at the address in Ann Arbor where Hayden and I lived. The poem he wrote later about his father recalls to me the discomfort and regrets of that time.

—Manly Johnson, 78, Retired Professor of American Studies, Tulsa, Oklahoma

When I first read it, I was immediately struck by the relationship the speaker has with his father, as it reminds me of the way my stepfather and I related during my youth. He was tough, had been a Marine, a football coach, and had been raised by an aloof, disapproving father himself. Not once in my life did he initiate an embrace, or say he loves me. I used to resent this lack of warmth, and his inability to express emotion or compassion. The last stanza of Hayden's poem opened up my heart to the ways my dad did show his love for me, and still does. Healing wisdom is the true purpose of poetry.

—Peter Frengel, 33, High School Teacher, Harrisburg, Pennsylvania

Until I read Hayden's poem (with its awful conclusion), I had not tried to understand my own father's severity—and let go of my subterranean anger. I thank the poet for that.

—Vilma Potter, 75, Professor, Pasadena, California

I first heard the poem about twenty years ago when I started working at the Library of Congress and Robert Hayden read at a gathering of former Poetry Consultants. The poem really struck me then and has haunted me ever since. It was around the time my son was born, too. But it reminds me of the relationship between my grandfather and my father and also somewhat of the relationship between my father and myself. My grandfather was an Irish immigrant who was a widower at an early age and raised six boys; my father was the oldest. I guess my grandfather, my uncles have told me, had to be particularly hard, even though he was very loving toward my father. My father later became a police lieutenant in New York City and although they're from an Irish-American background and Robert Hayden grew up in an African-American background, at these deep human levels, the particulars don't matter. My father and Robert Hayden were almost exact contemporaries. They were born and died within about a year of each other: 1912 and 1913 and 1980 and 1982.

—John Clarke, 54, Legislative Researcher, Chevy Chase, Maryland

Broke my heart and restored it.

—Phyllis Becker, Kansas City, Missouri

Those Winter Sundays

Sundays too my father got up early
and put his clothes on in the blueblack cold,

then with cracked hands that ached
from labor in the weekday weather made
banked fires blaze. No one ever thanked him.

I'd wake and hear the cold splintering, breaking.
When the rooms were warm, he'd call,
and slowly I would rise and dress,
fearing the chronic angers of that house,

Speaking indifferently to him,
who had driven out the cold
and polished my good shoes as well.
What did I know, what did I know
of love's austere and lonely offices?

Here is an African-American poet, in my world but not of it, who reveals his world of colors, vivid and transcendent, who takes me beyond our times into timelessness, who invites me into our common humanity of both joy and tears, whose gift is the beauty and the soul of poetry. This poem is especially meaningful to me because I have lived through the '60s and '70s civil rights struggle and violence and the Vietnam divisiveness. I am a Korean War Marine Corps veteran, a member of Veterans for Peace, Inc. My wife is a painter and we both have seen and admire Monet's work. I believe Hayden's poem to be a voice of peace. Hayden died much too soon.

—Max Money, 69, Retired, Centersville, Massachusetts

Monet's "Waterlilies"

(for Bill and Sonja)

Today as the news from Selma and Saigon
poisons the air like fallout,
    I come again to see
the serene great picture that I love
and flames disfigured once
    and efficient evil may yet destroy.

Here space and time exist in light
the eye like the eye of faith believes.
    The seen, the known
dissolve in irridescence, become

illusive flesh of light
    that was not, was, forever is.

O light beheld as through refracting tears.
Here is the aura of that world
    each of us has lost.
Here is the shadow of its joy.

SEAMUS HEANEY

IRELAND * B. 1939

It may seem kind of demented to enjoy a poem of this nature but, it reminds me of some-thing that happened a few years ago. While I was away at college my sophomore year my grandfather passed away. When I read this poem it reminds me of the good times that I shared with my grandfather. The boy in the poem states, "I was embarrassed by old men standing up to shake my hand." The same thing happened to me when I walked into the fu-neral home. I will never understand why these men did this, but it made me feel better. The boy in the poem also mentions that he had not seen his brother in six weeks. I had not seen my grandfather for a couple of months before his death and it really tore at my heart because I wasn't able to share his last moments with him. Even though this poem is about a child who was killed it remains lodged in my heart because of the memories it brings back about my grandftather. He was a great man and his memory remains living inside of me because of this poem.

—Chad Clark, 22, Student, Vermillion, South Dakota

Mid-Term Break

I sat all morning in the college sick bay
Counting bells knelling classes to a close.
At two o'clock our neighbours drove me home.

In the porch I met my father crying—
He had always taken funerals in his stride—
And Big Jim Evans saying it was a hard blow.

The baby cooed and laughed and rocked the pram
When I came in, and I was embarrassed
By old men standing up to shake my hand

And tell me they were 'sorry for my trouble.'
Whispers informed strangers I was the eldest,
Away at school, as my mother held my hand

In hers and coughed out angry tearless sighs.
At ten o'clock the ambulance arrived
With the corpse, stanched and bandaged by the nurses.

Next morning I went up into the room. Snowdrops
And candles soothed the bedside; I saw him
For the first time in six weeks. Paler now,

Wearing a poppy bruise on his left temple,
He lay in the four foot box as in his cot.
No gaudy scars, the bumper knocked him clear.

A four foot box, a foot for every year.

WILLIAM ERNEST HENLEY

ENGLAND • 1849–1903

It came to my mind during the attack on Pearl Harbor and nearby Hickam Field. I was a private stationed at Hickam. For two-and-a-half to three hours, a buddy and I dodged straf-ing, bombing, and the usual horrors of wounded and dead. Fearful of dying and in despair, I raised a clenched fist to the skies and 'master of my fate' took hold in my mind, and 'cap-tain of my soul' fortified my resolve. We hadn't lost; we had a God-given direction to turn to. Later I learned that I had recalled a part of "Invictus."

—Arthur Scevola, 80, Retired Optometrist, Debary, Florida

I am submitting this wonderful poem to the Favorite Poem Project. I am a forty-nine-year-old woman and I have been incarcerated for the past twenty-three years, serving a life sen-tence. I have never done violence to anyone, yet I have paid dearly for my mistakes in my youth. I have handled the nightmare of prison with dignity, courage, and maturity. There have been times of despair that I thought I couldn't go on, yet somehow I have. This beau-tiful poem has been an inspiration and a source of strength and comfort to me whenever I close my eyes and recite it to myself.

—Diane Metzger, 49, State Prisoner, Newcastle, Delaware

I am an aged exile from New England, confined at home after a stroke some eighteen years ago. I hold Henley's poem to be a true masterpiece of inspiration. On the night of the stroke, as my inert body was being wheeled by paramedics down the corridors of Mass General Hos-pital, my mind staved off panic by silently repeating this poem.

—Joe Sabia, 74, Corpus Christi, Texas

Invictus

Out of the night that covers me,
    Black as the Pit from pole to pole,
I thank whatever gods may be
    For my unconquerable soul.

In the fell clutch of circumstance
    I have not winced nor cried aloud.
Under the bludgeonings of chance
    My head is bloody, but unbowed.

Beyond this place of wrath and tears
    Looms but the horror of the shade,

And yet the menace of the years
   Finds, and shall find me, unafraid:

It matters not how strait the gate,
   How charged with punishments the scroll,
I am the master of my fate:
   I am the captain of my soul.

GEORGE HERBERT

ENGLAND • 1593–1633

Years ago, I was writing a song for George Herbert on an electric typewriter. I stopped to read it—and it was really terrible. I got incredibly depressed and I put my head in my hands and sat there groaning, "I can't write, I'll never get this, I'm a terrible person. . . ." Then I heard this very loud sound coming up from the table through my elbows and into my ears. It was the sound of the typewriter's motor, very low pitched and rumbling, and I thought, "That's it! I'm going to build a talking table!" So I built a big electronic table that has tape decks and very powerful drivers inside. It compressed the sound and drove it up steel rods so that when you sat with your elbows on the table and your hands to your ears, it was like wearing a pair of very powerful headphones. I made some songs for the table in which some of the round sounds of the bassline came into one ear while in the other ear an acoustic piano played the same part, then they'd slowly switch places. In another for violin, the bow seemed to be drawn through your head as the sounds panned. Finally I got words to work. I used a line from George Herbert "Now I in you without a bodie move," panning from side to side so you hear two words per ear at a time. The word "move" traveled very slowly through your head. I liked the physical gesture of listening to this, and putting my head in my hands was exactly what I was doing when I thought of it—except now it was a gesture about listening and concentration instead of depression. George Herbert was a music lover as well as a parson. His poem is a kind of love letter to music.

—Laurie Anderson, 51, Performing Artist, New York, New York

Church-musick

Sweetest of sweets, I thank you: when displeasure
        Did through my bodie wound my minde,
You took me thence, and in your house of pleasure
        A daintie lodging me assign'd.

Now I in you without a bodie move,
        Rising and falling with your wings:
We both together sweetly live and love,
        Yet say sometimes, *God help poore Kings.*

Comfort, 'Ile die; for if you poste from me,
        Sure I shall do so, and much more:
But if I travell in your companie,
        You know the way to heavens doore.

I read it at my father's funeral in 1987; he and my mother both died in the month of May and the spring imagery seemed right. I like the line about bidding "the rash gazer wipe his eye," and the quiet reference to "season'd timber" in the last verse.

—Hugh O'Donnel, 53, Legal Aid Attorney, St. Paul, Virginia

Vertue

Sweet day, so cool, so calm, so bright,
The bridall of the earth and skie:
The dew shall weep thy fall to night;
            For thou must die.

Sweet rose, whose hue angrie and brave
Bids the rash gazer wipe his eye:
Thy root is ever in its grave,
            And thou must die.

Sweet spring, full of sweet dayes and roses,
A box where sweets compacted lie;
My musick shows ye have your closes,
            And all must die.

Onely a sweet and vertuous soul,
Like season'd timber, never gives;
But though the whole world turn to coal,
            Then chiefly lives.

ZBIGNIEW HERBERT

POLAND • B. 1924

The poem represents to me a simplicity of vision about the world, which is something I strive for myself. With great economy of means, as opposed to the glut of verbiage all around us, the poet expresses an admirable humility before nature and a deep sense of its calm permanence in the face of human frailty. It is called "The pebble," but is really a gem.

—Basil DePinto, 68, Hospital Chaplain, Piedmont, California

The pebble

The pebble
is a perfect creature

equal to itself
mindful of its limits

filled exactly
with pebbly meaning

with a scent which does not remind one of anything
does not frighten anything away does not arouse desire

its ardour and coldness
are just and full of dignity

I feel a heavy remorse
when I hold it in my hand
and its noble body
is permeated by false warmth

> —Pebbles cannot be tamed
> to the end they will look at us
> with a calm and very clear eye

Translated from the Polish by Czeslaw Milosz and Peter Dale Scott

NAZIM HIKMET

TURKEY * *1902–1963*

I identify with this poem about imprisonment, censorship, longing, and belief in oneself more than with any other poem I have read. This poem needs to be heard! Please.

—Chad Menville, 24, Student, New York, New York

Things I Didn't Know I Loved

it's 1962 March 28th
I'm sitting by the window on the Prague-Berlin train
night is falling
I never knew I liked
night descending like a tired bird on a smoky wet plain
I don't like
comparing nightfall to a tired bird

I didn't know I loved the earth
can someone who hasn't worked the earth love it
I've never worked the earth
it must be my only Platonic love

and here I've loved rivers all this time
whether motionless like this they curl skirting the hills
European hills crowned with chateaus
or whether stretched out flat as far as the eye can see
I know you can't wash in the same river even once
I know the river will bring new lights you'll never see
I know we live slightly longer than a horse but not nearly as long
   as a crow
I know this has troubled people before
    and will trouble those after me
I know all this has been said a thousand times before
    and will be said after me

I didn't know I loved the sky
cloudy or clear
the blue vault Andrei studied on his back at Borodino
in prison I translated both volumes of *War and Peace* into Turkish
I hear voices

not from the blue vault but from the yard
the guards are beating someone again

I didn't know I loved trees
bare beeches near Moscow in Peredelkino
they come upon me in winter noble and modest
beeches are Russian the way poplars are Turkish
"the poplars of Izmir
losing their leaves . . .
they call me The Knife . . .
        lover like a young tree . . .
I blow stately mansions sky-high"
in the Ilgaz woods in 1920 I tied an embroidered linen handkerchief
        to a pine bough for luck

I never knew I loved roads
even the asphalt kind
Vera's behind the wheel we're driving from Moscow to the Crimea
        Koktebele
        formerly "Goktepé ili" in Turkish
the two of us inside a closed box
the world flows past on both sides distant and mute
I was never so close to anyone in my life
bandits stopped me on the red road between Bolu and Geredé
        when I was eighteen
apart from my life I didn't have anything in the wagon they could take
and at eighteen our lives are what we value least
I've written this somewhere before
wading through a dark muddy street I'm going to the shadow play
Ramazan night
a paper lantern leading the way
maybe nothing like this ever happened
maybe I read it somewhere an eight-year-old boy
        going to the shadow play
Ramazan night in Istanbul holding his grandfather's hand
    his grandfather has on a fez and is wearing the fur coat
        with a sable collar over his robe
    and there's a lantern in the servant's hand
    and I can't contain myself for joy

flowers come to mind for some reason
poppies cactuses jonquils

in the jonquil garden in Kadikoy Istanbul I kissed Marika
fresh almonds on her breath
I was seventeen
my heart on a swing touched the sky
I didn't know I loved flowers
friends sent me three red carnations in prison

I just remembered the stars
I love them too
whether I'm floored watching them from below
or whether I'm flying at their side

I have some questions for the cosmonauts
were the stars much bigger
did they look like huge jewels on black velvet
        or apricots on orange
did you feel proud to get closer to the stars
I saw color photos of the cosmos in *Ogonek* magazine now don't
    be upset comrades but nonfigurative shall we say or abstract
    well some of them looked just like such paintings which is to
    say they were terribly figurative and concrete
my heart was in my mouth looking at them
they are our endless desire to grasp things
seeing them I could even think of death and not feel at all sad
I never knew I loved the cosmos

snow flashes in front of my eyes
both heavy wet steady snow and the dry whirling kind
I didn't know I liked snow

I never knew I loved the sun
even when setting cherry-red as now
in Istanbul too it sometimes sets in postcard colors
but you aren't about to paint it that way
I didn't know I loved the sea
    except the Sea of Azov
or how much

I didn't know I loved clouds
whether I'm under or up above them
whether they look like giants or shaggy white beasts

moonlight the falsest the most languid the most petit-bourgeois
strikes me
I like it

I didn't know I liked rain
whether it falls like a fine net or splatters against the glass my
    heart leaves me tangled up in a net or trapped inside a drop
    and takes off for uncharted countries I didn't know I loved
    rain but why did I suddenly discover all these passions sitting
    by the window on the Prague-Berlin train
is it because I lit my sixth cigarette
one alone could kill me
is it because I'm half dead from thinking about someone back in
    Moscow
her hair straw-blond eyelashes blue

the train plunges on through the pitch-black night
I never knew I liked the night pitch-black
sparks fly from the engine
I didn't know I loved sparks
I didn't know I loved so many things and I had to wait until sixty
    to find it out sitting by the window on the Prague-Berlin train
    watching the world disappear as if on a journey of no return

Translated from the Turkish by Randy Blasing and Mutlu Konuk

HUGO VON HOFMANNSTHAL

AUSTRIA • 1874–1929

My father is from Germany, and I have a strong attachment to the literature in that language. The poem is by an Austrian poet. It's basically about homesickness and love. As a musician, the sounds and rhythms of words are as important to me as their meanings. This poem, in a language that is often considered ugly, is one of the most flowingly beautiful works I know, in sound as well as meaning. The music brings the poem close to my heart, as does the imagery: of seeing the warm lights of the small town nestled in a valley, and longing to be there.

—Tom Schnauber, 29, Musician/Graduate Student, Ann Arbor, Michigan

Do you see the town?

Do you see the town, how it rests over there,
whispering, it nestles in the cloak of night?
The moon pours her silvery silken stream
down upon it in magical splendor.

The gentle night wind wafts its breath from there,
so ghostly, a dying gentle sound:
It cries in dreams, it breathes deeply and heavily,
it whispers, mysterious, alluringly frightened . . .

The dark town, it sleeps in my heart
with brilliance and fire, with painfully colorful splendor:
But its reflection floats around you, flatters you,
Hushed to a whisper, gliding through the night.

Translated from the German by Anne Adams

HOMER

GREECE • *Mid Ninth Century* B.C.E.

Life dealt me some wild cards. In 1995, after many years of depression, I found myself in the psychiatric ward wondering what had happened. During the process of my recovery from assorted mental and physical maladies, my psychiatrist came in and stood with one foot upon a chair, and recited Rudyard Kipling's "Gunga Din" to me, with the deep resonance and cadence of a true foot soldier. It thrilled my soul, and revived my thirst for poetry. Dr Stanley challenged me to read Homer's Iliad, *assuring me I could do it. My favorite lines of the Iliad are 439 to 479 of Book Six. Amidst all the carnage and cruelty by gods and men, Hektor shows a thoughtful and tender love for his wife and child.*

—Teresita Glaze, 51, Retail, Sioux Falls, South Dakota

from the Iliad (*Book Six, 439-79*)

Then tall Hektor of the shining helm answered her: 'All these
things are in my mind also, lady; yet I would feel deep shame
before the Trojans, and the Trojan women with trailing garments,
if like a coward I were to shrink aside from the fighting;
and the spirit will not let me, since I have learned to be valiant
and to fight always among the foremost ranks of the Trojans,
winning for my own self great glory, and for my father.
For I know this thing well in my heart, and my mind knows it:
there will come a day when sacred Ilion shall perish,
and Priam, and the people of Priam of the strong ash spear.
But it is not so much the pain to come of the Trojans
that troubles me, not even of Priam the king not Hekabe,
not the thought of my brothers who in their numbers and valour
shall drop in the dust under the hands of men who hate them,
as troubles me the thought of you, when some bronze-armoured
Achaian leads you off, taking away your day of liberty,
in tears; and in Argos you must work at the loom of another,
and carry water from the spring Messeis or Hypereia,
all unwilling, but strong will be the necessity upon you;
and some day seeing you shedding tears a man will say of you;
"This is the wife of Hektor, who was ever the bravest fighter
of the Trojans, breakers of horses, in the days when they fought about Ilion."
So will one speak of you; and for you it will be yet a fresh grief,
to be widowed of such a man who could fight off the day of your slavery.
But may I be dead and the piled earth hide me under before I
hear you crying and know by this that they drag you captive.'

So speaking glorious Hektor held out his arms to his baby,
who shrank back to his fair-girdled nurse's bosom
screaming, and frightened at the aspect of his own father,
terrified as he saw the bronze and the crest with its horse-hair,
nodding dreadfully, as he thought, from the peak of the helmet.
Then his beloved father laughed out, and his honoured mother,
and at once glorious Hektor lifted from his head the helmet
and laid it in all its shining upon the ground. Then taking
up his dear son he tossed him about in his arms, and kissed him,
and lifted his voice in prayer to Zeus and the other immortals:
"Zeus, and you other immortals, grant that this boy, who is my son,
may be as I am, pre-eminent among the Trojans,
great in strength, as am I, and rule strongly over Ilion;
and some day let them say of him: "He is better by far than his father",

Translated from the Greek by Richmond Lattimore

GERARD MANLEY HOPKINS

ENGLAND • 1844–1889

I am a retired Jesuit Priest, approaching seventy-seven years of life on this planet I am currently enjoying my retirement years here in Los Gatos, California, where God's Grandeur is everywhere.

—J. Ripley Caldwell, 77, Retired Jesuit Priest, Los Gatos, California

I have loved Hopkins's poetry since my mother introduced me to it as a child. We lived on a farm seven miles from town, with no car, but mother saw to it that we were introduced to good reading, poetry, and music from the time we were born. I loved the unexpected way his poetry did not go as you anticipated and you dare not let your mind waver. The words "the soil is bare now, nor can foot feel, being shod" sang in my soul as I ran barefoot with my siblings all over the farm, stream, and fields, when not astride one horse or another. O the restraint that sentence conjured in mind for one used to total freedom. But the line that lives with me still is this "There lives the dearest freshness deep down things." It was my lodestar, my constant, when I lost an infant son, my dear sister, my parents, and only recently my beloved husband of fifty-two years. Nestled in between those losses, O, such joy! There is today, at 74, "the dearest freshness deep down things."

—Juanita Yates, 74, Journalist, Monroe City, Missouri

God's Grandeur

The world is charged with the grandeur of God.
    It will flame out, like shining from shook foil;
    It gathers to a greatness, like the ooze of oil
Crushed. Why do men then now not reck his rod?
Generations have trod, have trod, have trod;
    And all is seared with trade; bleared, smeared with toil;
    And wears man's smudge and shares man's smell: the soil
Is bare now, nor can foot feel, being shod.

And for all this, nature is never spent;
    There lives the dearest freshness deep down things;
And though the last lights off the black West went
    Oh, morning, at the brown brink eastward, springs—
Because the Holy Ghost over the bent
    World broods with warm breast and with ah! bright wings.

My fiancée is truly the most freckled woman in the Northern Hemisphere, which makes her all the more glowing.

—Josh Merlin, 29, Bookstore Employee, Jamaica Plain, Massachusetts

Whenever I get tangled up in everyday frustrations, this poem reminds me to look outside myself. The way the words roll off my tongue never fails to cheer me: "rose moles," "fresh-firecoal chestnut-falls," "couple-colour as a brinded cow." Oddly, I'm not at all religious—and this is a praise poem—yet I can't help but share the poet's reverence for specific, wondrous details of the world around us.

—Judith Constans, 57, Attorney, Edmonds, Washington

Pied Beauty

Glory be to God for dappled things—
    For skies of couple-colour as a brinded cow;
        For rose-moles all in stipple upon trout that swim;
Fresh-firecoal chestnut-falls; finches' wings;
    Landscape plotted and pieced—fold, fallow, and plough;
        And áll trádes, their gear and tackle and trim.

All things counter, original, spare, strange;
    Whatever is fickle, freckled (who knows how?)
        With swift, slow; sweet, sour; adazzle, dim;
He fathers-forth whose beauty is past change:
                Praise him.

I have always marveled at the airiness of the language employed by Hopkins to describe this detached and wild bird in full flight. I find this poem as arresting today as I did when I first read it at Pensacola in the summer of 1949 in navy flight school. Its naturalness, tempo, and mysticism express the beauty of flight. I would often recite the poem in the course of my 299 carrier landings in the Corsair while stationed in the Mediterranean. The poem brought comfort and solace at that dangerous time.

—Richard Greenwood, 71, Retired Circuit Court Judge, Green Bay, Wisconsin

I was nineteen, had just entered Fresno State College at mid-term and, in an English Lit class, discovered Gerard Manley Hopkins. The man was drunk with words! "The Wind-hover" blew me away. I read it aloud in my bedroom over and over. The words were chew-able. It was syncopated; it was Gershwin; it was Cole Porter; it was de-lovely. I had no idea what half the words meant and only the vaguest realization that it was about a bird that, to Hopkins, was a big deal. He had dedicated it "To Christ Our Lord." I was a Jew who had never been in a synagogue, but, hey, if that was Hopkins's cup of tea, mazel tov. I looked up the words in an unabridged dictionary, because some of the time he used archaic meanings. I finally pieced most of it together and understood enough of it to know that it was magnificent. How often in the decades of my life has my heart in hiding stirred for the achievement, the mastery of Hopkins: a faith that caused his "blue-bleak" life to "gash gold-vermilion." I believe there are other poets as good as he, but none finer in this or any other century. "The Windhover" is his dawn-drawn autobiography.

Don Levy, 73, Retired Teacher, Screenwriter and Actor, Lodi, California

The Windhover

To Christ Our Lord

I caught this morning morning's minion, kingdom
   of daylight's dauphin, dapple-dawn-drawn Falcon, in his riding
   Of the rolling level underneath him steady air, and striding
High there, how he rung upon the rein of a wimpling wing
In his ecstasy then off, off forth on swing,
   As a skate's heel sweeps smooth on a bow-bend: the hurl and gliding
   Rebuffed the big wind. My heart in hiding
Stirred for a bird,—the achieve of, the mastery of the thing!

Brute beauty and valour and act, oh, air, pride, plume, here
   Buckle, AND the fire that breaks from thee then, a billion
Times told lovelier, more dangerous, O my chevalier!

   No wonder of it: shéer plód makes plough down sillion
Shine, and blue-bleak embers, ah my dear,
   Fall, gall themselves, and gash gold-vermilion.

A. E. HOUSMAN

ENGLAND • 1859–1936

Because I cannot read it without shuddering with pleasure.

—William Maxwell, 90, Novelist, New York, New York

Diffugere Nives

Horace, Odes, iv, 7

The snows are fled away, leaves on the shaws
　　And grasses in the mead renew their birth,
The river to the river-bed withdraws,
　　And altered is the fashion of the earth.

The Nymphs and Graces three put off their fear
　　And unapparelled in the woodland play.
The swift hour and the brief prime of the year
　　Say to the soul, *Thou wast not born for aye.*

Thaw follows frost; hard on the heel of spring
　　Treads summer sure to die, for hard on hers
Comes autumn with his apples scattering;
　　Then back to wintertide, when nothing stirs.

But oh, whate'er the sky-led seasons mar,
　　Moon upon moon rebuilds it with her beams;
Come *we* where Tullus and where Ancus are
　　And good Aeneas, we are dust and dreams.

Torquatus, if the gods in heaven shall add
　　The morrow to the day, what tongue has told?
Feast then thy heart, for what thy heart has had
　　The fingers of no heir will ever hold.

When thou descendest once the shades among,
　　The stern assize and equal judgment o'er,
Not thy long lineage nor thy golden tongue,
　　No, nor thy righteousness, shall friend thee more.

Night holds Hippolytus the pure of stain,
    Diana steads him nothing, he must stay;
And Theseus leaves Pirithous in the chain
    The love of comrades cannot take away.

LANGSTON HUGHES

UNITED STATES • 1902–1967

My interpretation of this poem written by Langston Hughes may not be the same as his. But a poem is what I choose to make of it and this one is a description of me. It explains how I feel about life. I am a female Cambodian growing up in America, the "Land of the Free and the Home of the Brave," but still I am not free. I may be living in America but I am raised in the old-fashioned Cambodian ways. Asian tradition for daughters is very strict. It is so hard for me to see my friends having a sleep over and the only person missing is me. I walk around school with a big smile on my face but inside I am a caged bird just waiting to be free. Life has never been easy for me especially with my parents' problems. Their problems started during the Khmer Rouge Genocide in the early '70s. Two of their sons passed away in front of their faces, killed by the Khmer Rouge. They still had the courage to get out of Cambodia and find refuge for us in America. Growing up in America is also hard. We've lived in many poor neighborhoods and I've seen it all—spousal abuse, drug dealing, even murder. We have escaped that life now but it still haunts me. When I am finished with school I plan to join the Peace Corps.

—Pov Chin, 19, Student, Stockton, California

Minstrel Man

Because my mouth
Is wide with laughter
And my throat
Is deep with song,
You do not think
I suffer after
I have held my pain
So long?

Because my mouth
Is wide with laughter,
You do not hear
My inner cry?
Because my feet
Are gay with dancing,
You do not know
I die?

I am a native Atlantan. I was born and raised in the segregation of Atlanta. I've seen it all. From the crosses burning on stone mountains to the people spitting on me walking down the street here. As much as things have changed, they tend to remain the same. And sometimes I still feel that I can't ride on the merry-go-round. Part of that is on both sides of the fence—black and white. Because we don't take time to know each other. We work side by side, day in and day out, we go to lunch, but after 5:00 and on the weekends, how many of us—black or white—know each other's people? I have the same problems you do. I have a family. I bleed the same way. I served seven years in the service during Vietnam. But we don't take the time to know each other. As long as this happens, we will integrate this society but will never assimilate. Because we don't care enough about each other. We say "God loves everybody" but we don't do it. It ends up being almost a thing of saying it is the folkways of race and the mores of southern life. It's here. I want to ride that train one day. And the first step starts with me loving you.

—Howard Michael Henderson, 56, Community Involvement Coordinator, Chamblee, Georgia

Merry-Go-Round

COLORED CHILD AT CARNIVAL

Where is the Jim Crow section
On this merry-go-round,
Mister, cause I want to ride?
Down South where I come from
White and colored
Can't sit side by side.
Down South on the train
There's a Jim Crow car.
On the bus we're put in the back—
But there ain't no back
To a merry-go-round!
Where's the horse
For a kid that's black?

If my parents were to speak to me in prose about their life, they would use the words of this poem to express themselves. As a child of immigrant parents who arrived here 14 years ago, I can only now imagine their struggle as they began their life anew in a foreign country, the language of which they did not know. Yet they have thrived, providing me with an education perhaps beyond their means in their native country. When I see myself faltering or giving up or becoming complacent, I remind myself of their daily struggles and it gives me fuel for the road ahead.

—Yoon Elizabeth Ji, 24, Operations Manager, Honolulu, Hawaii

I have always loved this poem, but it became really significant for me in 1976 when I began to work in the adult literacy program in my community. Many of the students came back to school against great odds. They fought the put-downs of their family members for being "too stupid to complete school." They fought against poverty, poor self-esteem, welfare, and abuses of all kinds during their lives because they lacked an adequate education.

—Sheila Hightower Allen, 44, Adult Literacy Instructor, Augusta, Georgia

To me, this poem is a determination poem. It's saying that regardless of what happens or what gets in your way, you have to keep going to reach those goals.

—Lee Sanders, 19, Stock/Sales, Jackson, Mississippi

Mother to Son

Well, son, I'll tell you:
Life for me ain't been no crystal stair.
It's had tacks in it,
And splinters,
And boards torn up,
And places with no carpet on the floor—
Bare.
But all the time
I'se been a-climbin' on,
And reachin' landin's,
And turnin' corners,
And sometimes goin' in the dark
Where there ain't been no light.
So boy, don't you turn back.
Don't you set down on the steps
'Cause you finds it's kinder hard.
Don't you fall now—
For I'se still goin', honey,
I'se still climbin',
And life for me ain't been no crystal stair.

RICHARD HUGO

UNITED STATES • *1923–1982*

I am from Greece. My mom died of breast cancer in '89. My dad left after her death. So I really never knew home. I have lived in Greece, Germany, North Carolina, and in Morristown, Pennsylvania. Now I am in Montana. And I have found home. I love this poem so much because it reminds me of freedom, love, life, happiness, family, everyday life and stress. It's really more than what the words say. You have to read it between the lines to understand. Or maybe live in Montana. I still find it hard to believe that this simple poem made me understand that I'm home. It's 4:00 A.M. right now, and I am at one of my two jobs. I am a night watch at one of the dormitories at the University of Montana. I'm a journalism major, and even though I rarely get to sleep anymore, I'm happy. I have three magnificent siblings who live close to me. I really can't complain. I live in the most beautiful place on earth.

—Despina Kelessidou, 20, Student, Missoula, Montana

Driving Montana

The day is a woman who loves you. Open.
Deer drink close to the road and magpies
spray from your car. Miles from any town
your radio comes in strong, unlikely
Mozart from Belgrade, rock and roll
from Butte. Whatever the next number,
you want to hear it. Never has your Buick
found this forward a gear. Even
the tuna salad in Reedpoint is good.

Towns arrive ahead of imagined schedule.
Absorakee at one. Or arrive so late—
Silesia at nine—you recreate the day.
Where did you stop along the road
and have fun? Was there a runaway horse?
Did you park at that house, the one
alone in a void of grain, white with green
trim and red fence, where you know you lived
once? You remembered the ringing creek,
the soft brown forms of far off bison.
You must have stayed hours, then drove on.
In the motel you know you'd never seen it before.

Tomorrow will open again, the sky wide
as the mouth of a wild girl, friable
clouds you lose yourself to. You are lost
in miles of land without people, without
one fear of being found, in the dash
of rabbits, soar of antelope, swirl
merge and clatter of streams.

RANDALL JARRELL

UNITED STATES • 1914–1965

I first encountered this poem back when I was in graduate school and we were all very Bo-hemian in the '60s, and we would sit around and read poetry to one another. I first heard it read by the wife of a friend of mine. The guys were all saying "Oh, yeah, cool, Randall Jar-rell." This woman and I looked at each other; it was just this shock of recognition. Recently, when I went back to it, I thought "Whoa, it's so sad." But now that I'm of an age that's closer to the speaker of the poem it's just uncanny the things in it that I identify with now. I'm not as sad as this woman. I don't really feel lost and confused the way she does. But the fact is that the more things change the more they stay the same. Even though this is very much a woman of the '50s speaking, even now in the '90s you might have a good job, respect in your career, a wonderful husband, as I do, who thinks you're exciting, but there's still this messed up way that this culture looks at aging—especially women and aging. That's what hit me so about this poem. And the fact that a man wrote this poem: that was the thing that blew me away about it originally and still does.

—Kay Bonetti Callison, 58, General Manager of a Public Radio Station,
　Columbia, Missouri

Next Day

Moving from Cheer to Joy, from Joy to All,
I take a box
And add it to my wild rice, my Cornish game hens.
The slacked or shorted, basketed, identical
Food-gathering flocks
Are selves I overlook. Wisdom, said William James,

Is learning what to overlook. And I am wise
If that is wisdom.
Yet somehow, as I buy All from these shelves
And the boy takes it to my station wagon,
What I've become
Troubles me even if I shut my eyes.

When I was young and miserable and pretty
And poor, I'd wish
What all girls wish: to have a husband,
A house and children. Now that I'm old, my wish
Is womanish:
That the boy putting groceries in my car

See me. It bewilders me he doesn't see me.
For so many years
I was good enough to eat: the world looked at me
And its mouth watered. How often they have undressed me,
The eyes of strangers!
And, holding their flesh within my flesh, their vile

Imaginings within my imagining,
I too have taken
The chance of life. Now the boy pats my dog
And we start home. Now I am good.
The last mistaken,
Ecstatic, accidental bliss, the blind

Happiness that, bursting, leaves upon the palm
Some soap and water—
It was so long ago, back in some Gay
Twenties, Nineties, I don't know . . . Today I miss
My lovely daughter
Away at school, my sons away at school,

My husband away at work—I wish for them.
The dog, the maid,
And I go through the sure unvarying days
At home in them. As I look at my life,
I am afraid
Only that it will change, as I am changing:

I am afraid, this morning, of my face.
It looks at me
From the rear-view mirror, with the eyes I hate,
The smile I hate. Its plain, lined look
Of gray discovery
Repeats to me: "You're old." That's all, I'm old.

And yet I'm afraid, as I was at the funeral
I went to yesterday.
My friend's cold made-up face, granite among its flowers,
Her undressed, operated-on, dressed body
Were my face and body.
As I think of her I hear her telling me

How young I seem; I *am* exceptional;
I think of all I have.
But really no one is exceptional,
No one has anything, I'm anybody,
I stand beside my grave
Confused with my life, that is commonplace and solitary.

After a tour during WWII as a tail gunner on a B-24, I discovered this poem. For an uned-ucated, innocent, naïve adolescent, that experience as part of the bombing campaign over Europe had a most profound and lasting impact on me. To this day I often return to the lines of that poem as a symbol of the days of my youth.

—Kenneth Blake, 73, Retired, West Brookfield, Massachussets

Losses

It was not dying: everybody died.
It was not dying: we had died before
In the routine crashes—and our fields
Called up the papers, wrote home to our folks,
And the rates rose, all because of us.
We died on the wrong page of the almanac,
Scattered on mountains fifty miles away;
Diving on haystacks, fighting with a friend,
We blazed up on the lines we never saw.
We died like aunts or pets or foreigners.
(When we left high school nothing else had died
For us to figure we had died like.)

In our new planes, with our new crews, we bombed
The ranges by the desert or the shore,
Fired at towed targets, waited for our scores—
And turned into replacements and woke up
One morning, over England, operational.
It wasn't different: but if we died
It was not an accident but a mistake
(But an easy one for anyone to make).
We read our mail and counted up our missions—
In bombers named for girls, we burned
The cities we had learned about in school—
Till our lives wore out; our bodies lay among

The people we had killed and never seen.
When we lasted long enough they gave us medals;
When we died they said, "Our casualties were low."
They said, "Here are the maps"; we burned the cities.

It was not dying—no, not ever dying;
But the night I died I dreamed that I was dead,
And the cities said to me: "Why are you dying?
We are satisfied, if you are; but why did I die?"

ROBINSON JEFFERS

UNITED STATES • 1887–1962

I am forty-four years old, a native of California. I work part-time as a blood bank courier transporting blood along our circulatory system of highways, saving lives in my cellular way. For love and money, I have done many things, from navy frogman to day laborer—and not in the upwardly mobile sequence society would deem. I have stood on snowy Alaskan mountaintops, hunched hungover in the Ensenada jail, Aqua-Lunged above rainbow reefs in the Philippines, gone bankrupt, piloted a single-engine aircraft with precious human cargo through a jolting Sierra windstorm, trucked freight through LA rush-hour traffic, and lit fireworks at Battery Park on the Fourth of July. I have no scholastic degrees, nor have I attended prestigious institutions or received awards. I've been married to my wife Debra for seventeen years, no children, no nest egg. Who I am is who I will be. For your project I chose "The Purse-Seine" by Robinson Jeffers. I picked this special poem because, despite its fatalistic tone, it asserts truth through a beautiful, haunting metaphor. In this poem, I am able to both observe and, like one of the frantic, phosphorescent fish, thrash—as one in the population gathered, insulated from the earth, hauled in, dependent. When I read this poem I honestly sense that, like death, there is no escape; yet I undergo a great catharsis, and regain hope. I read it back when isolation, helplessness, and panic roil over me as I tread in our deep, defiled modern sea.

—Vaughn Clark, 44, Blood Bank Courier/Truck Driver, Carpinteria, California

The Purse-Seine

Our sardine fishermen work at night in the dark of the moon; daylight or moonlight
They could not tell where to spread the net, unable to see the phosphorescence of
    the shoals of fish.
They work northward from Monterey, coasting Santa Cruz; off New Year's Point or
    off Pigeon Point
The look-out man will see some lakes of milk-color light on the sea's night-purple;
    he points, and the helmsman
Turns the dark prow, the motorboat circles the gleaming shoal and drifts out her
    seine-net. They close the circle
And purse the bottom of the net, then with great labor haul it in.

                                                  I cannot tell you
How beautiful the scene is, and a little terrible, then, when the crowded fish
Know they are caught, and wildly beat from one wall to the other of their closing
    destiny the phosphorescent
Water to a pool of flame, each beautiful slender body sheeted with flame, like a live
    rocket

A comet's tail wake of clear yellow flame; while outside the narrowing
Floats and cordage of the net great sea-lions come up to watch, sighing in the dark;
    the vast walls of night
Stand erect to the stars.

                                            Lately I was looking from a night mountain-top
On a wide city, the colored splendor, galaxies of light: how could I help but recall
    the seine-net
Gathering the luminous fish? I cannot tell you how beautiful the city appeared, and
    a little terrible.
I thought, We have geared the machines and locked all together into interdepen-
    dence; we have built the great cities; now
There is no escape. We have gathered vast populations incapable of free survival,
    insulated
From the strong earth, each person in himself helpless, on all dependent.
    The circle is closed, and the net
Is being hauled in. They hardly feel the cords drawing, yet they shine already.
    The inevitable mass-disasters
Will not come in our time nor in our children's, but we and our children
Must watch the net draw narrower, government take all powers—or revolution, and
    the new government
Take more than all, add to kept bodies kept souls—or anarchy, the mass-disasters.

                            These things are Progress;
Do you marvel our verse is troubled or frowning, while it keeps its reason?
    Or it lets go, lets the mood flow
In the manner of the recent young men into mere hysteria, splintered gleams,
    crackled laughter. But they are quite wrong.
There is no reason for amazement: surely one always knew that cultures decay, and
    life's end is death.

JAMES WELDON JOHNSON

UNITED STATES • *1871–1938*

I have loved this poem since the seventh grade when my teacher, Mr. John Bean, taught me the difference between a poem read and a poem read aloud. Mr. Bean allowed his best readers (three little black girls) to perform the poem on stage before the whole school. I can still remember the hush between the moment I stopped reading and when the auditorium shook with applause. It still gives me goose bumps. The experience taught me so much. I learned to love to read poetry. I also learned that a child's voice can be powerful. This poem is so much a part of me that during a recent in-depth study of the Bible I was shocked to discover that so much of what I thought I knew about the creation story was not Genesis, but Johnson!

—Eve Riley, 43, Judge/Writer, St. Louis, Missouri

Many years ago when I was a small child, Sunday was truly a day for family. In the early evening, before and after dinner everyone was at home. One Sunday, my father's sister, her husband, and a young lady came to visit. My aunt and uncle did not know this young lady very well. She was a new neighbor and came with them just for the outing. After dinner, the conversation turned to books and literature. This young lady was asked about her favorite poem. She chose this poem. When asked if there was a particular verse, she replied, "All of it." She stood up in the middle of our living room and very dramatically and passionately recited verbatim the entire poem. I was in fourth grade at the time, and was quite impressed. Only later, after reading the poem, did I marvel that she was able to spontaneously recite a poem with such flair to a group of strangers.

—Natalie Borum, 60, Retired Reading Specialist, Fair Lawn, New Jersey

The Creation

(A Negro Sermon from GOD'S TROMBONES)

And God stepped out on space,
And he looked around and said:
I'm lonely—
I'll make me a world.

And far as the eye of God could see
Darkness covered everything,
Blacker than a hundred midnights
Down in a cypress swamp.

Then God smiled,
And the light broke,

And the darkness rolled up on one side,
And the light stood shining on the other,
And God said: That's good!

Then God reached out and took the light in His hands,
And God rolled the light around in His hands
Until He made the sun;
And He set that sun a-blazing in the heavens.
And the light that was left from making the sun
God gathered it up in a shining ball
And flung it against the darkness,

Spangling the night with the moon and stars.
Then down between
The darkness and the light
He hurled the world;
And God said: That's good!

Then God himself stepped down—
And the sun was on His right hand,
And the moon was on His left;
The stars were clustered about His head,
And the earth was under His feet.
And God walked, and where He trod
His footsteps hollowed the valleys out
And bulged the mountains up.

Then He stopped and looked and saw
That the earth was hot and barren.
So God stepped over to the edge of the world
And He spat out the seven seas—
He batted His eyes, and the lightnings flashed—
He clapped His hands, and the thunders rolled—
And the waters above the earth came down,
The cooling waters came down.

Then the green grass sprouted,
And the little red flowers blossomed,
The pine tree pointed his finger to the sky,
And the oak spread out his arms,
The lakes cuddled down in the hollows of the ground,
And the rivers ran down to the sea;

And God smiled again,
And the rainbow appeared,
And curled itself around His shoulder.

Then God raised His arm and He waved His hand
Over the sea and over the land,
And He said: Bring forth! Bring forth!
And quicker than God could drop His hand,
Fishes and fowls
And beasts and birds
Swam the rivers and the seas,
Roamed the forests and the woods,
And split the air with their wings.
And God said: That's good!

Then God walked around,
And God looked around
On all that He had made.
He looked at His sun,
And He looked at His moon,
And He looked at His little stars;
He looked on His world
With all its living things,
And God said: I'm lonely still.

Then God sat down—
On the side of a hill where He could think;
By a deep, wide river He sat down;
With His head in His hands,
God thought and thought,
Till He thought: I'll make me a man!

Up from the bed of the river
God scooped the clay;
And by the bank of the river
He kneeled Him down;

And there the great God Almighty
Who lit the sun and fixed it in the sky,
Who flung the stars to the most far corner of the night,
Who rounded the earth in the middle of His hand;
This Great God,

Like a mammy bending over her baby,
Kneeled down in the dust
Toiling over a lump of clay
Till He shaped it in His own image;

Then into it He blew the breath of life,
And man became a living soul.
Amen. Amen.

BEN JONSON

ENGLAND • 1573–1637

It is so meaningful to me because of feelings I have for my first love, who I was engaged to in my youth, but did not marry. The beauty of it is very moving to me now, as it was then.

—Verna Boutte, Lewisville, Texas

Song To Celia

Drink to me only with thine eyes,
   And I will pledge with mine;
Or leave a kiss but in the cup,
   And I'll not look for wine.
The thirst that from the soul doth rise
   Doth ask a drink divine;
But might I of Jove's nectar sup,
   I would not change for thine.

I sent thee late a rosy wreath,
   Not so much honoring thee
As giving it a hope that there
   It could not withered be.
But thou thereon didst only breathe,
   And sent'st it back to me;
Since when it grows, and smells, I swear,
   Not of itself but thee.

Because it compresses exquisitely the voices of a bereaved father, a guilty Christian, and a poet.

—John Pasanen, 61, Teacher, Burlington, Connecticut

On My First Son

Farewell, thou child of my right hand, and joy;
My sin was too much hope of thee, loved boy:
Seven years thou'wert lent to me, and I thee pay,
Exacted by thy fate, on the just day.
O could I lose all father now! for why

Will man lament the state he should envý,
To have so soon 'scaped world's and flesh's rage,
And, if no other misery, yet age?
Rest in soft peace, and asked, say, "Here doth lie
Ben Jonson his best piece of poetry."
For whose sake henceforth all his vows be such
As what he loves may never like too much.

JAMES JOYCE

IRELAND • 1882–1941

During my adolescent years, my father and I struggled through a stormy relationship. When I was twenty-two, just as we were making the transition to a more peaceful relationship, he died of a heart attack. A colleague brought this poem to my attention years ago. Now, when I see my father's smile in my daughter's face—and I look at a child from a parent's perspective—I wish my father were here to experience it with me.

—Alex Salachi, 45, Library Media Specialist/Teacher, Mansfield, Massachusetts

Ecce Puer

Of the dark past
A child is born;
With joy and grief
My heart is torn.

Calm in his cradle
The living lies.
May love and mercy
Unclose his eyes!

Young life is breathed
On the glass;
The world that was not
Comes to pass.

A child is sleeping:
An old man gone.
O, father forsaken,
Forgive your son!

JOHN KEATS

ENGLAND • 1795–1821

I've loved Keats since high school. Last year, on a difficult day my first fall of full-time teaching, "Ode to a Nightingale" struck my heart again. My students were struggling with Romantic poetry; their struggles were due in part to the mechanical way they read aloud at each class meeting. I looked at the page where Keats's ode lay waiting and, filled with un-teacherly feelings of hostility toward my students and defensive love of the poem, wrested, as I then thought, the class from itself and decided that I would read it. My voice broke on the first line. I read on; and I watched my students watching me with attention and emotion as together we heard the sorrow and isolation the poem expresses. My mistaken sense of my students became clear. Of course, I realized, they hadn't been reading poetry "right"—not because they couldn't, but because they hadn't really heard it read: my fault. In the rich tones of Keats's poem, whose theme I'd thought simply to claim for myself, together we moved a little toward his ideal, often dismissed, of sounding the intensity of sadness and finding its sweetness.

—Alyson Bardsley, 35, Teacher, Staten Island, New York

Ode to a Nightingale

I

My heart aches, and a drowsy numbness pains
  My sense, as though of hemlock I had drunk,
Or emptied some dull opiate to the drains
  One minute past, and Lethe-wards had sunk:
'Tis not through envy of thy happy lot,
  But being too happy in thine happiness—
    That thou, light-wingéd Dryad of the trees,
      In some melodious plot
  Of beechen green, and shadows numberless,
    Singest of summer in full-throated ease.

2

O, for a draught of vintage! that hath been
  Cooled a long age in the deep-delvéd earth,
Tasting of Flora and the country green,
  Dance, and Provençal song, and sunburnt mirth!
O for a beaker full of the warm South,
  Full of the true, the blushful Hippocrene,
    With beaded bubbles winking at the brim,
      And purple-stainéd mouth;

That I might drink, and leave the world unseen,
   And with thee fade away into the forest dim:

3

Fade far away, dissolve, and quite forget
   What thou among the leaves hast never known,
The weariness, the fever, and the fret
   Here, where men sit and hear each other groan;
Where palsy shakes a few, sad, last gray hairs,
   Where youth grows pale, and specter-thin, and dies,
     Where but to think is to be full of sorrow
       And leaden-eyed despairs,
   Where Beauty cannot keep her lustrous eyes,
    Or new Love pine at them beyond tomorrow.

4

Away! away! for I will fly to thee,
   Not charioted by Bacchus and his pards,
But on the viewless wings of Poesy,
   Though the dull brain perplexes and retards:
Already with thee! tender is the night,
   And haply the Queen-Moon is on her throne,
     Clustered around by all her starry Fays;
       But here there is no light,
   Save what from heaven is with the breezes blown
    Through verdurous glooms and winding mossy ways.

5

I cannot see what flowers are at my feet,
   Nor what soft incense hangs upon the boughs,
But, in embalméd darkness, guess each sweet
   Wherewith the seasonable month endows
The grass, the thicket, and the fruit tree wild;
   White hawthorn, and the pastoral eglantine,
     Fast fading violets covered up in leaves;
       And mid-May's eldest child,
   The coming musk-rose, full of dewy wine,
    The murmurous haunt of flies on summer eves.

6

Darkling I listen; and for many a time
   I have been half in love with easeful Death,
Called him soft names in many a muséd rhyme,
   To take into the air my quiet breath;
Now more than ever seems it rich to die,
   To cease upon the midnight with no pain,
      While thou art pouring forth thy soul abroad
         In such an ecstasy!
   Still wouldst thou sing, and I have ears in vain—
     To thy high requiem become a sod.

7

Thou wast not born for death, immortal Bird!
   No hungry generations tread thee down;
The voice I hear this passing night was heard
   In ancient days by emperor and clown:
Perhaps the selfsame song that found a path
   Through the sad heart of Ruth, when, sick for home,
      She stood in tears amid the alien corn;
         The same that ofttimes hath
   Charmed magic casements, opening on the foam
     Of perilous seas, in faery lands forlorn.

8

Forlorn! the very word is like a bell
   To toll me back from thee to my sole self!
Adieu! the fancy cannot cheat so well
   As she is famed to do, deceiving elf.
Adieu! adieu! thy plaintive anthem fades
   Past the near meadows, over the still stream,
      Up the hill side; and now 'tis buried deep
         In the next valley-glades:
   Was it a vision, or a waking dream?
     Fled is that music:—Do I wake or sleep?

I am an attorney in Dallas, Texas. I am married and have two small children. One of my greatest joys is hiking and backpacking with my friends. Some of the best moments of my life have been sharing a sense of solitude with others in the mountains. This is where I see God the clearest. Sharing a sense of solitude may seem like a paradox, but I think anyone who has spent time in the wilderness understands this. I think it is what Keats had in mind.

—William O. Holston Jr., 42, Attorney, Dallas, Texas

Sonnet VII

O Solitude! if I must with thee dwell,
   Let it not be among the jumbled heap
   Of murky buildings; climb with me the steep,—
Nature's observatory—whence the dell,
Its flowery slopes, its river's crystal swell,
   May seem a span; let me thy vigils keep
   'Mongst boughs pavillion'd, where the deer's swift leap
Startles the wild bee from the fox-glove bell.
But though I'll gladly trace these scenes with thee,
   Yet the sweet converse of an innocent mind,
Whose words are images of thoughts refin'd,
   Is my soul's pleasure; and it sure must be
Almost the highest bliss of human-kind,
   When to thy haunts two kindred spirits flee.

I love that long thrumming sentence which is nonetheless direct, piercing. I have always found this poem riveting, and riveting to any audience—that "you" like a stake through any listener. I also think the poem is prescient—almost a modern poem.

—Sally Ball, 30, Homemaker, St. Louis, Missouri

This Living Hand

This living hand, now warm and capable
Of earnest grasping, would, if it were cold
And in the icy silence of the tomb,
So haunt thy days and chill thy dreaming nights
That thou wouldst wish thine own heart dry of blood
So in my veins red life might stream again,
And thou be conscience-calmed—see here it is—
I hold it towards you.

JANE KENYON

UNITED STATES • 1947–1995

I live with cancer; I know there is an otherwise.

—Jamien Morehouse, 48, Artist, Rockport, Maine

Otherwise

I got out of bed
on two strong legs.
It might have been
otherwise. I ate
cereal, sweet
milk, ripe, flawless
peach. It might
have been otherwise.
I took the dog uphill
to the birch wood.
All morning I did
the work I love.

At noon I lay down
with my mate. It might
have been otherwise.
We ate dinner together
at a table with silver
candlesticks. It might
have been otherwise.
I slept in a bed
in a room with paintings
on the walls, and
planned another day
just like this day.
But one day, I know,
it will be otherwise.

GALWAY KINNELL

UNITED STATES • B. 1927

Over the years, this poem resonates deeper and deeper. Now I am caring for my eighty-four-year-old husband who has Alzheimer's. There is the danger of going through my life in a mindless, perfunctory way. This poem keeps me true to the holiness of everyday life.

—Sally Moore, 64, Retired Psychotherapist, Missoula, Montana

Such a great understanding of animal and human nature.

—Margery Cornwell, 63, Professor, Brooklyn, New York

I became familiar with this poem first by hearing it read on an audiotape from a talk by a Buddhist meditation teacher. She used the poem to introduce the concept of metta *which translates from Pali as "lovingkindness." I could not believe how perfectly it expressed just what I needed, and what I know most of us need, to be allowed to flower in one's own way from within, to benefit from self-blessing.*

—Barbara Dorfman, 49, Social Worker/Psychotherapist, Miller Place, New York

St. Francis and the Sow

The bud
stands for all things,
even for those things that don't flower,
for everything flowers, from within, of self-blessing;
though sometimes it is necessary
to reteach a thing its loveliness,
to put a hand on its brow
of the flower
and retell it in words and in touch
it is lovely
until it flowers again from within, of self-blessing;
as Saint Francis
put his hand on the creased forehead
of the sow, and told her in words and in touch
blessings of earth on the sow, and the sow
began remembering all down her thick length,
from the earthen snout all the way
through the fodder and slops to the spiritual curl of the tail,
from the hard spininess spiked out from the spine
down through the great broken heart

to the sheer blue milken dreaminess spurting and shuddering
from the fourteen teats into the fourteen mouths sucking and blowing beneath
    them;
the long, perfect loveliness of sow.

YUSEF KOMUNYAKAA

UNITED STATES • B. 1947

I served in Vietnam with a USAF tactical unit in 1965 and again in Saigon in '71. For years I could not face the Memorial "Wall." This poem opened my emotions and I always think of it when I visit the wall.

—Michael Lythgoe, 58, Foundation Director, Gainesville, Virginia

Facing It

My black face fades,
hiding inside the black granite.
I said I wouldn't,
dammit: No tears.
I'm stone. I'm flesh.
My clouded reflection eyes me
like a bird of prey, the profile of night
slanted against morning. I turn
this way—the stone lets me go.
I turn that way—I'm inside
the Vietnam Veterans Memorial
again, depending on the light
to make a difference.
I go down the 58,022 names,
half-expecting to find
my own in letters like smoke.
I touch the name Andrew Johnson;
I see the booby trap's white flash.
Names shimmer on a woman's blouse
but when she walks away
the names stay on the wall.
Brushstrokes flash, a red bird's
wings cutting across my stare.
The sky. A plane in the sky.
A white vet's image floats
closer to me, then his pale eyes
look through mine. I'm a window.
He's lost his right arm
inside the stone. In the black mirror
a woman's trying to erase names:
No, she's brushing a boy's hair.

STANLEY KUNITZ

UNITED STATES • B. 1905

I have been a lover of poetry since my mother bought me Robert Louis Stevenson's A Child's Garden of Verses *for a Christmas present when I was seven. I do not remember her teaching me nursery rhymes, although I must have learned them somewhere. She was not a poetry reader then or ever, so I do not know how it came about that she chose the book for me. When I was nine, I wrote my first poem, which she kept among her important papers until she died. I am not particularly well-educated and do not understand a lot of poetry. Sometimes this makes me feel angry and cheated. Sometimes it doesn't matter that I don't understand, when I am delighted by the sound and rhythm alone. I was not only delighted by the sound and rhythm of Stanley Kunitz's poem; I understood it immediately. Every time I read it, it makes me cry and it makes me laugh. It makes me recognize myself. I am in my early sixties; not so very old nor as old as I hope to become, but older than I've been before. Earnest and intense, I have always looked forward to being changed, exalted to a higher place, transformed. No therapy, religious dogma, or spiritual practice has succeeded in doing that. Stanley Kunitz's poem brings a satisfying acceptance of my hornworminess to me. Isn't poetry wonderful?*

—Donna Bickel, 62, Bookkeeper, Larkspur, California

Hornworm: Autumn Lamentation

Since that first morning when I crawled
into the world, a naked grubby thing,
and found the world unkind,
my dearest faith has been that this
is but a trial: I shall be changed.
In my imaginings I have already spent
my brooding winter underground,
unfolded silky powdered wings, and climbed
into the air, free as a puff of cloud
to sail over the steaming fields,
alighting anywhere I pleased,
thrusting into deep tubular flowers.

It is not so: there may be nectar
in those cups, but not for me.
All day, all night, I carry on my back
embedded in my flesh, two rows
of little white cocoons,
so neatly stacked

they look like eggs in a crate.
And I am eaten half away.

If I can gather strength enough
I'll try to burrow under a stone
and spin myself a purse
in which to sleep away the cold;
though when the sun kisses the earth
again, I know I won't be there.
Instead, out of my chrysalis
will break, like robbers from a tomb,
a swarm of parasitic flies,
leaving my wasted husk behind.

Sir, you with the red snippers
in your hand, hovering over me,
casting your shadow, I greet you,
whether you come as an angel of death
or of mercy. But tell me,
before you choose to slice me in two:
Who can understand the ways
of the Great Worm in the Sky?

LAO TZU

CHINA • CA. *Fourth to Third Centuries* B.C.E.

I like this part of the poem because it is short and simple, yet it carries a powerful message. I think the message is to have patience even if you want something. I can relate to it because I feel that I struggle with my own impatience with things I want. I am trying to learn to be more patient from the message in this poem.

—Alex DeCarli, 12, Student, East Northport, New York

from Tao te Ching

To understand others is to be knowledgeable;
To understand yourself is to be wise.
To conquer others is to have strength;
To conquer yourself is to be strong.
To know when you have enough is to be rich.
To go forward with strength is to have ambition.
To not lose your place is to last long.
To die but not be forgotten—that's true long life.

Translated from the Chinese by Robert G. Henricks

D. H. LAWRENCE

ENGLAND • 1885–1930

Snake

A snake came to my water trough
On a hot, hot day, and I in pajamas for the heat,
To drink there.

In the deep, strange-scented shade of the great dark carob tree
I came down the steps with my pitcher
And must wait, must stand and wait, for there he was at the trough before me.

He reached down from a fissure in the earth-wall in the gloom
And trailed his yellow-brown slackness soft-bellied down, over the edge of the stone
     trough
And rested his throat upon the stone bottom,
And where the water had dripped from the tap, in a small clearness,
He sipped with his straight mouth,
Softly drank through his straight gums, into his slack long body,
Silently.

Someone was before me at my water trough,
And I, like a second-comer, waiting.

He lifted his head from his drinking, as cattle do,
And looked at me vaguely, as drinking cattle do,
And flickered his two-forked tongue from his lips, and mused a moment.
And stooped and drank a little more,
Being earth-brown, earth-golden from the burning bowels of the earth
On the day of Sicilian July, with Etna smoking.

The voice of my education said to me
He must be killed,
For in Sicily the black black snakes are innocent, the gold are venomous.

And voices in me said, If you were a man
You would take a stick and break him now, and finish him off.

But must I confess how I liked him,
How glad I was he had come like a guest in quiet, to drink at my water trough
And depart peaceful, pacified, and thankless
Into the burning bowels of this earth?

Was it cowardice, that I dared not kill him?
Was it perversity, that I longed to talk to him?
Was it humility, to feel so honored?
I felt so honored.

And yet those voices:
If you were not afraid, you would kill him!

And truly I was afraid, I was most afraid,
But even so, honored still more
That he should seek my hospitality
From out the dark door of the secret earth.

He drank enough
And lifted his head, dreamily, as one who has drunken,
And flickered his tongue like a forked night on the air, so black,
Seeming to lick his lips,
And looked around like a god, unseeing, into the air,
And slowly turned his head,
And slowly, very slowly, as if thrice adream
Proceeded to draw his slow length curving round
And climb the broken bank of my wall-face.

And as he put his head into that dreadful hole,
And as he slowly drew up, snake-easing his shoulders, and entered further,
A sort of horror, a sort of protest against his withdrawing into that horrid black hole,
Deliberately going into the blackness, and slowly drawing himself after,
Overcame me now his back was turned.
I looked round, I put down my pitcher,

I picked up a clumsy log
And threw it at the water trough with a clatter.

I think it did not hit him;
But suddenly that part of him that was left behind convulsed in undignified haste,
Writhed like lightning, and was gone
Into the black hole, the earth-lipped fissure in the wall-front
At which, in the intense still noon, I stared with fascination.

And immediately I regretted it.
I thought how paltry, how vulgar, what a mean act!
I despised myself and the voices of my accursed human education.

And I thought of the albatross,
And I wished he would come back, my snake.

For he seemed to me again like a king,
Like a king in exile, uncrowned in the underworld,
Now due to be crowned again.

And so, I missed my chance with one of the lords
Of life.
And I have something to expiate:
A pettiness.

EMMA LAZARUS

UNITED STATES • 1849–1887

"The New Colossus" by Emma Lazarus, inscribed on the pedestal of the Statue of Liberty, has been my favorite poem since I was a little girl growing up in Queens. Many was the time I took the Staten Island Ferry for fifteen cents to go to the statue and read the famous poem on its base. The plaque where the poem is written was placed there in 1901. I love this poem not only because it captures the hopes and dream of our nation's immigrants in this century, but because my grandfather, Big Daddy, loved it as well. His grandparents sent their four young sons over on steerage after the Great Famine in Ireland. The greatest legacy I have from him is my love of America and Ireland. This poem tells our family's story. I recently took my thirteen-year-old son to Big Daddy's ancestral village of Carramore. On our way back, I took him by ferry to the Statue of Liberty, where we read this poem together. We learned more about Emma Lazarus—that she was Jewish and wrote the poem to raise funds for the pedestal. That she was not only a poet but an activist, raising funds and opening schools for Russian immigrants driven here by pogroms. The poem forever echoes the hopes of millions of Americans who passed through the "golden door."

—Mary Korr, 49, Freelance Journalist, Barrington, Rhode Island

The New Colossus

Not like the brazen giant of Greek fame,
With conquering limbs astride from land to land;
Here at our sea-washed, sunset gates shall stand
A mighty woman with a torch, whose flame
Is the imprisoned lightning, and her name
Mother of Exiles. From her beacon-hand
Glows world-wide welcome; her mild eyes command
The air-bridged harbor that twin cities frame.
"Keep, ancient lands, your storied pomp!" cries she
With silent lips. "Give me your tired, your poor,
Your huddled masses yearning to breathe free,
The wretched refuse of your teeming shore.
Send these, the homeless, tempest-tost to me,
I lift my lamp beside the golden door!"

DENISE LEVERTOV

UNITED STATES • 1923–1997

For me, that instant when a poem distills a truth I half-knew but couldn't quite see on my own is such a liberation: it always has a sharp, freeing effect and gives me a sense of relief. I used to feel guilty about not striving to analyze poems that felt obscure and dry to me, but gradually I realized that such thoughts were foolish—like feeling apologetic toward an orange because you were in the mood to eat an apple instead. For me "Come into Animal Presence" is a powerful reminder that the sacred is always with us, right here in this room, and not in some distant, hard-to-achieve location we can only reach through esoteric discipline. I am a park ranger. I spend a lot of time walking around several deserted beaches on the southern Oregon coast in case a tourist shows up and gets too close to the Snowy Plover nesting grounds. This work suits me, but even in wild places there are pressures to focus only on the visible and the pragmatic. The biologists I work with are faithful caretakers of threatened species, but I can't seem to get with their program as far as counting animals and recording wind conditions. Hell, I can't even remember the jillions of names of all these species—the scientific brass tacks of categorizing nature. It's enough for me that they're here, and I'll admit it. I'm mostly interested in their beauty and what they teach me about my own humanity. This poem coaxes me closer to the heart of things, and that's really what I want most.

—Leslie Mraz, 47, Park Ranger, Coos Bay, Oregon

Come into Animal Presence

Come into animal presence.
No man is so guileless as
the serpent. The lonely white
rabbit on the roof is a star
twitching its ears at the rain.
The llama intricately
folding its hind legs to be seated
not disdains but mildly
disregards human approval.
What joy when the insouciant
armadillo glances at us and doesn't
quicken his trotting
across the track into the palm brush.

What is this joy? That no animal
falters, but knows what it must do?
That the snake has no blemish,

164   Denise Levertov

that the rabbit inspects his strange surroundings
in white star-silence? The llama
rests in dignity, the armadillo
has some intention to pursue in the palm-forest.
Those who were sacred have remained so,
holiness does not dissolve, it is a presence
of bronze, only the sight that saw it
faltered and turned from it.
An old joy returns in holy presence.

PHILIP LEVINE

UNITED STATES • B. 1928

When I first read this poem, I realized that to be a blue-collar worker in the United States didn't mean I had to be ignorant. Since my parents only went to the eighth grade, and since, at the time, there was a real possibility that I would have to follow my father into the steel mill, this was an important discovery.

—Tim Skeen, 40, Community College Teacher, Prestonburg, Kentucky

You Can Have It

My brother comes home from work
and climbs the stairs to our room.
I can hear the bed groan and his shoes drop
one by one. You can have it, he says.

The moonlight streams in the window
and his unshaven face is whitened
like the face of the moon. He will sleep
long after noon and waken to find me gone.

Thirty years will pass before I remember
that moment when suddenly I knew each man
has one brother who dies when he sleeps
and sleeps when he rises to face this life,

and that together they are only one man
sharing a heart that always labors, hands
yellowed and cracked, a mouth that gasps
for breath and asks, Am I gonna make it?

All night at the ice plant he had fed
the chute its silvery blocks, and then I
stacked cases of orange soda for the children
of Kentucky, one gray boxcar at a time

with always two more waiting. We were twenty
for such a short time and always in
the wrong clothes, crusted with dirt
and sweat. I think now we were never twenty.

In 1948 in the city of Detroit, founded
by de la Mothe Cadillac for the distant purposes
of Henry Ford, no one wakened or died,
no one walked the streets or stoked a furnace,

for there was no such year, and now
that year has fallen off all the old newspapers,
calendars, doctors' appointments, bonds,
wedding certificates, drivers licenses.

The city slept. The snow turned to ice.
The ice to standing pools or rivers
racing in the gutters. Then bright grass rose
between the thousands of cracked squares,

and that grass died. I give you back 1948.
I give you all the years from then
to the coming one. Give me back the moon
with its frail light falling across a face.

Give me back my young brother, hard
and furious, with wide shoulders and a curse
for God and burning eyes that look upon
all creation and say, You can have it.

HENRY WADSWORTH LONGFELLOW

UNITED STATES • 1807–1882

I was born in Roxbury at the crossing. My parents came as immigrants, African-Caribbean immigrants, to Roxbury. They purchased a little cottage on a little street that was dominated by Irish and Jewish families. And then the crash came—the Great Depression. I needed inspiration. I needed challenge. I needed a philosophy to live by. And in junior high school an Irish teacher kept quoting the seventh stanza of a poem by a person she called "The New England Poet." Later on, at Boston English High School, another teacher had us learn all the stanzas of the same poem—Longfellow's "A Psalm of Life." In 1989, by that time a minister, I took critically ill with a life-threatening affliction. I turned to this bit of poetry again—for inspiration, for challenge, for philosophy, and even for a theological contemplation. In my preparation for the inevitable, I scribbled on paper some funeral notations, even an inscription for a gravestone. But I got well. Some time later, a rumor spread through Roxbury that Michael Haynes was indeed dead. The rumor said that there was a gravestone in Forest Hills Cemetery. I discovered that the cemetery had made a mistake and had installed the gravestone that was supposed to be stored in a warehouse; on the stone, the second stanza of "A Psalm of Life."

—Reverend Michael Haynes, 71, Minister, Roxbury, Massachusetts

A Psalm of Life

> *Life that shall send*
> *A challenge to its end,*
> *And when it comes, say, 'Welcome, friend.'* *

WHAT THE HEART OF THE YOUNG MAN SAID TO THE PSALMIST

I

Tell me not, in mournful numbers,
   Life is but an empty dream!
For the soul is dead that slumbers,
   And things are not what they seem.

2

Life is real—life is earnest—
   And the grave is not its goal:

---

* Slightly misquoted from *Wishes to His Supposed Mistress* by the English poet Richard Crashaw (ca. 1613–1649).

Dust thou art, to dust returnest,
  Was not spoken of the soul.

   3

Not enjoyment, and not sorrow,
  Is our destin'd end or way;
But to *act,* that each to-morrow
  Find us farther than to-day.

   4

Art is long, and time is fleeting,
  And our hearts, though stout and brave,
Still, like muffled drums, are beating
Funeral marches to the grave.

   5

In the world's broad field of battle,
  In the bivouac of Life,
Be not like dumb, driven cattle!
  Be a hero in the strife!

   6

Trust no Future, howe'er pleasant!
  Let the dead Past bury its dead!
Act—act in the glorious Present!
  Heart within, and God o'er head!

   7

Lives of great men all remind us
  We can make *our* lives sublime,
And, departing, leave behind us
  Footsteps on the sands of time.

   8

Footsteps, that, perhaps another,
  Sailing o'er life's solemn main,
A forlorn and shipwreck'd brother,
  Seeing, shall take heart again.

9

Let us then be up and doing,
    With a heart for any fate;
Still achieving, still pursuing,
    Learn to labor and to wait.

FEDERICO GARCIA LORCA

SPAIN • *1898–1936*

Like most people, I am much moved by a full-moonrise, especially over the lake we live on. Put that together with the magic of Lorca's Andalusian, slightly surreal imagery and his mirrorings of shapes and colors, and the result is eternally both haunting and comforting. Buena suerte.

—Sheldon Flory, 71, Retired Teacher/Priest, Naples, New York

The Moon Sails Out

When the moon sails out
the church bells die away
and the paths overgrown
with brush appear.

When the moon sails out
the waters cover the earth
and the heart feels it is
a little island in the infinite.

No one eats oranges
under the full moon.
The right things are fruits
green and chilled.

When the moon sails out
with a hundred faces all the same,
the coins made of silver
break out in sobs in the pocket.

Translated from the Spanish by Robert Bly

When I first encountered it, I was pierced. Lorca to me is the poet of interiority. He gets into your bones. I was shaken by its beauty, its steely brilliance. Like all of his poems it is full of fire—dark fire—and music. To quote Cyranno, "Greater than love's power to love."

—Walter Howard, 67, Retired Professor, Natick, Massachusetts

Song of the Barren Orange Tree

Woodcutter.
Cut my shadow from me.
Free me from the torment
of seeing myself without fruit.

Why was I born among mirrors?
The day walks in circles around me,
and the night copies me
in all its stars.

I want to live without seeing myself.
And I will dream that ants
and thistleburrs are my
leaves and my birds.

Woodcutter.
Cut my shadow from me.
Free me from the torment
of seeing myself without fruit.

Translated from the Spanish by W. S. Merwin

AMY LOWELL

UNITED STATES • 1874–1925

When I was very young, in 1918, my cousin was killed in the trenches of France. He was survived by a grieving girlfriend, Bertha. Bertha never married and became a romantic symbol of the personal tragic heartache caused by a "pattern called a war."

—Doris Levin, 82, Retired Librarian, Lakewood, New York

It is a challenge to all we do in life. It is deep in its artistry. It moves the soul. Especially in music, we seek to comprehend this most ephemeral of the arts by seeing and feeling its patterns of rhythm, harmony, melodic line, and variation. This poem, so strong, so deep, was written by a woman. Imagine, if you can, growing up in the United States in the '40s, '50s and '60s. The artists were men, Degas, Rembrandt, Picasso; the violinists were men, Heifitz, Stern, Menuhin; the writers have always been men, Shakespeare, Dickens, Poe, Frost.

—Kathleen Barraclough, 59, Symphony Conductor/Violinist, Bellingham, Washington

It was summertime in the '50s. I was twelve years old. My favorite aunt sat me down and read me "Patterns." I was never the same again. From then on, there would be an awareness of life's designs. Some patterns would be rejected, some enforced. Oh, the challenge of examination!

—Phoebe Underwood, 62, Medical Researcher, Albuquerque, New Mexico

Patterns

I walk down the garden paths,
And all the daffodils
Are blowing, and the bright blue squills.
I walk down the patterned garden paths
In my stiff, brocaded gown.
With my powdered hair and jeweled fan,
I too am a rare
Pattern. As I wander down
The garden paths.

My dress is richly figured,
And the train
Makes a pink and silver stain
On the gravel, and the thrift
Of the borders.
Just a plate of current fashion,
Tripping by in high-heeled, ribboned shoes.

Not a softness anywhere about me,
Only whale-bone and brocade.
And I sink on a seat in the shade
Of a lime tree. For my passion
Wars against the stiff brocade.
The daffodils and squills
Flutter in the breeze
As they please.   •
And I weep;
For the lime tree is in blossom
And one small flower has dropped upon my bosom.

And the plashing of waterdrops
In the marble fountain
Comes down the garden paths.
The dripping never stops.
Underneath my stiffened gown
Is the softness of a woman bathing in a marble basin,
A basin in the midst of hedges grown
So thick, she cannot see her lover hiding,
But she guesses he is near,
And the sliding of the water
Seems the stroking of a dear
Hand upon her.
I should like to see it lying in a heap upon the ground,
All the pink and silver crumpled up on the ground.

I would be the pink and silver as I ran along the paths,
And he would stumble after,
Bewildered by my laughter.
I should see the sun flashing from his sword hilt and the buckles on his shoes.
I would choose
To lead him in a maze along the patterned paths,
A bright and laughing maze for my heavy-booted lover,
Till he caught me in the shade,
And the buttons of his waistcoat bruised my body as he clasped me,
Aching, melting, unafraid.
With the shadows of the leaves and the sundrops,
And the plopping of the waterdrops,
All about us in the open afternoon—
I am very like to swoon

With the weight of this brocade,
For the sun sifts through the shade.

Underneath the fallen blossom
In my bosom,
Is a letter I have hid.
It was brought to me this morning by a rider from the Duke.
"Madam, we regret to inform you that Lord Hartwell
Died in action Thursday se'n night."
As I read it in the white, morning sunlight,
The letters squirmed like snakes.
"Any answer, Madam," said my footman.
"No," I told him.
"See that the messenger takes some refreshment.
No, no answer."
And I walked into the garden,
Up and down the patterned paths,
In my stiff, correct brocade.
The blue and yellow flowers stood up proudly in the sun,
Each one.
I stood upright too,
Held rigid to the pattern
By the stiffness of my gown.
Up and down I walked,
Up and down.

In a month he would have been my husband.
In a month, here, underneath this lime,
We would have broke the pattern;
He for me, and I for him,
He as Colonel, I as Lady,
On this shady seat.
He had a whim
That sunlight carried blessing.
And I answered, "It shall be as you have said."
Now he is dead.
In Summer and in Winter I shall walk
Up and down
The patterned garden paths
In my stiff, brocaded gown.
The squills and daffodils
Will give place to pillared roses, and to asters, and to snow.

I shall go
Up and down,
In my gown.
Gorgeously arrayed,
Boned and stayed.
And the softness of my body will be guarded from embrace
By each button, hook, and lace.
For the man who should loose me is dead,
Fighting with the Duke in Flanders,
In a pattern called a war.
Christ! What are patterns for?

JAMES RUSSELL LOWELL

UNITED STATES • 1819–1891

My father was the first one to wake up in our house. He was eager to greet each day. One of his great pleasures was to announce an overnight snowstorm by reciting, "The snow had begun in the gloaming." Then he would watch his five children leap from bed and run to the window to see for themselves. Early one winter morning in later years I received a wake-up call. I answered the phone groggily and heard my father's voice: "The snow had begun in the gloaming." My father has been gone for seven years. There have been many snowfalls since then, but I still get tears in my eyes when I wake up to a white world without his voice reciting James Russell Lowell's 'The First Snow-Fall.'

—Dorothy Stanaitis, 60+, Retired Librarian, Gloucester, New Jersey

The First Snow-Fall

The snow had begun in the gloaming,
And busily all the night
Had been heaping field and highway
With a silence deep and white.

Every pine and fir and hemlock
Wore ermine too dear for an earl,
And the poorest twig on the elm tree
Was ridged inch deep with pearl.

From sheds new-roofed with Carrara
Came Chanticleer's muffled crow,
The stiff rails softened to swan's-down,
And still fluttered down the snow.

I stood and watched by the window
The noiseless work of the sky,
And the sudden flurries of snow-birds,
Like brown leaves whirling by.

I thought of a mound in sweet Auburn
Where a little headstone stood;
How the flakes were folding it gently,
As did robins the babes in the wood.

Up spoke our own little Mable,
Saying, "Father, who makes it snow?"
And I told of the good All-Father
Who cares for us here below.

Again I looked at the snowfall,
And thought of the leaden sky
That arched o'er our first great sorrow,
When that mound was heaped so high.

I remember that gradual patience
That fell from that cloud like snow,
Flake by flake, healing and hiding
The scar that renewed our woe.

And again to the child I whispered,
"The snow that husheth all,
Darling, the merciful Father
Alone can make it fall!"

Then, with eyes that saw not, I kissed her;
And she, kissing back, could not know
That my kiss was given to her sister,
Folded close under deepening snow.

ROBERT LOWELL

UNITED STATES • 1917–1977

This poem is significant to me because it takes place at McLean Hospital, where I've worked since 1982. I run a couple of poetry groups for psychiatric patients. Every patient I've talked to can relate to Lowell's line "each of us holds a locked razor." The poem captures the privileged milieu of Brahmin mental patients at a very elite hospital in the 1950s. I am stunned by the contrast with the present-day environment. This poem presents men in their most vulnerable condition, despite all the patrician posturing and trappings.

—Doug Holder, 43, Hospital Counselor, Somerville, Massachusetts

Waking in the Blue

The night attendant, a B. U. sophomore,
rouses from the mare's-nest of his drowsy head
propped on *The Meaning of Meaning*.
He catwalks down our corridor.
Azure day
makes my agonized blue window bleaker.
Crows maunder on the petrified fairway.
Absence! My heart grows tense
as though a harpoon were sparring for the kill.
(This is the house for the 'mentally ill'.)

What use is my sense of humour?
I grin at 'Stanley', now sunk in his sixties,
once a Harvard all-American fullback,
(if such were possible!)
still hoarding the build of a boy in his twenties,
as he soaks, a ramrod
with the muscle of a seal
in his long tub,
vaguely urinous from the Victorian plumbing.
A kingly granite profile in a crimson golf-cap,
worn all day, all night,
he thinks only of his figure,
of slimming on sherbet and ginger ale—
more cut off from words than a seal.

This is the way day breaks in Bowditch Hall at McLean's;
the hooded night lights bring out 'Bobbie',

Porcellian '29,
a replica of Louis XVI
without the wig—
redolent and roly-poly as a sperm whale,
as he swashbuckles about in his birthday suit
and horses at chairs.

These victorious figures of bravado ossified young.

In between the limits of day,
hours and hours go by under the crew haircuts
and slightly too little nonsensical bachelor twinkle
of the Roman Catholic attendants.
(There are no Mayflower
screwballs in the Catholic Church.)

After a hearty New England breakfast,
I weigh two hundred pounds
this morning. Cock of the walk,
I strut in my turtle-necked French sailor's jersey
before the metal shaving mirrors,
and see the shaky future grow familiar
in the pinched, indigenous faces
of these thoroughbred mental cases,
twice my age and half my weight.
We are all old-timers,
each of us holds a locked razor.

HAKI R. MADHUBUTI

UNITED STATES • B. 1942

My name is Jessica Laughlin. I have a favorite poem. It has meant a lot to me because I have always been very against racism. Or very for the idea of complete freedom from the judgment of others. I feel that this poem, "Big Momma," is kind of what I have had to deal with lately. I moved to a small town with basically one black family and one Hispanic family. So most of my classmates are very prejudiced. I have tried my hardest to stick up for people that they joke about, but I don't think it is helping. This poem reminded me that other people are sticking up for them, too, it makes me feel like I am not the only one that is trying to make people aware of equal and fair treatment of everyone.

—Jessica Laughlin, 15, Student, Ashland, Nebraska

Big Momma

finally retired   pensionless
from cleaning somebody else's house
she remained home to clean
the one she didn't own.

in her kitchen where we often talked
the *chicago tribune* served as a tablecloth
for the two cups of tomato soup that went
along with my weekly visit & talkingto.

she was in a seriously-funny mood
& from the get-go she was down, realdown:

>   roaches around here are like
>   letters on a newspaper
>   or
>   u gonta be a writer, hunh
>   when u gone write me some writen
>   or
>   the way niggers act around here
>   if talk cd kill we'd all be dead.

she's somewhat confused about all this *blackness*
but said that it's good when negroes start putting themselves
first and added: we've always shopped at the colored stores,
         & the way niggers cut each other up round

here every weekend that whiteman don't
haveta
worry bout no revolution specially when he's
gonta haveta pay for it too, anyhow all he's
gotta do is drop a truck load of *dope* out
there
on 43rd st. & all the niggers & yr
revolutionaries
be too busy getten high & then they'll turn
round
and fight each other over who got the mostest.

we finished our soup and i moved to excuse myself,
as we walked to the front door she made a last comment:
   now *luther* i knows you done changed a lots but if
   you can think back, we never did eat too much pork
   round here anyways, it was bad for the belly.
I shared her smile and agreed.

touching the snow lightly i headed for 43rd st.
at the corner i saw a brother crying while
trying to hold up a lamp post,
thru his watery eyes i cd see big momma's words.

at sixty-eight
she moves freely, is often right
and when there is food
eats joyously with her own
real teeth.

ANDREW MARVELL

ENGLAND • 1621–1678

I have always loved the rhythms of this poem. As a young woman, I identified with the mistress. There I was with hair down to my waist and great legs, listening to a chorus line of intelligent, importuning, horny young men. Logic and lust—what a seductive cocktail. As I hit fifty, I began to identify more with the poet, particularly when he hears "time's wingéd chariot." I can see that sweet and sour chariot, loaded up with all my unlived life and my unfinished business. It looks like a runaway T bus, but the poem provides the laughter and energy I need to hop on board shouting, "I'm not dead yet."

—Kathleen Rogers, 51, Writer, Hull, Massachusetts

Although the poem embraces a sexual meaning, I try to live my life by the underlying theme, which encourages you to live each day as though it were your last. I, too, believe that we should take advantage of life and all it has to offer and not inflict limitations on ourselves. —Thomas Scaife, 18, Cadet, West Point, New York

I fell in love with the man who recited it to me.

—Debra Sudy, 40, Student, Brunswick, Ohio

I don't care if I read this poem a million times. It always gives me chills the way it suddenly turns the corner and stares stone cold at death.

—Ellen Brenneman, 41, Greeting Card Writer, Kansas City, Missouri

I am eighty years old. I discovered this remarkable poem when I was twenty and have read it regularly ever since. Along with its sensuality, its gorgeous imagery cloaked in logic, and the impact of its pure sound appeal, it carries one of the all-powerful messages of life: the steady inexorable passage of time.

—Herbert Shultz, 80, Fundraising Consultant, Kingston, New York

To His Coy Mistress

   Had we but world enough, and time,
This coyness, lady, were no crime.
We would sit down, and think which way
To walk, and pass our long love's day.
Thou by the Indian Ganges' side
Shoudst rubies find; I by the tide
Of Humber would complain. I would
Love you ten years before the flood,
And you should, if you please, refuse

Till the conversion of the Jews.
My vegetable love should grow
Vaster than empires and more slow;
An hundred years should go to praise
Thine eyes, and on thy forehead gaze;
Two hundred to adore each breast,
But thirty thousand to the rest;
An age at least to every part,
And the last age should show your heart.
For, lady, you deserve this state,
Nor would I love at lower rate.

    But at my back I always hear
Time's wingéd chariot hurrying near;
And yonder all before us lie
Deserts of vast eternity.
Thy beauty shall no more be found;
Nor, in thy marble vault, shall sound
My echoing song; then worms shall try
That long-preserved virginity,
And your quaint honor turn to dust,
And into ashes all my lust:
The grave's a fine and private place,
But none, I think, do there embrace.

    Now therefore, while the youthful hue
Sits on thy skin like morning glow,
And while thy willing soul transpires
At every pore with instant fires,
Now let us sport us while we may,
And now, like amorous birds of prey,
Rather at once our time devour
Than languish in his slow-chapped power.
Let us roll all our strength and all
Our sweetness up into one ball,
And tear our pleasures with rough strife
Thorough the iron gates of life:
Thus, though we cannot make our sun
Stand still, yet we will make him run.

HERMAN MELVILLE

UNITED STATES • 1819–1891

It is the offspring of a creative mind. It holds no bounds, only endless possibilities. It reflects whole countries, nations, more importantly, individuality. I believe on a moonlit night, Herman Melville reached his mind out toward the stars. What he found was pure art. What he shares is a reflection of common ingenuity.

—Adam Evans, 17, Student, Strongville, Ohio

Art

In placid hours well-pleased we dream
Of many a brave unbodied scheme.
But form to lend, pulsed life create,
What unlike things must meet and mate:
A flame to melt—a wind to freeze;
Sad patience—joyous energies;
Humility—yet pride and scorn;
Instinct and study; love and hate;
Audacity—reverence. These must mate,
And fuse with Jacob's mystic heart,
To wrestle with the angel—Art.

W. S. MERWIN

UNITED STATES • B. 1927

This poem reminds me of my parents, long dead, who grew up in small towns in Kentucky where the land itself contributed nearly everything that sustained their lives and the lives of their people. Then, the poem reminds me of my younger days when I was lucky enough to experience on summer mornings the sound of strawberry vendors in our neighborhood. These past qualities of our lives won't come again, but they appear to me in my dreams and memories. Merwin's poem parallels my dreams and my memories.

—Allan McGuffey, 46, Technical Writer, Louisville, Kentucky

Strawberries

When my father died I saw   a narrow valley

it looked as though it began   across the river
from the landing where he was born   but there was no river

I was hoeing the sand   of a small vegetable plot
for my mother   in deepening twilight
and looked up in time   to see a farm wagon
dry and gray   horse already hidden
and no driver   going into the valley
carrying a casket

          and another wagon
coming out of the valley   behind a gray horse
with a boy driving   and a high load
of two kinds of berries   one of them strawberries

that night when I slept   I dreamed of things
wrong in the house   all of them signs
the water of the shower   running brackish
and an insect of a kind   I had seen him kill
climbing around   the walls of his bathroom
up in the morning   I stopped on the stairs
my mother was awake   already and asked me
if I wanted a shower   before breakfast
and for breakfast she said   we have strawberries

EDNA ST. VINCENT MILLAY

UNITED STATES • 1892–1950

In our early twenties, my friend Deborah and I developed a wonderful relationship over several years where we connected in a hitherto unexperienced sense of oneness. We communicated in glances and smiles as well as through our love of poetry. I delighted in going to the mailbox and finding an oversize letter, bulging, and written on solid stationery shaded lavender or pale gray. It was sure to be a new bundle of poems that Deborah had found and written down to share with me! The poems reflected our sense of connectedness. We seemed to share the same aesthetic sense of what was beautiful and of poems that led to undiscovered dimensions of the heart. We spent all of our free time together, traveled, and shared many new experiences. During these years I did not realize how meaningful this time was. Our passion, however, remained on some higher almost spiritual level and eventually left us unfulfilled in the earthly realm. After a long and awkward period of trying to distance ourselves, we eventually went on to develop lives with other people. Going through this change was one of the most painful times in my life. I knew that there could never be another person like this in my life and had never felt such pains of separation. This sonnet is from Deborah's book and was one we both loved.

—Larry Bauer, 42, Psychiatric Registered Nurse, Rockville, Maryland

Sonnet XXIV

When you, that at this moment are to me
Dearer than words on paper, shall depart,
And be no more the warder of my heart,
Whereof again myself shall hold the key;
And be no more—what now you seem to be—
The sun, from which all excellences start
In a round nimbus, nor a broken dart
Of moonlight, even, splintered on the sea;
I shall remember only of this hour—
And weep somewhat, as now you see me weep—
The pathos of your love, that, like a flower,
Fearful of death yet amorous of sleep,
Droops for a moment and beholds, dismayed,
The wind whereon its petals shall be laid.

I first heard this poem at a gay rights rally during a memorial service for our friends who had died from AIDS. The poem still haunts me. It states the unspeakable sense of loss and anger and exhaustion I feel when I look back at what has happened to my generation of gay men. This poem honors my friends and contemporaries who did not have a fair chance at a full life—sort of the only way to make sense of it: "I know. But I do not approve. And I am not resigned."

—John Yelton, 36, Graphic Designer, Asheville, North Carolina

Dirge Without Music

I am not resigned to the shutting away of loving hearts in the hard ground.
So it is, and so it will be, for so it has been, time out of mind:
Into the darkness they go, the wise and the lovely. Crowned
With lilies and with laurel they go; but I am not resigned.

Lovers and thinkers, into the earth with you.
Be one with the dull, the indiscriminate dust.
A fragment of what you felt, of what you knew,
A formula, a phrase remains,—but the best is lost.

The answers quick and keen, the honest look, the laughter, the love,—
They are gone. They are gone to feed the roses. Elegant and curled
Is the blossom. Fragrant is the blossom. I know. But I do not approve.
More precious was the light in your eyes than all the roses in the world.

Down, down, down into the darkness of the grave
Gently they go, the beautiful, the tender, the kind;
Quietly they go, the intelligent, the witty, the brave.
I know. But I do not approve. And I am not resigned.

A. A. MILNE

ENGLAND • 1882–1956

When I was very young, my mother would read the poems of A. A. Milne to me. One poem became my favorite and I made her read it to me again and again. I memorized it and I was probably driving her nuts so at one point she handed me the book and told me to read it myself. I don't remember how old I was, maybe five, but I would hold the book up in front of me and pretend I was reading as I recited it over and over. One day (and I remember this clearly) I was sitting on my bed "reading" and I realized the words I was saying were those on the page. From that moment I started picking the words from my poem and finding them in other poems in the book, in other books, or anywhere there were printed words. I could read—and from that point on I've never stopped. My mother died when I was eighteen but the love of books I inherited from her is the greatest gift I ever received. It all started with a tiny little poem that I didn't even know the title of until I was nearly thirty. The poem is called "Happiness" and the happiness it's brought me is immeasurable.

—Vanessa Metam, 37, Book Store Employee, Ann Arbor, Michigan

Happiness

John had
Great Big
Waterproof
Boots on;
John had a
Great Big
Waterproof
Hat;
John had a
Great Big
Waterproof
Mackintosh—
And that
(Said John)
Is
That.

CZESLAW MILOSZ

POLAND * B. *1911*

Great poems to me raise my flesh. I get goose bumps. This one, always and without fail, does it. It is mysterious, yet familiar somehow to the part of myself that needs comfort and reassurance. It is a reminder of how big and also how small it is to be human.

—Carol Edelstein, 43, Social Worker, Northampton, Massachusetts

On Pilgrimage

May the smell of thyme and lavender accompany us on our journey
To a province that does not know how lucky it is
For it was, among all the hidden corners of the earth,
The only one chosen and visited.

We tended toward the Place but no signs led there.
Till it revealed itself in a pastoral valley
Between mountains that look older than memory,
By a narrow river humming at the grotto.

May the taste of wine and roast meat stay with us
As it did when we used to feast in the clearings,
Searching, not finding, gathering rumors,
Always comforted by the brightness of the day.

May the gentle mountains and the bells of the flocks
Remind us of everything we have lost,
For we have seen on our way and fallen in love
With the world that will pass in a twinkling.

Translated from the Polish by Czeslaw Milosz and Robert Hass

JOHN MILTON

ENGLAND • 1608–1674

My father, who normally read no fiction, no poetry, no essays—just the daily newspapers—remembered, and loved, this poem. He never attended college, so he must have read it in high school. He used to recite this and parts of Paradise Lost *to me, and the family often wondered why this particular poem stayed with him. I have frequently had some of the lines of "Lycidas" go through my mind when things seemed grim—or I saw them as grim. Perhaps that's the same feeling he had. A great uplift of spirit after a real down.*

—Joan Thuebel, 68, Retired, Chatham, New Jersey

Lycidas

> *In this Monody the author bewails a learned friend, unfortunately drowned in his passage from Chester on the Irish seas, 1637. And by occasion foretells the ruin of our corrupted clergy, then in their height.*

Yet once more, O ye laurels and once more
Ye myrtles brown, with ivy never sere,
I come to pluck your berries harsh and crude,
And with forced fingers rude,
Shatter your leaves before the mellowing year.
Bitter constraint, and sad occasion dear,
Compels me to disturb your season due;
For Lycidas is dead, dead ere his prime,
Young Lycidas, and hath not left his peer.
Who would not sing for Lycidas? He knew
Himself to sing, and build the lofty rhyme.
He must not float upon his watery bier
Unwept, and welter to the parching wind,
Without the meed of some melodious tear.
Begin then, sisters of the sacred well
That from beneath the seat of Jove doth spring,
Begin, and somewhat loudly sweep the string.
Hence with denial vain, and coy excuse;
So may some gentle Muse
With lucky words favor my destined urn,
And as he passes turn,
And bid fair peace be to my sable shroud.
For we were nursed upon the selfsame hill,
Fed the same flock, by fountain, shade, and rill.

Together both, ere the high lawns appeared
Under the opening eyelids of the morn,
We drove afield, and both together heard
What time the grayfly winds her sultry horn,
Battening our flocks with the fresh dews of night,
Oft till the star that rose at evening bright
Toward Heaven's descent had sloped his westering wheel.
Meanwhile the rural ditties were not mute,
Tempered to th' oaten flute,
Rough satyrs danced, and fauns with cloven heel
From the glad sound would not be absent long,
And old Damoetas loved to hear our song.
    But O the heavy change, now thou art gone,
Now thou art gone, and never must return!
Thee, shepherd, thee the woods and desert caves,
With wild thyme and the gadding vine o'ergrown,
And all their echoes mourn.
The willows and the hazel copses green
Shall now no more be seen,
Fanning their joyous leaves to thy soft lays.
As killing as the canker to the rose,
Or taint-worm to the weanling herds that graze,
Or frost to flowers that their gay wardrobe wear,
When first the white thorn blows;
Such, Lycidas, thy loss to shepherd's ear.
    Where were ye, nymphs, when the remorseless deep
Closed o'er the head of your loved Lycidas?
For neither were ye playing on the steep,
Where your old Bards, the famous Druids lie,
Nor on the shaggy top of Mona high,
Nor yet where Deva spreads her wizard stream:
Ay me! I fondly dream—
Had ye been there—for what could that have done?
What could the Muse herself that Orpheus bore,
The Muse herself, for her inchanting son
Whom universal Nature did lament,
When by the rout that made the hideous roar,
His gory visage down the stream was sent,
Down the swift Hebrus to the Lesbian shore?
    Alas! What boots it with uncessant care
To tend the homely slighted shepherd's trade,
And strictly meditate the thankless Muse?

Were it not better done as others use,
To sport with Amaryllis in the shade,
Or with the tangles of Neaera's hair?
Fame is the spur that the clear spirit doth raise
(That last infirmity of noble mind)
To scorn delights, and live laborious days;
But the fair guerdon when we hope to find,
And think to burst out into sudden blaze,
Comes the blind Fury with th' abhorréd shears,
And slits the thin spun life. "But not the praise,"
Phoebus replied, and touched my trembling ears;
"Fame is no plant that grows on mortal soil,
Nor in the glistering foil
Set off to th' world, nor in broad rumor lies,
But lives and spreads aloft by those pure eyes,
And perfect witness of all-judging Jove;
As he pronounces lastly on each deed,
Of so much fame in Heaven expect thy meed."
   O fountain Arethuse, and thou honored flood,
Smooth-sliding Mincius, crowned with vocal reeds,
That strain I heard was of a higher mood. ·
But now my oat proceeds,
And listens to the herald of the sea
That came in Neptune's plea.
He asked the waves, and asked the felon winds,
"What hard mishap hath doomed this gentle swain?"
And questioned every gust of rugged wings
That blows from off each beakéd promontory;
They knew not of his story,
And sage Hippotades their answer brings,
That not a blast was from his dungeon strayed,
The air was calm, and on the level brine,
Sleek Panope with all her sisters played.
It was that fatal and perfidious bark
Built in th' eclipse, and rigged with curses dark,
That sunk so low that sacred head of thine.
   Next Camus, reverend sire, went footing slow,
His mantle hairy, and his bonnet sedge,
Inwrought with figures dim, and on the edge
Like to that sanguine flower inscribed with woe.
"Ah! who hath reft," quoth he, "my dearest pledge?"
Last came and last did go

The pilot of the Galilean lake,
Two massy keys he bore of metals twain
(The golden opes, the iron shuts amain).
He shook his mitered locks, and stern bespake:
"How well could I have spared for thee, young swain,
Enow of such as for their bellies' sake,
Creep and intrude, and climb into the fold!
Of other care they little reckoning make,
Than how to scramble at the shearers' feast,
And shove away the worthy bidden guest.
Blind mouths! That scarce themselves know how to hold
A sheep-hook, or have learned aught else the least
That to the faithful herdsman's art belongs!
What recks it them? What need they? They are sped;
And when they list, their lean and flashy songs
Grate on their scrannel pipes of wretched straw.
The hungry sheep look up, and are not fed,
But swoln with wind, and the rank mist they draw,
Rot inwardly, and foul contagion spread,
Besides what the grim wolf with privy paw
Daily devours apace, and nothing said.
But that two-handed engine at the door
Stands ready to smite once, and smite no more."
    Return, Alpheus, the dread voice is past,
That shrunk thy streams; return, Sicilian muse,
And call the vales, and bid them hither cast
Their bells and flowerets of a thousand hues.
Ye valleys low where the mild whispers use,
Of shades and wanton winds, and gushing brooks,
On whose fresh lap the swart star sparely looks,
Throw hither all your quaint enameled eyes,
That on the green turf suck the honeyed showers,
And purple all the ground with vernal flowers.
Bring the rathe primrose that forsaken dies,
The tufted crow-toe, and pale jessamine,
The white pink, and the pansy freaked with jet,
The glowing violet,
The musk-rose, and the well attired woodbine.
With cowslips wan that hang the pensive head,
And every flower that sad embroidery wears:
Bid amaranthus all his beauty shed,
And daffadillies fill their cups with tears,
To strew the laureate hearse where Lycid lies.

For so to interpose a little ease,
Let our frail thoughts dally with false surmise.
Ay me! Whilst thee the shores and sounding seas
Wash far away, where'er thy bones are hurled,
Whether beyond the stormy Hebrides,
Where thou perhaps under the whelming tide
Visit'st the bottom of the monstrous world;
Or whether thou, to our moist vows denied,
Sleep'st by the fable of Bellerus old,
Where the great vision of the guarded mount
Looks toward Namancos and Bayona's hold;
Look homeward angel now, and melt with ruth:
And, O ye dolphins, waft the hapless youth.
   Weep no more, woeful shepherds, weep no more,
For Lycidas your sorrow is not dead,
Sunk though he be beneath the watery floor,
So sinks the day-star in the ocean bed,
And yet anon repairs his drooping head,
And tricks his beams, and with new-spangled ore,
Flames in the forehead of the morning sky:
So Lycidas sunk low, but mounted high,
Through the dear might of him that walked the waves,
Where other groves, and other streams along,
With nectar pure his oozy locks he laves,
And hears the unexpressive nuptial song,
In the blest kingdoms meek of joy and love.
There entertain him all the saints above,
In solemn troops and sweet societies
That sing, and singing in their glory move,
And wipe the tears forever from his eyes.
Now, Lycidas, the shepherds weep no more;
Henceforth thou art the genius of the shore,
In thy large recompense, and shalt be good
To all that wander in that perilous flood.
   Thus sang the uncouth swain to th' oaks and rills,
While the still morn went out with sandals gray;
He touched the tender stops of various quills,
With eager thought warbling his Doric lay:
And now the sun had stretched out all the hills,
And now was dropped into the western bay;
At last he rose, and twitched his mantle blue:
Tomorrow to fresh woods, and pastures new.

WILLIAM VAUGHN MOODY

UNITED STATES • 1869–1910

As a seventeen-year-old piano student, I play mostly classical-type pieces. An old man recently came to tune our piano and began to play several ragtime and jazz pieces. It may have been the newly-tuned piano that made this music sound so nice, but, listening to him play "The Girl from Ipanema" on the piano, I think it sounded better simply because it was a different, stimulating sound coming from my old piano. It certainly had more expression and direction than a drawn-out concerto. Just as Moody wrote that he thought he knew his harp's "secrets through and through," I also thought I knew all the sounds of my instrument. The old man in the poem who creates a "clear gold note" reminds me of my piano tuner's jazz songs that sounded so clear and expressive.

—Nancy Keuss, 17, Student, Plano, Texas

Harmonics

This string upon my harp was best beloved:
I thought I knew its secrets through and through;
Till an old man, whose young eyes lightened blue
'Neath his white hair, bent over me and moved
His fingers up and down, and broke the wire
To such a laddered music, rung on rung,
As from the patriarch's pillow skyward sprung
Crowded with wide-flung wings and feet of fire.

O vibrant heart! so metely tuned and strung
That any untaught hand can draw from thee
One clear gold note that makes the tired years young—
What of the time when Love had whispered me
Where slept thy nodes, and my hand pausefully
Gave to the dim harmonics voice and tongue?

MARIANNE MOORE

UNITED STATES • 1887–1972

As a scientist trained in molecular genetics, I find truth in many things, including my data.
I like this poem because it expresses in emotional terms the connection I see between my
work and life.

—Angela Baldo, 33, Geneticist, Henderson, Nevada

Poetry

I, too, dislike it: there are things that are important beyond all this fiddle.
   Reading it, however, with a perfect contempt for it, one discovers in
   it after all, a place for the genuine.
      Hands that can grasp, eyes
      that can dilate, hair that can rise
         if it must, these things are important not because a

high-sounding interpretation can be put upon them but because they are
   useful. When they become so derivative as to become unintelligible,
   the same thing may be said for all of us, that we
      do not admire what
      we cannot understand: the bat
         holding on upside down or in quest of something to

eat, elephants pushing, a wild horse taking a roll, a tireless wolf under
   a tree, the immovable critic twitching his skin like a horse that feels a flea,
         the base-
   ball fan, the statistician—
      nor is it valid
         to discriminate against "business documents and

school-books"; all these phenomena are important. One must make a
         distinction
   however: when dragged into prominence by half poets, the result is not
         poetry,
   nor till the poets among us can be
      "literalists of
      the imagination"—above
         insolence and triviality and can present

for inspection, "imaginary gardens with real toads in them," shall we have
   it. In the meantime, if you demand on the one hand,
     the raw material of poetry in
       all its rawness and
       that which is on the other hand
         genuine, you are interested in poetry.

It took on a special meaning when my doctor was diagnosing my cancer and said, "If it is what I think it is, I give you less than six months to live." I went home, taped the poem to my bathroom mirror, and lived it every day of my treatment. That was twenty-eight months ago. Thanks for the opportunity for closeted poetry lovers to come out. Two years, Cancer free.

—Douglas Shaffer, 35, Restaurant Manager, Des Moines, Iowa

I May, I Might, I Must

If you will tell me why the fen
appears impassable, I then
will tell you why I think that I
can get across it if I try.

THOMAS MOORE

IRELAND • 1779–1852

This poem for the most part describes me. My life is based on the women in it and I like it that way.

—Luke Trowbridge, Vermillion, South Dakota

The Time I've Lost in Wooing

The time I've lost in wooing,
In watching and pursuing
   The light that lies
   In woman's eyes,
Has been my heart's undoing.
Though Wisdom oft has sought me,
I scorn'd the lore she brought me,
   My only books
   Were woman's looks,
And folly's all they've taught me.

Her smile when Beauty granted,
I hung with gaze enchanted,
   Like him, the Sprite,
   Whom maids by night
Oft meet in glen that's haunted.
Like him, too, Beauty won me,
But while her eyes were on me:
   If once their ray
   Was turn'd away,
Oh, winds could not outrun me.

PABLO NERUDA

CHILE * 1904–1973

I have knitted socks.

—Emily Wilson Orzechowski, 59, Teacher, Oneanta, New York

Ode to My Socks

Maru Mori brought me
a pair
of socks
which she knitted herself
with her sheep-herder's hands,
two socks as soft
as rabbits.
I slipped my feet
into them
as though into
two
cases
knitted
with threads of
twilight
and goatskin.
Violent socks,
my feet were
two fish made
of wool,
two long sharks
seablue, shot
through
by one golden thread,
two immense blackbirds,
two cannons,
my feet
were honored
in this way
by
these
heavenly

socks.
They were
so handsome
for the first time
my feet seemed to me
unacceptable
like two decrepit
firemen, firemen
unworthy
of that woven
fire,
of those glowing
socks.

Nevertheless
I resisted
the sharp temptation
to save them somewhere
as schoolboys
keep
fireflies,
as learned men
collect
sacred texts,
I resisted
the mad impulse
to put them
in a golden
cage
and each day give them
birdseed
and pieces of pink melon.
Like explorers
in the jungle who hand
over the very rare
green deer
to the spit
and eat it
with remorse,
I stretched out
my feet
and pulled on

the magnificent
socks
and then my shoes.

The moral
of my ode is this:
beauty is twice
beauty
and what is good is doubly
good
when it is a matter of two socks
made of wool
in winter.

Translated from the Spanish by Stephen Mitchell

JACOB NIBENEGENASÁBE

CANADA • 1900–1977

This is a Swampy Cree Indian narrative poem that was gathered and translated by Howard A. Norman. I love this poem because it is an affirmation of the rhythms and tides of life that we all feel. It is also a wonderful metaphor about the creative life.

—Pat Braus, 45, Small Press Printer/Book Artist, Seattle, Washington

Quiet Until the Thaw

Her name tells of how
it was with her.

The truth is, she did not speak
in winter.
Everyone learned not to
ask her questions in winter,
once this was known about her.

The first winter this happened
we looked in her mouth to see
if something was frozen. Her tongue
maybe, or something else in there.

But after the thaw she spoke again
and told us it was fine for her that way.

So each spring we
looked forward to that.

Translated from the Cree by Howard A. Norman

FRANK O'HARA

UNITED STATES • 1926–1966

This poem catches you in a casual, breezy, atmosphere into which the poet injects a beautifully tragic realization of the fleetingness of life, relationships, and desire.

—Vincent Katz, 38, Writer, New York, New York

A True Account of Talking to the Sun at Fire Island

The Sun woke me this morning loud
and clear, saying "Hey! I've been
trying to wake you up for fifteen
minutes. Don't be so rude, you are
only the second poet I've ever chosen
to speak to personally
                              so why
aren't you more attentive? If I could
burn you through the window I would
to wake you up. I can't hang around
here all day."
                    "Sorry, Sun, I stayed
up late last night talking to Hal."

"When I woke up Mayakovsky he was
a lot more prompt" the Sun said
petulantly. "Most people are up
already waiting to see if I'm going
to put in an appearance."
                              I tried
to apologize "I missed you yesterday."
"That's better" he said. "I didn't
know you'd come out." "You may be
wondering why I've come so close?"
"Yes" I said beginning to feel hot
wondering if maybe he wasn't burning me
anyway.
          "Frankly I wanted to tell you
I like your poetry. I see a lot
on my rounds and you're okay. You may
not be the greatest thing on earth, but

you're different. Now, I've heard some
say you're crazy, they being excessively
calm themselves to my mind, and other
crazy poets think that you're a boring
reactionary. Not me.
                            Just keep on
like I do and pay no attention. You'll
find that people always will complain
about the atmosphere, either too hot
or too cold too bright or too dark, days
too short or too long.
                            If you don't appear
at all one day they think you're lazy
or dead. Just keep right on, I like it.

And don't worry about your lineage
poetic or natural. The Sun shines on
the jungle, you know, on the tundra
the sea, the ghetto. Wherever you were
I knew it and saw you moving. I was waiting
for you to get to work.

                            And now that you
are making your own days, so to speak,
even if no one reads you but me
you won't be depressed. Not
everyone can look up, even at me. It
hurts their eyes."
                            "Oh Sun, I'm so grateful to you!"

"Thanks and remember I'm watching. It's
easier for me to speak to you out
here. I don't have to slide down
between buildings to get your ear.
I know you love Manhattan, but
you ought to look up more often.
                                            And
always embrace things, people earth
sky stars, as I do, freely and with
the appropriate sense of space. That
is your inclination, known in the heavens
and you should follow it to hell, if

necessary, which I doubt.
                            Maybe we'll
speak again in Africa, of which I too
am specially fond. Go back to sleep now
Frank, and I may leave a tiny poem
in that brain of yours as my farewell."

"Sun, don't go!" I was awake
at last. "No, go I must, they're calling
me."
            "Who are they?"
                            Rising he said "Some
day you'll know. They're calling to you
too." Darkly he rose, and then I slept.

MARY OLIVER

UNITED STATES • B. 1953

Now an author of children's books, I grew up in Houston in the shadow of the oil refineries. Both of my grandfathers worked in the industry, one for Sinclair and one for Shell—a blue-collar environment for sure. However, my father was and still is a true fan of Kipling and Longfellow and I know that when I write my own books I hear those two rhymers in my head as I go. Most of my books are in fact in rhyme, but my favorite poem is not rhymed at all. I have this poem taped on the wall beside my desk and I read it every day, sometimes several times. I make copies of it for friends. I read it to people over the phone. Mostly, I ask myself the question Oliver poses at the end of the poem. I don't have the answer, I don't think I need one, but the question itself challenges me to revel in the search.

—Kathi Appelt, 44, Children's Book Author, College Station, Texas

The Summer Day

Who made the world?
Who made the swan, and the black bear?
Who made the grasshopper?
This grasshopper, I mean—
the one who has flung herself out of the grass,
the one who is eating sugar out of my hand,
who is moving her jaws back and forth instead of up and down—
who is gazing around with her enormous and complicated eyes.
Now she lifts her pale forearms and thoroughly washes her face.
Now she snaps her wings open, and floats away.
I don't know exactly what a prayer is.
I do know how to pay attention, how to fall down
into the grass, how to kneel down in the grass,
how to be idle and blessed, how to stroll through the fields,
which is what I have been doing all day.
Tell me, what else should I have done?
Doesn't everything die at last, and too soon?
Tell me, what is it you plan to do
with your one wild and precious life?

WILFRED OWEN

ENGLAND • *1893–1918*

In the poem mustard gas is dropped in behind the fatigued soldiers. As they walk through the sludge they hear the bottles of mustard gas opening and letting the gas out. One man doesn't get his mask on and, unfortunately, he is killed. The third and fourth stanzas were the ones that really got me going. This poem connected to me by means of life itself.

—Mike Gleason, 12, Student, East Northport, New York

I first read this poem for a seventh-grade English class assignment in 1972. My father was blinded by an exploding shell on Okinawa during World War II, and he never discussed his wartime experiences with me in spite of my questions. Although this poem pertains to a different war, it made me aware of the sacrifice that my father made, and even more amazed than I already was at his ability to live his life as if this terrible event had never occurred. He was different from other parents. He was funnier than they were. He treated me fairly and with respect. He had to raise the three of us without my mother's help, after she died when I was nine. The description of one soldier witnessing the death of another due to mustard gas was the most graphic thing I had ever read at the age of twelve. The poem made me realize that my perception of my parents' lives was based on the short time I had known them, and that they had a prior life about which I would never know.

—Mary McWhorter, 39, Accounting Manager, Stockton, California

Dulce et Decorum Est

Bent double, like old beggars under sacks,
Knock-kneed, coughing like hags, we cursed through sludge,
Till on the haunting flares we turned our backs
And towards our distant rest began to trudge.
Men marched asleep. Many had lost their boots
But limped on, blood-shod. All went lame; all blind;
Drunk with fatigue; deaf even to the hoots
Of tired, outstripped Five-Nines that dropped behind.

Gas! Gas! Quick, boys!—An ecstasy of fumbling,
Fitting the clumsy helmets just in time;
But someone still was yelling out and stumbling
And flound'ring like a man in fire or lime . . .
Dim, through the misty panes and thick green light,
As under a green sea, I saw him drowning.

In all my dreams, before my helpless sight,
He plunges at me, guttering, choking, drowning.

If in some smothering dreams you too could pace
Behind the wagon that we flung him in,
And watch the white eyes writhing in his face,
His hanging face, like a devil's sick of sin;
If you could hear, at every jolt, the blood
Come gargling from the froth-corrupted lungs,
Obscene as cancer, bitter as the cud
Of vile, incurable sores on innocent tongues,—
My friend, you would not tell with such high zest
To children ardent for some desperate glory,
The old Lie: Dulce et decorum est
Pro patria mori.

PHAM TIEN DUAT

VIETNAM • B. 1941

It means a lot to me and to us because Mr. Pham is a veteran of the American war in Vietnam and his work has been translated by Ngo Vinh Hai, who's a citizen of Vietnam and by Kevin Bowen, the director of the William Joiner Center where we work. He's also a veteran of the American war in Vietnam, and I think that Kevin is right when he states, as he has, that, if we're going to build a bridge of reconciliation between the United States and Vietnam, we can do it with poetry and literature, and he's been working to translate Vietnamese poetry and literature for about ten years now. The poem also represents something that we think is important, which is a desire to return to a level of sincerity that we think is lacking today.

—Edith Shillue, Adjunct Professor, Boston, Massachusetts
   Trong Chinh Nguyen, Student, Boston, Massachusetts

To Return to the Urges Unconscious of Their Beginnings

I want to return to the first urges, those urges that seemed so unconscious of their
    beginnings.
Urges that were eager to admire the first pen in my life my mother brought me
    when I was a child.
Urges that were the radiant new shirt of days in my poor village.
I want to return to those urges so unconscious of their beginnings.
Urges that were my astonishment at seeing the first feeding breast and the 1001st
    nostalgia that seemed almost too much to bear.
Urges that were the first naive and truthful song a soldier of the 308th division
    taught me in his loving arms.
Urges that were my first sensations at seeing my poems in print. How happy and
    anxious my heart that moment seeing the small creatures of handwriting
    incarnated into the dragons of type.
Urges that were the first insult about my poems that I heard from the mouth of one
    who didn't know me.
I want to return to those first urges so unconscious of their origins.
So I need no longer know which urges are introverted and which are extroverted.
So I need no longer know which poetry must be connected to policy and which
    must be away from policy.
So I need no longer know which poetry must be in established patterns as in "North
    of the River," or must be in free fashion as in "Cochinchina."
And last, so I need no longer know, can poems be sold, and can they be sold at a
    profit.

Translated from the Vietnamese by Ngo Vinh Hai and Kevin Bowen

CARL PHILLIPS

UNITED STATES • B. 1959

As a painter, I am fascinated by the interweaving of arts, like that which is often displayed in theater. Perhaps that's why one of my favorite poems is "Luncheon on the Grass" by Carl Phillips. The poet writes about Manet's painting Dejeuner sur l'herbe. *Not only are the two art forms, poetry and oil painting, different, but the two artists are from entirely different places and times. The most interesting aspect is the raw feeling that Phillips is able to extract when he looks at the painting. When I present artwork, I am excited when someone is able to grasp the feelings in the painting like Phillips.*

—Stephanie Giddings, 20, Student, Vermillion, South Dakota

Luncheon on the Grass

They're a curious lot, Manet's scandalous
lunch partners. The two men, lost
in cant and full dress, their legs sprawled
subway-style, as men's legs invariably are, seem
remarkably unruffled, all but oblivious to their nude
female companion. Her nudity is puzzling and
correct; clothes for her are surely only needed
to shrug a shoulder out of. She herself appears
baldly there-for-the-ride; her eyes, moving out
toward the viewer, are wide with the most banal,
detached surprise, as if to say, "where's
the *real* party?"

Now, in a comparable state of outdoor
undress, I'm beginning to have a fair idea
of what's going on in that scene. Watching
you, in clothes, remove one boot to work your
finger toward an itch in your athletic sock,
I look for any similarities between art
and our afternoon here on abandoned
property. The bather in the painting's
background, presumably there for a certain
balance of composition, is for us an ungainly,
rusted green dumpster, rising from overgrown
weeds that provide a contrast only remotely
pastoral. We are two to Manet's main group
of three, but the hum of the odd car or truck

on the highway below us offers a transient third.
Like the nude, I don't seem especially hungry,
partly because it's difficult eating naked when
everyone else is clothed, partly because
you didn't remember I hate chicken salad.
The beer you opened for me sits untouched,
going flat in the sun. I stroke the wet bottle
fitfully, to remind myself just how far
we've come or more probably have always been
from the shape of romance. My dear,
this is not art, we're not anywhere close
to Arcadia.

SYLVIA PLATH

UNITED STATES • 1932–1963

*About a year after I graduated from college, I moved to Paris. I often checked out reading
material from the British Institute and the American Library. I recall at one point checking
out a cassette of Sylvia Plath reading her poetry and listening to it in my tiny chambre de
bonne. During this time, I was suffering from a disastrous love affair and so I particularly
related to her, finding a great deal of comfort in the following poem. Even though this poem
is about her baby son, it encapsulates for me the quality of loving intensely, the magnitude
of such an energy, and how it must exist somehow, somewhere, in some form that doesn't
die. Later as a young mother, feeding and comforting a child in the solitude of night, and
uncertain about the future, I related to her poems again. It seemed to me I could feel their
fevers, the blood and the milk coursing through them. The power of her poetry does not di-
minish for me.*

—Amy Foster, 43, Legal Document Specialist, Berkeley, California

The Night Dances

A smile fell in the grass.
Irretrievable!

And how will your night dances
Lose themselves. In mathematics?

Such pure leaps and spirals——
Surely they travel

The world forever, I shall not entirely
Sit emptied of beauties, the gift

Of your small breath, the drenched grass
Smell of your sleeps, lilies, lilies.

Their flesh bears no relation.
Cold folds of ego, the calla,

And the tiger, embellishing itself——
Spots, and a spread of hot petals.

The comets
Have such a space to cross.

Such coldness, forgetfulness.
So your gestures flake off——

Warm and human, then their pink light
Bleeding and peeling

Through the black amnesias of heaven.
Why am I given

These lamps, these planets
Failing like blessings, like flakes

Six-sided, white
On my eyes, my lips, my hair

Touching and melting.
Nowhere.

This is the first poem that made me feel what poetry can do. There I was, a seventeen-year-old boy from Jamaica opening a book written by a white woman so far away from me, and yet she spoke my own life. I love that she did that for me. I love that poetry still does that.

—Seph Rodney, 27, Proofreader/Photographer, Bronx, New York

Lady Lazarus

I have done it again.
One year in every ten
I manage it——

A sort of walking miracle, my skin
Bright as a Nazi lampshade,
My right foot

A paperweight,
My face a featureless, fine
Jew linen.

Peel off the napkin
O my enemy.
Do I terrify?——

The nose, the eye pits, the full set of teeth?
The sour breath
Will vanish in a day.

Soon, soon the flesh
The grave cave ate will be
At home on me

And I a smiling woman.
I am only thirty.
And like the cat I have nine times to die.

This is Number Three.
What a trash
To annihilate each decade.

What a million filaments.
The peanut-crunching crowd
Shoves in to see

Them unwrap me hand and foot——
The big strip tease.
Gentlemen, ladies

These are my hands
My knees.
I may be skin and bone,

Nevertheless, I am the same, identical woman.
The first time it happened I was ten.
It was an accident.

The second time I meant
To last it out and not come back at all.
I rocked shut

As a seashell.
They had to call and call
And pick the worms off me like sticky pearls.

Dying
Is an art, like everything else.
I do it exceptionally well.

I do it so it feels like hell.
I do it so it feels real.
I guess you could say I've a call.

It's easy enough to do it in a cell.
It's easy enough to do it and stay put.
It's the theatrical

Comeback in broad day
To the same place, the same face, the same brute
Amused shout:

'A miracle!'
That knocks me out.
There is a charge

For the eyeing of my scars, there is a charge
For the hearing of my heart——
It really goes.

And there is a charge, a very large charge
For a word or a touch
Or a bit of blood

Or a piece of my hair or my clothes.
So, so, Herr Doktor.
So, Herr Enemy.

I am your opus,
I am your valuable,
The pure gold baby

That melts to a shriek.
I turn and burn.
Do not think I underestimate your great concern.

Ash, ash—
You poke and stir.
Flesh, bone, there is nothing there——

A cake of soap,
A wedding ring,
A gold filling.

Herr God, Herr Lucifer
Beware
Beware.

Out of the ash
I rise with my red hair
And I eat men like air.

A couple of years ago, this poem, which I had not known before, emerged into my life in a nearly magical way. There are two parts to this story. First, in 1991, my wife and I visited our daughter Polly in an art class. The immediate project involved the drawing or painting of trees. Polly took some pastels and, on a large piece of paper, she drew a tree. She worked very fast, and was finished in a very few minutes, as though the drawing emerged, fully formed, from her, like a birth. The drawing was like Polly herself: beautiful, luminous, mysterious. In 1996, Polly died suddenly of an asthma attack. She was twenty-four years old. It was by far the worst tragedy of my life, and I have known a few. The second part of this story happened the following spring. My son Jaik, Polly's older brother, was working in Maine and he stayed over at a friend's home. Jaik's friend showed him a copy of the collected poems of Sylvia Plath, and leafing through the book, he was quickly drawn to the title of the poem "Polly's Tree." Soon after, at a family gathering, he read it to us all. We were stunned and thrilled. The poem was about Polly's pastel. It told the story of that work, although the poem had been written in 1959, thirteen years before Polly was born.

—Martin Miller, 67, Clinical Psychologist, High Falls, New York

Polly's Tree

A dream tree, Polly's tree:
   a thicket of sticks,
      each speckled twig

ending in a thin-paned
   leaf unlike any
      other on it

or in a ghost flower
   flat as paper and
      of a color

vaporish as frost-breath,
     more finical than
          any silk fan

the Chinese ladies use
     to stir robin's egg
          air. The silver-

haired seed of the milkweed
     comes to roost there, frail
          as the halo

rayed round a candle flame,
     a will-o'-the-wisp
          nimbus, or puff

of cloud-stuff, tipping her
     queer candelabrum.
          Palely lit by

snuff-ruffed dandelions,
     white daisy wheels and
          a tiger-faced

pansy, it glows. O it's
     no family tree,
          Polly's tree, nor

a tree of heaven, though
     it marry quartz-flake,
          feather and rose.

It sprang from her pillow
     whole as a cobweb,
          ribbed like a hand,

a dream tree. Polly's tree
     wears a valentine
          arc of tear-pearled

bleeding hearts on its sleeve
     and, crowning it, one
          blue larkspur star.

HYAM PLUTZIK

UNITED STATES • 1911–1962

I am a sixty-seven year old, retired professor of electrical engineering at the University of Rochester. Hyam Plutzik was the Deane Professor of Rhetoric and Poetry when he died of cancer in 1962 at the age of fifty. I joined the university in 1967, so I never knew Plutzik. As a cancer survivor myself, I regret the life cut short. This poem is vivid and powerful in its description of cancer, in the metaphor of the bursting nova, in the way the victim is presented.

—Sidney Shapiro, 67, Retired Engineering Professor, Rochester, New York

Cancer and Nova

The star exploding in the body;
The creeping thing, growing in the brain or the bone;
The hectic cannibal, the obscene mouth.

The mouths along the meridian sought him,
Soft as moths, many a moon and sun,
Until one
In a pale fleeing dream caught him.

Waking, he did not know himself undone,
Nor walking, smiling, reading that the news was good,
The star exploding in his blood.

ALEXANDER POPE

ENGLAND • *1688–1744*

This poem exemplifies Pope's humor, conciseness, and ego, while using the range of his skills. His feelings are not emotions recollected in tranquility, but emotions right from the pulse.

—Richard Reynolds, 69, Retired Professor, Storrs, Connecticut

from Epistle to Dr. Arbuthnot

Shut, shut the door, good John! (fatigued, I said),
Tie up the knocker, say I'm sick, I'm dead.
The Dog Star rages! nay 'tis past a doubt
All Bedlam, or Parnassus, is let out:
Fire in each eye, and papers in each hand,
They rave, recite, and madden round the land.
What walls can guard me, or what shades can hide?
They pierce my thickets, through my grot they glide,
By land, by water, they renew the charge,
They stop the chariot, and they board the barge.
No place is sacred, not the church is free;
Even Sunday shines no Sabbath day to me:
Then from the Mint walks forth the man of rhyme,
Happy to catch me just at dinner time.
Is there a parson, much bemused in beer,
A maudlin poetess, a rhyming peer,
A clerk foredoomed his father's soul to cross,
Who pens a stanza when he should engross?
Is there who, locked from ink and paper, scrawls
With desperate charcoal round his darkened walls?
All fly to Twit'nam, and in humble strain
Apply to me to keep them mad or vain.
Arthur, whose giddy son neglects the laws,
Imputes to me and my damned works the cause:
Poor Cornus sees his frantic wife elope,
And curses wit, and poetry, and Pope.
Friend to my life (which did not you prolong,
The world had wanted many an idle song)
What drop or nostrum can this plague remove?
Or which must end me, a fool's wrath or love?

A dire dilemma! either way I'm sped,
If foes, they write, if friends, they read me dead.
Seized and tied down to judge, how wretched I!
Who can't be silent, and who will not lie.
To laugh were want of goodness and of grace,
And to be grave exceeds all power of face.
I sit with sad civility, I read
With honest anguish and an aching head,
And drop at last, but in unwilling ears,
This saving counsel, "Keep your piece nine years."
    "Nine years!" cries he, who high in Drury Lane,
Lulled by soft zephyrs through the broken pane,
Rhymes ere he wakes, and prints before term ends,
Obliged by hunger and request of friends:
"The piece, you think, is incorrect? why, take it,
I'm all submission, what you'd have it, make it."
    Three things another's modest wishes bound,
My friendship, and a prologue, and ten pound.
    Pitholeon sends to me: "You know his Grace,
I want a patron; ask him for a place."
Pitholeon libeled me—"but here's a letter
Informs you, sir, 'twas when he knew no better.
Dare you refuse him? Curll invites to dine.

He'll write a *Journal,* or he'll turn divine."
Bless me! a packet—" 'Tis a stranger sues,
A virgin tragedy, an orphan Muse."
If I dislike it, "Furies, death, and rage!"
If I approve, "Commend it to the stage."
There (thank my stars) my whole commission ends,
The players and I are, luckily, no friends.
Fired that the house reject him, " 'Sdeath, I'll print it,
And shame the fools—Your interest, sir, with Lintot!"
Lintot, dull rogue, will think your price too much.
"Not, sir, if you revise it, and retouch."
All my demurs but double his attacks;
At last he whispers, "Do; and we go snacks."
Glad of a quarrel, straight I clap the door,
"Sir, let me see your works and you no more."

EZRA POUND

UNITED STATES • 1885–1972

Rarely has a poem so beautifully captured the heart of a woman.
—Margaret Moller, ESL Instructor, Ann Arbor, Michigan

The River-Merchant's Wife: A Letter

after Li Po

While my hair was still cut straight across my forehead
I played about the front gate, pulling flowers.
You came by on bamboo stilts, playing horse,
You walked about my seat, playing with blue plums.
And we went on living in the village of Chokan:
Two small people, without dislike or suspicion.

At fourteen I married My Lord you.
I never laughed, being bashful.
Lowering my head, I looked at the wall.
Called to, a thousand times, I never looked back.

At fifteen I stopped scowling,
I desired my dust to be mingled with yours
Forever and forever and forever.
Why should I climb the look out?

At sixteen you departed,
You went into far Ku-to-yen, by the river of swirling eddies,
And you have been gone five months.
The monkeys make sorrowful noise overhead.

You dragged your feet when you went out.
By the gate now, the moss is grown, the different mosses,
Too deep to clear them away!
The leaves fall early this autumn, in wind.
The paired butterflies are already yellow with August
Over the grass in the West garden;
They hurt me. I grow older.

If you are coming down through the narrows of the river Kiang,
Please let me know beforehand,
And I will come out to meet you
                As far as Cho-fu-Sa.

ALEXANDER PUSHKIN

RUSSIA • 1799–1837

Every woman dreams about such love.

—Zhanna Matserat, 65, Teacher, San Jose, California

I loved you

I loved you; and perhaps I love you still,
The flame, perhaps, is not extinguished; yet
It burns so quietly within my soul,
No longer should you feel distressed by it.
Silently and hopelessly I loved you,
At times too jealous and at times too shy.
God grant you find another who will love you
As tenderly and truthfully as I.

Translated from the Russian by D. M. Thomas

FRANCISCO DE QUEVEDO

SPAIN • *1580–1645*

The writer Octavio Paz loved the sixteenth-century Spanish writer, Francisco de Quevedo, whose works in their entirety have yet to be translated fully into English—one of the great scandals of our time. Quevedo is as important to the Spanish-speaking world and indeed to world literature as Shakespeare, but a name still too little known here. This was Octavio Paz's favorite poem.

—Steve Wasserman, 46, Editor, Los Angeles, California

Love Constant Beyond Death

The final shadow that will close my eyes
will in its darkness take me from white day
and instantly untie the soul from lies
and flattery of death, and find its way,
and yet my soul won't leave its memory
of love there on the shore where it has burned:
my flame can swim cold water and has learned
to lose respect for laws' severity.
My soul, whom a God made his prison of,
my veins, which a liquid humor fed to fire,
my marrows, which have gloriously flamed,
will leave their body, never their desire;
they will be ash but ash in feeling framed;
they will be dust but will be dust in love.

Translated from the Spanish by Willis Barnstone

SIR WALTER RALEIGH

ENGLAND • CA. 1552–1618

I like this poem because it is a really caddish response to Marlowe's over-quoted poem "The Passionate Shepherd to His Love." It is a response my generation (The "X" one) has had to learn the hard way through the discourse of AIDS.

—Julie Reiser, 30, Graduate Student, Silver Spring, Maryland

The Nymph's Reply to the Shepherd

If all the world and love were young,
And truth in every shepherd's tongue,
These pretty pleasures might me move
To live with thee and be thy love.

Time drives the flocks from field to fold
When rivers rage and rocks grow cold,
And Philomel becometh dumb;
The rest complains of cares to come.

The flowers do fade, and wanton fields
To wayward winter reckoning yields;
A honey tongue, a heart of gall,
Is fancy's spring, but sorrow's fall.

Thy gowns, thy shoes, thy beds of roses,
Thy cap, thy kirtle, and thy posies
Soon break, soon wither, soon forgotten—
In fully ripe, in reason rotten.

Thy belt of straw and ivy buds,
Thy coral clasps and amber studs,
All these in me no means can move
To come to thee and be thy love.

But could youth last and love still breed,
Had joys no date nor age no need,
Then these delights my mind might move
To live with thee and be thy love.

HENRY REED

ENGLAND • *1914–1986*

I was an army nurse in WWII, and at one point they made us disassemble, clean, and put together an M-1 rifle! We sat round a table with gunnery sergeants standing behind us in case we needed help. Initially we had to do it in so many seconds. Everyone got finished, but I was struggling with one last part and I couldn't find where it fit. The sergeant behind me stepped forward and said, sarcastically, "Lieutenant, that's the cap off the grease tube!" This poem made me think of it. It is such a gentle ironic statement about war and violence and lethal weapons—while we are surrounded by beauty, which speaks more strongly and beguiles us in spite of those ugly things.

—Helen Rubar, Retired Nurse, Bath, New York

Naming of Parts

Today we have naming of parts. Yesterday,
We had daily cleaning. And tomorrow morning,
We shall have what to do after firing. But today,
Today we have naming of parts. Japonica
Glistens like coral in all of the neighbouring gardens,
      And today we have naming of parts.

This is the lower sling swivel. And this
Is the upper sling swivel, whose use you will see,
When you are given your slings. And this is the piling swivel,
Which in your case you have not got. The branches
Hold in the gardens their silent, eloquent gestures,
      Which in our case we have not got.

This is the safety-catch, which is always released
With an easy flick of the thumb. And please do not let me
See anyone using his finger. You can do it quite easy
If you have any strength in your thumb. The blossoms
Are fragile and motionless, never letting anyone see
      Any of them using their finger.

And this you can see is the bolt. The purpose of this
Is to open the breech, as you see. We can slide it
Rapidly backwards and forwards: we call this
Easing the spring. And rapidly backwards and forwards

The early bees are assaulting and fumbling the flowers:
     They call it easing the Spring.

They call it easing the Spring: it is perfectly easy
If you have any strength in your thumb: like the bolt,
And the breech, and the cocking-piece, and the point of balance,
Which in our case we have not got; and the almond-blossom
Silent in all of the gardens and the bees going backwards and forwards,
     For today we have naming of parts.

ADRIENNE RICH

UNITED STATES • B. 1929

I recently returned from working for two years as a Peace Corps volunteer in Jamaica. Throughout all of the struggles and changes I went through, reading poetry kept me sane and helped me clarify the person I was becoming. This poem in particular jumped out at me, because it spoke to me simply and clearly of what all poetry seems to be about—what it means to be human.

—Niki Mathias, 26, Teacher, Powell, Ohio

To the Days

From you I want more than I've ever asked,
all of it—the newscasts' terrible stories
of life in my time, the knowing it's worse than that,
much worse—the knowing what it means to be lied to.

Fog in the mornings, hunger for clarity,
coffee and bread with sour plum jam.
Numbness of soul in placid neighborhoods.
Lives ticking on as if.

A typewriter's torrent, suddenly still.
Blue soaking through fog, two dragonflies wheeling.
Acceptable levels of cruelty, steadily rising.
Whatever you bring in your hands, I need to see it.

Suddenly I understand the verb without tenses.
To smell another woman's hair, to taste her skin.
To know the bodies drifting underwater.
To be human, said Rosa—I can't teach you that.

A cat drinks from a bowl of marigolds—his moment.
Surely the love of life is never-ending,
the failure of nerve, a charred fuse?
I want more from you than I ever knew to ask.

Wild pink lilies erupting, tasseled stalks of corn
in the Mexican gardens, corn and roses.
Shortening days, strawberry fields in ferment
with tossed-aside, bruised fruit.

I lost my younger brother, Sam Nickles, in 1995, after his having lived seven years with AIDS. The experience was devastating on many different levels. He was my brother, my best friend, in many ways my son. We lived together all but four of his thirty-six years on this earth. This poem brought me great comfort.

—Susan Nickles, 43, National Accreditation Director, Department of Mental Health, Columbia, South Carolina

Prospective Immigrants Please Note

Either you will
go through this door
or you will not go through.

If you go through
there is always the risk
of remembering your name.

Things look at you doubly
and you must look back
and let them happen.

If you do not go through
it is possible
to live worthily

to maintain your attitudes
to hold your position
to die bravely

but much will blind you,
much will evade you,
at what cost who knows?

The door itself
makes no promises.
It is only a door.

RAINER MARIA RILKE

AUSTRIA • 1875–1926

This poem was given to me by Christian Yavorsky, my first love, five years after we had broken up. We had not spoken for most of those years, and on his twenty-fourth birthday I sent him a card that rekindled our friendship. I also sent him a copy of my favorite book, and he sent me the book of Rilke's poetry. At the time I was living in Portland, Maine, by myself and was working at a newspaper. My memories of my year in Maine consist mainly of riding my bicycle down Commercial Street at a high speed, hoping I would get hurt so that, as in combat, I would be sent home. It was always cold and I was too lonely to leave my apartment apart from going to work. When the Rilke book arrived, I decided to try to make poetry into something I could understand, as it had always intimidated me to the point where I never indulged in it. When I opened the book, the first poem shouted to me from the pages, and from Rilke's pen, and from Sheffield, England, where Christian lived at the time and was struggling with cold and solitude, the same two difficulties as me.

—Liz Schultz, 24, Photographer, Fairfax Station, Virginia

Entrance

Whoever you are: in the evening step out
of your room, where you know everything;
yours is the last house before the far-off:
whoever you are.
With your eyes, which in their weariness
barely free themselves from the worn-out threshold,
you lift very slowly one black tree
and place it against the sky: slender, alone.
And you have made the world. And it is huge
and like a word which grows ripe in silence.
And as your will seizes on its meaning,
tenderly your eyes let it go . . .

Translated from the German by Edward Snow

ARTHUR RIMBAUD

FRANCE • 1854–1891

"Nobody's serious when they're seventeen" begins this poem which I discovered at the too-serious age of seventeen. The misery of high school was tempered by French poetry, by Rimbaud and Baudelaire. At lunch I would sit alone in front of my locker and read their words and try to translate them.

—Deborah Wassertzug, 26, Librarian, New York, New York

Romance

I

Nobody's serious when they're seventeen.
On a nice night, the hell with beer and lemonade
And the café and the noisy atmosphere!
You walk beneath the linden trees on the promenade.

The lindens smell lovely on a night in June!
The air is so sweet that your eyelids close.
The breeze is full of sounds—they come from the town—
And the scent of beer, and the vine, and the rose . . .

2

You look up and see a little scrap of sky,
Dark blue and far off in the night,
Stuck with a lopsided star that drifts by
With little shivers, very small and white . . .

A night in June! Seventeen! Getting drunk is fun.
Sap like champagne knocks your head awry . . .
Your mind drifts; a kiss rises to your lips
And flutters like a little butterfly . . .

3

Your heart Crusoes madly through novels, anywhere,
When through the pale pool beneath a street light,
A girl goes by with the *most* charming air,
In the grim shadow of her father's dark coat.

And since she finds you marvelously naïve,
While her little heels keep tapping along
She turns, with a quick bright look . . .
And on your lips, despairing, dies your song.

   4

You are in love. Rented out till fall.
You are in love. Poetic fires ignite you.
Your friends laugh; they won't talk to you at all.
Then one night, the goddess deigns to write you!

That night . . . you go back to the café, to the noisy atmosphere;
You sit and order beer, or lemonade . . .
Nobody's serious when they're seventeen,
And there are linden trees on the promenade.

Translated from the French by Paul Schmidt

YANNIS RITSOS

GREECE • 1909-1990

I am the daughter of Greek immigrants. It is my parents' story.

—Dena Spanos-Hawkey, 49, Literacy Services Director, Claremont, California

Our Land

We climbed the hill to look over our land:
fields poor and few, stones, olive trees.
Vineyards head toward the sea. Beside the plow
a small fire smoulders. We shaped the old man's clothes
into a scarecrow against the ravens. Our days
are making their way toward a little bread and great sunshine.
Under the poplars a straw hat beams.
The rooster on the fence. The cow in yellow.
How did we manage to put our house and our life in order
with a hand made of stone? Up on the lintel
there's soot from the Easter candles, year by year:
tiny black crosses marked there by the dead
returning from the Resurrection Service. This land is much loved
with patience and dignity. Every night, out of the dry well,
the statues emerge cautiously and climb the trees.

Translated from the Greek by Edmund Keeley

EDWIN ARLINGTON ROBINSON

UNITED STATES • 1869–1935

I discovered the poem many years ago as a newly married girl living in a small town, which in fact possesses a harborside. My husband had an intractable (it seemed then) drug and alcohol problem and was away a lot for his job. I didn't have a job at the time, knew no one, and spent many days in solitude, riding my bike, reading, and reflecting on what my life had become since my decision to marry. I did not then comprehend what the line "for they that with a god have striven" meant. I just recognized completely the state of wishing to be united with a man because of what I knew or thought I knew of days and the onward years. I lived then and now in an ancient house left me by my father, whose father left it to him, whose father left it to him. It is one mile from the ocean, surrounded by old trees. These facts made up no small part of my husband's decision to marry me. I copied that poem into the journal I kept then and it sits before me on the table as I write. I have always felt the woman was as I was. The knowledge that I've gained about "the god" has lent a retrospective dignity to events experienced as utter failure. The discovery of the poem, with its eerily large number of coincidences with my own situation, was like a gift, or maybe a clue in a giant game of charades, from "the god" himself, who saw he had perhaps misjudged his opponent.

—Anonymous

Eros Turannos

She fears him, and will always ask
   What fated her to choose him;
She meets in his engaging mask
   All reasons to refuse him;
But what she meets and what she fears
Are less than are the downward years,
Drawn slowly to the foamless weirs
   Of age, were she to lose him.

Between a blurred sagacity
   That once had power to sound him,
And Love, that will not let him be
   The Judas that she found him,
Her pride assuages her almost,
As if it were alone the cost.—
He sees that he will not be lost,
   And waits and looks around him.

A sense of ocean and old trees
   Envelops and allures him;

Tradition, touching all he sees,
    Beguiles and reassures him;
And all her doubts of what he says
Are dimmed with what she knows of days—
Till even prejudice delays
    And fades, and she secures him.

The falling leaf inaugurates
    The reign of her confusion:
The pounding wave reverberates
    The dirge of her illusion;
And home, where passion lived and died,
Becomes a place where she can hide,
While all the town and harbor side
    Vibrate with her seclusion.

We tell you, tapping on our brows,
    The story as it should be,—
As if the story of a house
    Were told, or ever could be;
We'll have no kindly veil between
Her visions and those we have seen,—
As if we guessed what hers have been,
    Or what they are or would be.

Meanwhile we do no harm; for they
    That with a god have striven,
Not hearing much of what we say,
    Take what the god has given;
Though like waves breaking it may be,
Or like a changed familiar tree,
Or like a stairway to the sea
    Where down the blind are driven.

I grew up in Northeastern Vermont. All of my relations were working class men and women of few words, often heavy drinkers. As I grew older, I watched these people become less and less important to the local economy; farms and warehouses closed, and towns emptied of people between the ages of eighteen and fifty. Regret and fear were not given words. You didn't talk or remonstrate, but you did brood. Mr. Flood had once been an important person; these men had once been important to themselves, their families, and their towns. Now they had trouble earning a living. Some of these marginalized men frightened me,

Mr. Flood's Party

Old Eben Flood, climbing alone one night
Over the hill between the town below
And the forsaken upland hermitage
That held as much as he should ever know
On earth again of home, paused warily.
The road was his with not a native near;
And Eben, having leisure, said aloud,
For no man else in Tilbury Town to hear:

"Well, Mr. Flood, we have the harvest moon
Again, and we may not have many more;
The bird is on the wing, the poet says,
And you and I have said it here before.
Drink to the bird." He raised up to the light
The jug that he had gone so far to fill,
And answered huskily: "Well, Mr. Flood,
Since you propose it, I believe I will."

Alone, as if enduring to the end
A valiant armor of scarred hopes outworn,
He stood there in the middle of the road
Like Roland's ghost winding a silent horn.
Below him, in the town among the trees,
Where friends of other days had honored him,
A phantom salutation of the dead
Rang thinly till old Eben's eyes were dim.

Then, as a mother lays her sleeping child
Down tenderly, fearing it may awake,
He set the jug down slowly at his feet
With trembling care, knowing that most things break;
And only when assured that on firm earth
It stood, as the uncertain lives of men

Assuredly did not, he paced away,
And with his hand extended paused again:

"Well, Mr. Flood, we have not met like this
In a long time; and many a change has come
To both of us, I fear, since last it was
We had a drop together. Welcome home!"
Convivially returning with himself,
Again he raised the jug up to the light;
And with an acquiescent quaver said:
"Well, Mr. Flood, if you insist, I might.

"Only a very little, Mr. Flood—
For auld lang syne. No more, sir; that will do."
So, for the time, apparently it did,
And Eben evidently thought so too;
For soon amid the silver loneliness
Of night he lifted up his voice and sang,
Secure, with only two moons listening,
Until the whole harmonious landscape rang—

"For auld lang syne." The weary throat gave out,
The last word wavered, and the song was done.
He raised again the jug regretfully
And shook his head, and was again alone.
There was not much that was ahead of him,
And there was nothing in the town below—
Where strangers would have shut the many doors
That many friends had opened long ago.

THEODORE ROETHKE

UNITED STATES • 1908–1963

My eight kids have loved to rassle with me, just as I loved to tussle with my dad. The poem evokes precious memories of my dad's return home from work, dirty and tired from labor; and often a belly full of stew and dumplings, a shot or two of Early Times and playing with me, just as the boy in the poem. I am aware of the darker interpretation in the poem, but it just doesn't hit me that way. I remember a loving dad, who sometimes earned his wife's consternation for roughhousing.

—William Van Fields, 54, Retired, Stockton, California

It is a perfect poem—a waltz poem in Waltz rhythm. I was often waltzed around the house like this by a much larger person, a man I dated who was 6'6" and 240-plus pounds. When he would come home, sometimes drunk, I was picked up and we danced. I was exhilarated and scared at the same time, like the boy in the poem.

—Barbara McIntyre, 53, Librarian, Casselberry, Florida

My Papa's Waltz

The whiskey on your breath
Could make a small boy dizzy;
But I hung on like death:
Such waltzing was not easy.

We romped until the pans
Slid from the kitchen shelf;
My mother's countenance
Could not unfrown itself.

The hand that held my wrist
Was battered on one knuckle;
At every step you missed
My right ear scraped a buckle.

You beat time on my head
With a palm caked hard by dirt,
Then waltzed me off to bed
Still clinging to your shirt.

When I was a college student in New Jersey, and later, for several years when I lived and worked in Washington, D.C., I would take the Amtrak Crescent from my family home in

Danville, Virginia, north. Always my mother and sometimes my sisters or a brother would wait with me at the station until 4:00 A.M. or even later until I was packed aboard a dark and slumbering coach. I love this poem because even though Roethke's speaker is traveling west, he captures that feeling of being alone and alive in the moving darkness, the feeling of spiritual and physical transport. I think I was just out of school when I discovered this poem that held so much of what I felt, laying awake, gazing out the train windows at the Blue Ridge Mountains, hip and waist, shoulder and thigh, like giant sleeping Amazons. The mountains were always so amazing and beautiful that they made me forget my crying for home. Sitting here in California, I reread "Night Journey" and cry for the mountains and for home.

—Teresa Moore, 36, Reporter, San Francisco, California

Night Journey

Now as the train bears west,
Its rhythm rocks the earth,
And from my Pullman berth
I stare into the night
While others take their rest.
Bridges of iron lace,
A suddenness of trees,
A lap of mountain mist
All cross my line of sight,
Then a bleak wasted place,
And a lake below my knees.
Full on my neck I feel
The straining at a curve;
My muscles move with steel,
I wake in every nerve.
I watch a beacon swing
From dark to blazing bright;
We thunder through ravines
And gullies washed with light.
Beyond the mountain pass
Mist deepens on the pane;
We rush into a rain
That rattles double glass.
Wheels shake the roadbed stone,
The pistons jerk and shove,
I stay up half the night
To see the land I love.

The first verse of this poem helped me deal with having leukemia and a bone marrow trans-plant about three and a half years ago. Total recovery—no sign of cancer as of last test in June 1998.

—Tracy Hartley, 36, Furniture Builder, Atlanta, Georgia

Ten years ago, on 21 December, 1988, my sister, Karen Lee Hunt, was killed on Pan Am Flight 103—the result of a terrorist bombing. During her last months of life, she studied in London as part of Syracuse University's study abroad program. When my family received her possessions, we discovered a journal she kept while in London. The final entry inscribed in the journal is an excerpt taken from this poem. It reads, "I wake to sleep, and take my waking slow. I feel my fate in what I cannot fear. I learn by going where I have to go." My family feels that my sister was speaking to us through this poem, and it gives us great com-fort to know that she sensed her fate and accepted it.

—Robyn Hunt, 23, Student, Webster, New York

Now in my forty-eighth year I have experienced the tugs and collisions, the losses and up-endings of mid-life when nothing is as it was and nothing is predictable. I have moved from knowing what to make of life to not knowing anything. I no longer plan, and have no illu-sions that I am in control of anything but the details of my day. In other words, I am freer and more alive than I have ever been. I know truly what the poet means.

—Ruth Cherry, 48, Clinical Psychologist, San Diego, California

The Waking

I wake to sleep, and take my waking slow.
I feel my fate in what I cannot fear.
I learn by going where I have to go.

We think by feeling. What is there to know?
I hear my being dance from ear to ear.
I wake to sleep, and take my waking slow.

Of those so close beside me, which are you?
God bless the Ground! I shall walk softly there,
And learn by going where I have to go.

Light takes the Tree; but who can tell us how?
The lowly worm climbs up a winding stair;
I wake to sleep, and take my waking slow.

Great Nature has another thing to do
To you and me; so take the lively air,
And, lovely, learn by going where to go.

This shaking keeps me steady. I should know.
What falls away is always. And is near.
I wake to sleep, and take my waking slow.
I learn by going where I have to go.

JALAL AL-DIN RUMI

PERSIA/TURKEY • 1207–1273

This poem speaks to a space inside me that causes my life to be in its proper perspective. I can't live without it and I can die with it.

—Andrew Nagen, 48, Antique Navajo Textile, Dealer Corrales, New Mexico

Who Says Words with My Mouth

All day I think about it, then at night I say it.
Where did I come from, and what am I supposed to be doing?
I have no idea.
My soul is from elsewhere, I'm sure of that,
and I intend to end up there.

This drunkenness began in some other tavern.
When I get back around to that place,
I'll be completely sober. Meanwhile,
I'm like a bird from another continent, sitting in this aviary.

The day is coming when I fly off,
but who is it now in my ear, who hears my voice?
Who says words with my mouth?

Who looks out with my eyes? What is the soul?
I cannot stop asking.
If I could taste one sip of an answer,
I could break out of this prison for drunks.
I didn't come here of my own accord, and I can't leave that way.
Whoever brought me here will have to take me back.

This poetry. I never know what I'm going to say.
I don't plan it.
When I'm outside the saying of it,
I get very quiet and rarely speak at all.

Translated from the Persian by John Moyne and Coleman Barks

CARL SANDBURG

UNITED STATES • 1878–1967

Sandburg has captured the rhythms of the streetlights' vacillation, the lurid, sordid essence—and the pride that essence generates—of my hometown. Though we are no longer butcher nor toolmaker, nor wheat stacker nor freight handler to the nation, are we not still a tall, bold slugger? And do our big shoulders not shake with the laughter of youth?

—Allison Amend, 24, Student, Iowa City, Iowa

Chicago

> Hog Butcher for the World,
> Tool Maker, Stacker of Wheat,
> Player with Railroads and the Nation's Freight Handler;
> Stormy, husky, brawling,
> City of the Big Shoulders:

They tell me you are wicked and I believe them, for I have seen your painted
    women under the gas lamps luring the farm boys.
And they tell me you are crooked and I answer: Yes, it is true I have seen the
    gunman kill and go free to kill again.
And they tell me you are brutal and my reply is: On the faces of women and
    children I have seen the marks of wanton hunger.
And having answered so I turn once more to those who sneer at this my city,
    and I give them back the sneer and say to them:
Come and show me another city with lifted head singing so proud to be alive
    and coarse and strong and cunning.
Flinging magnetic curses amid the toil of piling job on job, here is a tall bold
    slugger set vivid against the little soft cities;
Fierce as a dog with tongue lapping for action, cunning as a savage pitted
    against the wilderness,
> Bareheaded,
> Shoveling,
> Wrecking,
> Planning,
> Building, breaking, rebuilding,

Under the smoke, dust all over his mouth, laughing with white teeth,
Under the terrible burden of destiny laughing as a young man laughs,
Laughing even as an ignorant fighter laughs who has never lost a battle,
Bragging and laughing that under his wrist is the pulse, and under his ribs the

heart of the people,
    Laughing!
Laughing the stormy, husky, brawling laughter of Youth, half-naked, sweating, proud to be Hog Butcher, Tool Maker, Stacker of Wheat, Player with Railroads and Freight Handler to the Nation.

SAPPHO

GREECE • 612 B.C.E.–?

In this dark time, when Eros herself is under fire of all sorts (and not least the dreary fire of legalese), I choose the following favorite poem.

—G. P. Skratz, 50, Epidimeology Coordinator, Oakland, California

Equal to the gods

Equal to the gods
is the man who sits
in front of you leaning closely
and hears you sweetly speaking
and the lust-licking laughter
of your mouth, oh it makes my
heart beat in flutters!

When I look at you
Brochea, not a part of my
voice comes out,
but my tongue breaks,
and right away
a delicate fire runs just beneath
my skin,

I see a dizzy nothing,
my ears ring with noise,
the sweat runs down
upon me, and a trembling
that I can not stop
seizes me limb and loin,
oh I am greener than grass, and
death seems so near. . . .

Translated from the Greek by Ed Sanders

GEORGE SEFERIS

GREECE • 1900–1971

*Like Seferis, I once lived alongside the Nile. I, too, embraced the river as a metaphor of my
own spiritual history and have measured the trivialities of life against its eternal flow.*

—Lewis Ware, 58, Professor of Middle East Studies, Maxwell Air Force Base, Alabama

An Old Man on the River Bank

To Nani Panayiotopoulo

And yet we should consider how we go forward.
To feel is not enough, nor to think, nor to move
nor to put your body in danger in front of an old loophole
when scalding oil and molten lead furrow the walls.

And yet we should consider towards what we go forward,
not as our pain would have it, and our hungry children
and the chasm between us and the companions calling from the opposite
    shore;
nor the whispering of the bluish light in an improvised hospital,
the pharmaceutic glimmer on the pillow of the youth operated upon at noon;
but it should be in some other way, I would say like
the long river that emerges from the great lakes enclosed deep in Africa,
that was once a god and then became a road and a benefactor, a judge and a
    delta;
that is never the same, as the ancient wise men taught,
and yet always remains the same body, the same bed, and the same Sign,
the same orientation.

I want no more than to speak simply, to be granted that grace.
Because we've loaded even our songs with so much music that they're slowly
    sinking
and we've decorated our art so much that its features have been eaten away
    by gold
and it's time to say our few words because tomorrow the soul sets sail.
If pain is human we are not human beings merely to suffer pain;
that's why I think so much these days about the great river,
that symbol which moves forward among herbs and greenery

and beasts that graze and drink, men who sow and harvest,
great tombs even and small habitations of the dead.
That current which goes its way and which is not so different from the blood
    of men,
from the eyes of men when they look straight ahead without fear in their
    hearts,
without the daily tremor for trivialities or even for important things;
when they look straight ahead like the traveler who is used to gauging his way
    by the stars,
not like us, the other day, gazing at the enclosed garden of a sleepy Arab
    house,
behind the lattices the cool garden changing shape, growing larger and
    smaller,
we too changing, as we gazed, the shape of our desire and our hearts,
at the tip of midday, we the patient dough of a world that throws us out and
    kneads us,
caught in the embroidered nets of a life that was whole and then became dust
    and sank into the sands
leaving behind it only that vague dizzying sway of a tall palm-tree.

Translated from the Greek by Edmund Keeley and Phillip Sherrard

WILLIAM SHAKESPEARE

ENGLAND • 1564–1616

I like poems that make you feel deeply inside and I could feel the romance in this poem. I could picture myself as the girl that the poem is being recited to. I could see a handsome young man reciting this poem to his true love, hoping that she would fall in love with him or go out on a date.

—Lauren Dimisa, 11, Student, East Northport, New York

I found this poem in a poetry book at my school book fair. My parents thought this book would be too old for me, but little did they know it helped develop a great taste in English literature. It gave me great ideas to write my own poems in Shakespeare's style.

—Diana Sands, 10, Student, Farmington, Connecticut

Sonnet 18

Shall I compare thee to a summer's day?
Thou art more lovely and more temperate:
Rough winds do shake the darling buds of May,
And summer's lease hath all too short a date:
Sometime too hot the eye of heaven shines
And often is his gold complexion dimmed;
And every fair from fair sometimes declines,
By chance or nature's changing course untrimmed;
But thy eternal summer shall not fade.
Nor lose possession of that fair thou ow'st;
Nor shall death brag thou wander'st in his shade,
When in eternal lines to time thou grow'st:
    So long as men can breathe, or eyes can see,
    So long lives this, and this gives life to thee.

I first read this poem in junior high school English class. As one recently out of an orphanage, I felt the desperateness of the statement "I all alone beweep my outcast state." When I came to the metaphor of the lark, my voice quivered with exultation at recovery of the grace of fortune. The love element then meant less to me than the reversal of fortune, but later I would recite this sonnet in that sense. In boot camp during WW II, I walked on guard duty from midnight to 4:00 A.M. on a freezing winter night, and to distract myself from the cold, went over all the poems I knew. Shakespeare's lark reminded me of Shelley's "To a Sky-Lark" and then I went on to Poe's "The Raven," and when I ran out of birds, I turned to

*Edna Millay. The time passed, the chilling wind not diminished but less noticeable. Poetry
helped.*

—Daniel McCall, 80, Retired Teacher, Boston, Massachusetts

Sonnet 29

When, in disgrace with fortune and men's eyes,
I all alone beweep my outcast state,
And trouble deaf heaven with my bootless cries,
And look upon myself, and curse my fate,
Wishing me like to one more rich in hope,
Featured like him, like him with friends possessed,
Desiring this man's art and that man's scope,
With what I most enjoy contented least;
Yet in these thoughts myself almost despising,
Haply I think on thee—and then my state,
Like to the lark at break of day arising
From sullen earth, sings hymns at heaven's gate;
For thy sweet love remembered such wealth brings
That then I scorn to change my state with kings.

—————————

*I am a typesetter for the Government Printing Office and I love reciting Shakespeare's son-
nets. The idea that simple lies as well as truths make up a relationship reminds me of my
twenty years with my wife. I find there is no logic to love. For me, mature love is not the ra-
tional sum of good versus the bad parts. Our love is there in full view of the everyday faults
we have. I believe that anyone can love a perfect being; not everyone can love the imperfect
ones, too.*

—John Bartoli, 51, Typesetter, College Park, Maryland

Sonnet 138

When my love swears that she is made of truth,
I do believe her, though I know she lies,
That she might think me some untutored youth,
Unlearnèd in the world's false subtleties.
Thus vainly thinking that she thinks me young,
Although she knows my days are past the best,
Simply I credit her false-speaking tongue:
On both sides thus is simple truth suppressed.

But wherefore says she not she is unjust?
And wherefore say not I that I am old?
Oh, love's best habit is in seeming trust,
And age in love loves not to have years told.
    Therefore I lie with her and she with me,
    And in our faults by lies we flattered be.

STEVIE SMITH

ENGLAND • 1902–1971

Here in southeast Alaska the winters are hard, and it's not unheard of for people to fall into a depression. Last winter, it was my turn. I think this poem spoke to me because its theme is isolation. One feature of depression is just that. You feel cut off from other people. You can see them out there mouthing words at you but it's like they're speaking through frosted glass. I think this poem crystalizes that feeling just exactly. Another thing I like is the water images. They seem to come into mind when you're going through a depression. Drowning, thrashing, going down, all of that. But what I liked about it that was hopeful, is that it has a little bit of a tone of defiance and bravery, a kind of chirpiness. It also helped me to share this poem with other people as a way to work out of the isolation. It encouraged me to keep thrashing, and to keep waving. It helped me.

—Bridgit Stearns, 50, Librarian, Ketchikan, Alaska

Not Waving But Drowning

Nobody heard him, the dead man,
But still he lay moaning:
I was much further out than you thought
And not waving but drowning.

Poor chap, he always loved larking
And now he's dead
It must have been too cold for him his heart gave way,
They said.

Oh, no no no, it was too cold always
(Still the dead one lay moaning)
I was much too far out all my life
And not waving but drowning.

WILLIAM STAFFORD

UNITED STATES • B. 1914

I have a thin jagged scar on my cheek, which I got while shaving at the age of two—trying to emulate my father. I have four brothers. None of them ever tried it.

—Lisa Frye Kinkel, 33, Administrative Assistant, Nashville, Tennessee

Scars

They tell how it was, and how time
came along, and how it happened
again and again. They tell
the slant life takes when it turns
and slashes your face as a friend.

Any wound is real. In church
a woman lets the sun find
her cheek, and we see the lesson:
there are years in that book; there are sorrows
a choir can't reach when they sing.

Rows of children lift their faces of promise,
places where the scars will be.

WALLACE STEVENS

UNITED STATES • 1879–1955

Several years ago illness switched off my short-term memory and all but obliterated my ability to read. Nothing new stays with me. What I have left are the poems that burned themselves into my being long ago, before the illness struck. They sustain me still. I'd like to submit Stevens's poem because for me it best realizes the way in which well-made words can transform and even redeem the chaos of the world. This passage in particular captures for me the power of the imagination to satisfy that "blessed rage for order" I think we all feel.

—Kathy Weiss, 50, Former Technical Writer, Asbury Park, New Jersey

This is a poem that I have loved for, as I was calculating it this evening, thirty-seven years, since I first read it. That's easy to say. It's harder for me to say exactly why it has been so important to me. But it is, I think, a splendid statement about the power of the human imagination and the human intellect, and how those powers, set against the powers of nature, create meaning in what otherwise might be chaos. For those who don't know the poem, the setting is simple. The poet and a friend, at Key West, at sunset, watch a woman walking along the edge of the ocean, singing.

—Jon Westling, 56, University President, Boston, Massachusetts

The Idea of Order at Key West

She sang beyond the genius of the sea.
The water never formed to mind or voice,
Like a body wholly body, fluttering
Its empty sleeves; and yet its mimic motion
Made constant cry, caused constantly a cry,
That was not ours although we understood,
Inhuman, of the veritable ocean.

The sea was not a mask. No more was she.
The song and water were not medleyed sound
Even if what she sang was what she heard,
Since what she sang was uttered word by word.
It may be that in all her phrases stirred
The grinding water and the gasping wind;
But it was she and not the sea we heard.
For she was the maker of the song she sang.
The ever-hooded, tragic-gestured sea
Was merely a place by which she walked to sing.
Whose spirit is this? we said, because we knew

It was the spirit that we sought and knew
That we should ask this often as she sang.

If it was only the dark voice of the sea
That rose, or even colored by many waves;
If it was only the outer voice of sky
And cloud, of the sunken coral water-walled,
However clear, it would have been deep air,
The heaving speech of air, a summer sound
Repeated in a summer without end
And sound alone. But it was more than that,
More even than her voice, and ours, among
The meaningless plungings of water and the wind,
Theatrical distances, bronze shadows heaped
On high horizons, mountainous atmospheres
Of sky and sea.
        It was her voice that made
The sky acutest at its vanishing.
She measured to the hour its solitude.
She was the single artificer of the world
In which she sang. And when she sang, the sea,
Whatever self it had, became the self
That was her song, for she was the maker. Then we,
As we beheld her striding there alone,
Knew that there never was a world for her
Except the one she sang and, singing, made.

Ramon Fernandez, tell me, if you know,
Why, when the singing ended and we turned
Toward the town, tell why the glassy lights,
The lights in the fishing boats at anchor there,
As the night descended, tilting in the air,
Mastered the night and portioned out the sea,
Fixing emblazoned zones and fiery poles,
Arranging, deepening, enchanting night.

Oh! Blessed rage for order, pale Ramon,
The maker's rage to order words of the sea,
Words of the fragrant portals, dimly-starred,
And of ourselves and of our origins,
In ghostlier demarcations, keener sounds.

The Snow Man

One must have a mind of winter
To regard the frost and the boughs
Of the pine-trees crusted with snow;

And have been cold a long time
To behold the junipers shagged with ice,
The spruces rough in the distant glitter

Of the January sun; and not to think
Of any misery in the sound of the wind,
In the sound of a few leaves,

Which is the sound of the land
Full of the same wind
That is blowing in the same bare place

For the listener, who listens in the snow,
And, nothing himself, beholds
Nothing that is not there and the nothing that is.

Tea at the Palaz of Hoon

Not less because in purple I descended
The western day through what you called
The loneliest air, not less was I myself.

What was the ointment sprinkled on my beard?
What were the hymns that buzzed beside my ears?
What was the sea whose tide swept through me there?

Out of my mind the golden ointment rained,
And my ears made the blowing hymns they heard.
I was myself the compass of that sea:

I was the world in which I walked, and what I saw
Or heard or felt came not but from myself;
And there I found myself more truly and more strange.

I am a Mississipian come north for study and cooler climes. The poem evokes memories of the pungent air of my Mississippi summers moving sluggishly over my body, pushed by the attic fan in a July that never seemed to end. Stevens captures that physical discomfort and the signal it sends: of no more easy nights; of the desperate physical ache of and for the bodies that move at rest in the nights around us.

—Andrew Johnson, 23, Student, Amherst, Massachusetts

Girl in a Nightgown

Lights out. Shades up.
A look at the weather.
There has been a booming all the spring,
A refrain from the end of the boulevards.

This is the silence of night,
This is what could not be shaken,
Full of stars and the images of stars—
And that booming wintry and dull,

Like a tottering, a falling and an end,
Again and again, always there,
Massive drums and leaden trumpets,
Perceived by feeling instead of sense,

A revolution of things colliding.
Phrases! But of fear and of fate.
The night should be warm and fluters' fortune
Should play in the trees when morning comes.

Once it was, the repose of night,
Was a place, strong place, in which to sleep.
It is shaken now. It will burst into flames,
Either now or tomorrow or the day after that.

ROBERT LOUIS STEVENSON

SCOTLAND • 1850–1894

I love building tall cities and houses. The poem reminds me of my little brother that I love. I try to build tall things but he always wrecks them. That's okay because I can always build something else. I studied medieval times in school a lot and liked it. This poem is about castles and kings.

—Andrew Toporoff, 7, Student, Yorktown Heights, New York

Block City

What are you able to build with your blocks?
Castles and palaces, temples and docks.
Rain may keep raining, and others go roam,
But I can be happy and building at home.

Let the sofa be mountains, the carpet be sea,
There I'll establish a city for me:
A kirk and a mill and a palace beside,
And a harbor as well where my vessels may ride.

Great is the palace with pillar and wall,
A sort of a tower on the top of it all,
And steps coming down in an orderly way
To where my toy vessels lie safe in the bay.

This one is sailing and that one is moored:
Hark to the song of the sailors on board!
And see on the steps of my palace, the kings
Coming and going with presents and things!

When I read this poem it is as if my father and I, one, then the other, appear in the words. For the last two years I have grieved his death. Two years ago, I received a call at the school where I work saying that he had committed suicide. My loss and sadness were great and seemed to take on universal proportions. His life magnified itself, especially what I know about his childhood and home-place. Dad shared his early experience often with me when I was a child. I was taken twice a month to visit my grandmother at the farm where he was raised. Grandma Ida always had a chicken dinner ready, cooked on her wood burning stove. We ate at the old table of my dad and his nine siblings. After the dishes were washed, my father made a fire in the fireplace. There we visited, with only firelight for illumination. My

father's family emphasized visiting, and many before me sat at that fire for conversation, cof-
fee, bread, and pie. I know the nature and culture of my dad's home-place and understand
what it meant to him. I want to carry on this value and affinity.

—Kay Israel, 58, Counselor/Teacher, Zanesville, Ohio

Home No More Home to Me, Whither Must I Wander?

(To the tune of "Wandering Willie")

Home no more home to me, whither must I wander?
   Hunger my driver, I go where I must.
Cold blows the winter wind over hill and heather;
   Thick drives the rain, and my roof is in the dust.
Loved of wise men was the shade of my roof-tree.
   The true word of welcome was spoken in the door—
Dear days of old, with the faces in the firelight,
   Kind folks of old, you come again no more.

Home was home then, my dear, full of kindly faces,
   Home was home then, my dear, happy for the child.
Fire and the windows bright glittered on the moorland;
   Song, tuneful song, built a palace in the wild.
Now, when day dawns on the brow of the moorland,
   Lone stands the house, and the chimney-stone is cold.
Lone let it stand, now the friends are all departed,
   The kind hearts, the true hearts, that loved the place of old.

Spring shall come, come again, calling up the moor-fowl,
   Spring shall bring the sun and rain, bring the bees and flowers;
Red shall the heather bloom over hill and valley,
   Soft flow the stream through the even-flowing hours;
Fair the day shine as it shone on my childhood—
   Fair shine the day on the house with open door;
Birds come and cry there and twitter in the chimney—
   But I go for ever and come again no more.

MARK STRAND

UNITED STATES * B. 1934

Eating is something we all do. Sometimes the experience can be totally gratifying. Most of the time we barely remember doing it. This poem reminds me how powerful and evocative this little daily ritual can be.

—Julie Matney, 46, Social Worker/Writer, Sarasota, Florida

Pot Roast

I gaze upon the roast,
that is sliced and laid out
on my plate
and over it
I spoon the juices
of carrot and onion.
And for once I do not regret
the passage of time.

I sit by a window
that looks
on the soot-stained brick of buildings
and do not care that I see
no living thing—not a bird,
not a branch in bloom,
not a soul moving
in the rooms
behind the dark panes.
These days when there is little
to love or to praise
one could do worse
than yield
to the power of food.
So I bend

to inhale
the steam that rises
from my plate, and I think
of the first time
I tasted a roast

like this.
It was years ago
in Seabright,
Nova Scotia;
my mother leaned
over my dish and filled it
and when I finished
filled it again.
I remember the gravy,
its odor of garlic and celery,
and sopping it up
with pieces of bread.

And now
I taste it again.
The meat of memory.
The meat of no change.
I raise my fork in praise,
and I eat.

WISLAWA SZYMBORSKA

POLAND • B. 1923

Someone gave me Szymborska's book at a time when my partner, Steve, was very sick with AIDS. This poem immediately appealed to me, made me feel better. I love the plainness of her language, the casual, matter-of-fact quality, and the very simple things she lists: "Wednesday, bread and alphabets." She shows the things one treasures when life seems confusing and hard and out of order. I'm delighted by the image of this elderly Polish poet—cigarette in hand—on a trek through the Himalayas. "We've inherited hope, the gift of forgetting. You'll see how we give birth among the ruins." Gorgeous!

—Bill Hayes, 38, Writer, San Francisco, California

Notes from a Nonexistent Himalayan Expedition

So these are the Himalayas.
Mountains racing to the moon.
The moment of their start recorded
on the startling, ripped canvas of the sky.
Holes punched in a desert of clouds.
Thrust into nothing.
Echo—a white mute.
Quiet.

Yeti, down there we've got Wednesday,
bread and alphabets.
Two times two is four.
Roses are red there,
and violets are blue.

Yeti, crime is not all
we're up to down there.
Yeti, not every sentence there
means death.

We've inherited hope—
the gift of forgetting.
You'll see how we give
birth among the ruins.

Yeti, we've got Shakespeare there.
Yeti, we play solitaire

and violin. At nightfall,
we turn lights on, Yeti.

Up here it's neither moon nor earth.
Tears freeze.
Oh Yeti, semi-moonman,
turn back, think again!

I called this to the Yeti
inside four walls of avalanche,
stomping my feet for warmth
on the everlasting
snow.

Translated from the Polish by Stanislaw Baranczak and Clare Cavanaugh

RABINDRANATH TAGORE

INDIA • 1861–1941

I spent five months last year volunteering as a nurse and doing health research in a Tibetan refugee settlement in northern India. While I was there, I also met a young Tibetan man who is now my close friend. When it came time to leave, I wanted to give him something to remember me by, but not just anything—something that would perfectly convey what our friendship means to me. This was more difficult than I originally imagined, because there is always more room for misinterpretation when you're communicating across cultures. I thought about my lucky ring, or a photograph, or some music, but nothing seemed appropriate—not until I was leafing through a collection of work by the great Bengali poet Rabindranath Tagore. And there it was, the perfect "Gift." The poem captures our inability to make our love something visible, tangible, permanent.

—D'Arcy Richardson, 37, Nurse, Berkeley, California

Gift

O my love, what gift of mine
Shall I give you this dawn?
A morning song?
But morning does not last long—
The heat of the sun
Wilts it like a flower
And songs that tire
Are done.

O friend, when you come to my gate
At dusk
What is it you ask?
What shall I bring you?
A light?
A lamp from a secret corner of my silent house?
But will you want to take it with you
Down the crowded street?
Alas,
The wind will blow it out.

Whatever gifts are in my power to give you,
Be they flowers,
Be they gems for your neck,
How can they please you

If in time they must surely wither,
Crack,
Lose lustre?
All that my hands can place in yours
Will slip through your fingers
And fall forgotten to the dust
To turn into dust.

Rather,
When you have leisure,
Wander idly through my garden in spring
And let an unknown, hidden flower's scent startle you
Into sudden wondering—
Let that displaced moment
Be my gift.
Or if, as you peer your way down a shady avenue,
Suddenly, spilled
From the thick gathered tresses of evening
A single shivering fleck of sunset-light stops you,
Turns your daydreams to gold,
Let that light be an innocent
Gift.

Truest treasure is fleeting;
It sparkles for a moment, then goes.
It does not tell its name; its tune
Stops us in our tracks, its dance disappears
At the toss of an anklet.
I know no way to it—
No hand, nor word can reach it.
Friend, whatever you take of it,
On your own,
Without asking, without knowing, let that
Be yours.
Anything I can give you is trifling—
Be it a flower, or a song.

Translated from the Bengali by William Radice

ALFRED, LORD TENNYSON

ENGLAND • 1809–1892

Like most, I was introduced to the poem in high school. In my case, by Miss Rosa Mae Mahaffey, a self-proclaimed flapper, as I recall, still fond of shimmery dresses, and the first person I ever heard who read Chaucer in Old English. In the fall of 1961, I set sail in Ulysses's path, so to speak. First in military service, then with the Peace Corps, and later in other pursuits, I crossed oceans by ship or aircraft, contended with strange people in stranger cultures, and learned of our common humanity. In those travels I'm sure I have met Circe in several of her guises, if not some of the lesser gods. I have eaten the lotus fruit and seen the walls of my enemies fall, been among the Amazon women and waxed my ears against siren's calls. If I am fortunate enough, I'll have more opportunities to set my sails for the sunset (or the sunrise). When my time comes to die, I want to be facing forward, not looking back.

—Charles Griffin, 55, Writer/Photographer, San Antonio, Texas

Ulysses

It little profits that an idle king,
By this still hearth, among these barren crags,
Match'd with an aged wife, I mete and dole
Unequal laws unto a savage race,
That hoard, and sleep, and feed, and know not me.
I cannot rest from travel; I will drink
Life to the lees. All times I have enjoy'd
Greatly, have suffer'd greatly, both with those
That loved me, and alone; on shore, and when
Thro' scudding drifts the rainy Hyades
Vext the dim sea. I am become a name;
For always roaming with a hungry heart
Much have I seen and known,—cities of men
And manners, climates, councils, governments,
Myself not least, but honor'd of them all,—
And drunk delight of battle with my peers,
Far on the ringing plains of windy Troy.
I am a part of all that I have met;
Yet all experience is an arch wherethro'
Gleams that untravell'd world whose margin fades
For ever and for ever when I move.
How dull it is to pause, to make an end,
To rust unburnish'd, not to shine in use!
As tho' to breathe were life! Life piled on life

Were all too little, and of one to me
Little remains; but every hour is saved
From that eternal silence, something more,
A bringer of new things; and vile it were
For some three suns to store and hoard myself,
And this gray spirit yearning in desire
To follow knowledge like a sinking star,
Beyond the utmost bound of human thought.
   This is my son, mine own Telemachus,
To whom I leave the sceptre and the isle,—
Well-loved of me, discerning to fulfil
This labor, by slow prudence to make mild
A rugged people, and thro' soft degrees
Subdue them to the useful and the good.
Most blameless is he, centred in the sphere
Of common duties, decent not to fail
In offices of tenderness, and pay
Meet adoration to my household gods,
When I am gone. He works his work, I mine.
   There lies the port; the vessel puffs her sail;
There gloom the dark, broad seas. My mariners,
Souls that have toil'd, and wrought, and thought with me,—
That ever with a frolic welcome took
The thunder and the sunshine, and opposed
Free hearts, free foreheads,—you and I are old;
Old age hath yet his honor and his toil.
Death closes all; but something ere the end,
Some work of noble note, may yet be done,
Not unbecoming men that strove with Gods.
The lights begin to twinkle from the rocks;
The long day wanes; the slow moon climbs; the deep
Moans round with many voices. Come, my friends.
'T is not too late to seek a newer world.
Push off, and sitting well in order smite
The sounding furrows; for my purpose holds
To sail beyond the sunset, and the baths
Of all the western stars, until I die.
It may be that the gulfs will wash us down;
It may be we shall touch the Happy Isles,
And see the great Achilles, whom we knew.
Tho' much is taken, much abides; and tho'
We are not now that strength which in old days

Moved earth and heaven, that which we are, we are,—
One equal temper of heroic hearts,
Made weak by time and fate, but strong in will
To strive, to seek, to find, and not to yield.

ERNEST LAWRENCE THAYER

UNITED STATES • 1863–1940

It all started in the mid-1930s when I was a boy of seven or eight. We lived in an upstairs apartment in my grandfather's house. Both my parents worked; my father on the W.P.A and my mother in a glove factory. School would let out at 3:00 P.M. every day and I would hurry home, where at 3:15 P.M. the ballgames would come on the radio. Grandpa was a great baseball fan. We could get the Yankees, Giants, and Dodgers, and if the weather was right, the Athletics or Phillies from Philadelphia. We both knew all the players' names and their batting averages. These were some of the happiest times of my entire life. My other love, besides baseball, was Big Band music, and my parents had a record player. I started collecting records in 1936. Sometime in the late 1930s or early 1940s, Decca Records put out a 78 R.P.M. album entitled "Take Me Out to the Ballgame." On it was a recording of "Casey at the Bat" read by Harry Hirschfield. I memorized that poem and recited it just about every day until I went in the navy in 1943. While in the navy, I used to recite it into my headphones to the other guys on the midnight to 4:10 A.M. watch. Sometimes they would ask me to recite it on other watches. Took a cruise a few years back and recited it in a Passenger Talent Night on board ship.

—Paul Cornell, 72, Retired, Scottsdale, Arizona

I am a complete baseball fanatic. I learned to read from sorting through my many, many baseball cards. I love the history of baseball. In this poem, Casey is the star hitter and a show-off and he ends up striking out. I play in Little League and I see this happen all the time. One of the things I love about baseball is that games can turn around so quickly.

—Lee Samuel, 11, Student, Atlanta, Georgia

Casey at the Bat

The outlook wasn't brilliant for the Mudville nine that day:
The score stood four to two, with but one inning more to play,
And then when Cooney died at first, and Barrows did the same,
A pall-like silence fell upon the patrons of the game.

A straggling few got up to go in deep despair. The rest
Clung to that hope which springs eternal in the human breast;
They thought, "If only Casey could but get a whack at that—
We'd put up even money now, with Casey at the bat."

But Flynn preceded Casey, as did also Jimmy Blake,
And the former was a hoodoo, while the latter was a cake;
So upon that stricken multitude grim melancholy sat,
For there seemed but little chance of Casey getting to the bat.

But Flynn let drive a single, to the wonderment of all,
And Blake, the much despisèd, tore the cover off the ball;
And when the dust had lifted, and men saw what had occurred,
There was Jimmy safe at second and Flynn a-hugging third.

Then from five thousand throats and more there rose a lusty yell;
It rumbled through the valley, it rattled in the dell;
It pounded on the mountain and recoiled upon the flat,
For Casey, mighty Casey, was advancing to the bat.

There was ease in Casey's manner as he stepped into his place;
There was pride in Casey's bearing and a smile lit Casey's face.
And when, responding to the cheers, he lightly doffed his hat,
No stranger in the crowd could doubt 'twas Casey at the bat.

Ten thousand eyes were on him as he rubbed his hands with dirt;
Five thousand tongues applauded when he wiped them on his shirt;
Then while the writhing pitcher ground the ball into his hip,
Defiance flashed in Casey's eye, a sneer curled Casey's lip.

And now the leather-covered sphere came hurtling through the air,
And Casey stood a-watching it in haughty grandeur there.
Close by the sturdy batsman the ball unheeded sped—
"That ain't my style," said Casey. "Strike one!" the umpire said.

From the benches, black with people, there went up a muffled roar,
Like the beating of the storm-waves on a stern and distant shore;
"Kill him! Kill the umpire!" shouted someone on the stand;
And it's likely they'd have killed him had not Casey raised his hand.

With a smile of Christian charity great Casey's visage shone;
He stilled the rising tumult; he bade the game go on;
He signaled to the pitcher, and once more the dun sphere flew;
But Casey still ignored it and the umpire said, "Strike two!"

"Fraud!" cried the maddened thousands, and echo answered "Fraud!"
But one scornful look from Casey and the audience was awed.
They saw his face grow stern and cold, they saw his muscles strain,
And they knew that Casey wouldn't let that ball go by again.

The sneer is gone from Casey's lip, his teeth are clenched in hate,
He pounds with cruel violence his bat upon the plate;

And now the pitcher holds the ball, and now he lets it go,
And now the air is shattered by the force of Casey's blow.

Oh, somewhere in this favoured land the sun is shining bright,
The band is playing somewhere, and somewhere hearts are light;
And somewhere men are laughing, and somewhere children shout,
But there is no joy in Mudville—mighty Casey has struck out.

DYLAN THOMAS

WALES • 1914–1953

Five years Medical-Surgical Nursing. Sixteen years in Critical Care: bedside and adminis-
trative responsibility of nursing care given to patients in 102 monitored beds. Six years On-
cology (Cancer). Death was very familiar in those years, so this poem was significant,
magnificent, and meaningful as we worked acutely, critically, and raged "against the dying
of the light." We used powerful medicines, equipment, electricity, and people. Lines of po-
etry were tossed about, some from this poem.

—Jane Simpson, 63, Retired Registered Nurse, Toivola, Michigan

I have always been what most people consider a big, tough guy. I grew up in a fairly large
city where acting tough was the only way to get home from Catholic school without being
followed and harassed by the neighborhood bully. I have an unconventional look, with a
shaved head, six earrings and a few body piercings. This may all seem inconsequential to my
affection for poetry but it makes a poignant preface to the first reason this is my favorite
poem. It makes me cry. The poem has a very personal side for me as well. Several years ago
my mother had contracted cancer. My mother and I are very close. She has always nurtured
my loves especially when it came to poetry. Her cancer had led to surgery, which caused
complications and eventually a minor stroke and the amputation of half her left arm. I was
away at college when this began and my father and sister, while holding down full-time
jobs, were taking care of my mom. After my semester was over, I moved home to help take
care of her. My family was exhausted. She went through intensive chemotherapy and few
people thought she would live for more than a few months. Day after day she would lie and
suffer. She forever had a love for life which was being sapped by this dreadful disease and
draining cure. I read this poem to her often at night. My mother raged and fought the dying
of the light for months. Now, four years later, and after another battle with this ailment, my
mother is alive and well and my family continues to share with each other all that life has
for us.

—Billy Dall, 29, Emergency Medical Technician/Computer Consultant, North Bergen,
  New Jersey

Do Not Go Gentle into That Good Night

Do not go gentle into that good night,
Old age should burn and rave at close of day;
Rage, rage against the dying of the light.

Though wise men at their end know dark is right,
Because their words had forked no lightning they
Do not go gentle into that good night.

Good men, the last wave by, crying how bright
Their frail deeds might have danced in a green bay,
Rage, rage against the dying of the light.

Wild men who caught and sang the sun in flight,
And learn, too late, they grieved it on its way,
Do not go gentle into that good night.

Grave men, near death, who see with blinding sight
Blind eyes could blaze like meteors and be gay,
Rage, rage against the dying of the light.

And you, my father, there on the sad height,
Curse, bless, me now with your fierce tears, I pray.
Do not go gentle into that good night.
Rage, rage against the dying of the light.

<hr>

*I started memorizing poetry as a test of sobriety. (If I could remember the words, I wasn't too
drunk.) And I mentally called back favorite poems to assist me through painful times, both
physical and emotional. I repeated "When to the sessions . . ." when I was in labor with my
son. This Thomas poem has become something of a talisman for me. It inspires me to go on.*

—Marjorie Pokorny, 48, Clerk, Sherman, Texas

In My Craft or Sullen Art

In my craft or sullen art
Exercised in the still night
When only the moon rages
And the lovers lie abed
With all their griefs in their arms,
I labour by singing light
Not for ambition or bread
Or the strut and trade of charms
On the ivory stages
But for the common wages
Of their most secret heart.

Nor for the proud man apart
From the raging moon I write
On these spindrift pages

Nor for the towering dead
With their nightingales and psalms
But for the lovers, their arms
Round the griefs of the ages,
Who pay no praise or wages
Nor heed my craft or art.

This poem, to me, is a spoken memory of my own happy childhood on my grandmother's farm. I spent more hours there, with my siblings and cousins, than I did in my own home. I was raised in that same green corner of Wales where Dylan lived and is buried. The poem is a lyrical evocation of the glories of a happy childhood, spent in a beautiful place, yet it underscores the sadness of childhood's ephemerality.

—Elizabeth Davies, 72, Retired Teacher, San Diego, California

Fern Hill

Now as I was young and easy under the apple boughs
About the tilting house and happy as the grass was green,
    The night above the dingle starry,
        Time let me hail and climb
    Golden in the heydays of his eyes,
And honoured among wagons I was prince of the apple towns
And once below a time I lordly had the trees and leaves
        Trail with daisies and barley
    Down the rivers of the windfall light.

And as I was green and carefree, famous among the barns
About the happy yard and singing as the farm was home,
    In the sun that is young once only,
        Time let me play and be
    Golden in the mercy of his means,
And green and golden I was huntsman and herdsman, the calves
Sang to my horn, the foxes on the hills barked clear and cold,
        And the sabbath rang slowly
    In the pebbles of the holy streams.

All the sun long it was running, it was lovely, the hay
Fields high as the house, the tunes from the chimneys, it was air
    And playing, lovely and watery
        And fire green as grass.

And nightly under the simple stars
As I rode to sleep the owls were bearing the farm away,
All the moon long I heard, blessed among stables, the nightjars
   Flying with the ricks, and the horses
      Flushing into the dark.

And then to awake, and the farm, like a wanderer white
With the dew, come back, the cock on his shoulder: it was all
   Shining, it was Adam and maiden,
      The sky gathered again
   And the sun grew round that very day.
So it must have been after the birth of the simple light
In the first, spinning place, the spellbound horses walking warm
   Out of the whinnying green stable
      On to the fields of praise.

And honoured among foxes and pheasants by the gay house
Under the new made clouds and happy as the heart was long,
   In the sun born over and over,
      I ran my heedless ways,
   My wishes raced through the house high hay
And nothing I cared, at my sky blue trades, that time allows
In all his tuneful turning so few and such morning songs
   Before the children green and golden
      Follow him out of grace,

Nothing I cared, in the lamb white days, that time would take me
Up to the swallow thronged loft by the shadow of my hand,
   In the moon that is always rising,
      Nor that riding to sleep
   I should hear him fly with the high fields
And wake to the farm forever fled from the childless land.
Oh as I was young and easy in the mercy of his means,
      Time held me green and dying
   Though I sang in my chains like the sea.

CHIDIOCK TICHBORNE

ENGLAND • CA. 1558–1586

This poem is about "I have lived and I haven't lived." So think what that guy went through, and what we go through, okay? That poem touched me deeply.

—Andrew Bostjanaia, 11, Student, Pittsburg, Pennsylvania

Tichborne's Elegy

Written with his own hand in the Tower before his execution

My prime of youth is but a frost of cares,
My feast of joy is but a dish of pain,
My crop of corn is but a field of tares,
And all my good is but vain hope of gain;
The day is past, and yet I saw no sun,
And now I live, and now my life is done.

My tale was heard and yet it was not told,
My fruit is fallen and yet my leaves are green,
My youth is spent and yet I am not old,
I saw the world and yet I was not seen;
My thread is cut and yet it is not spun,
And now I live, and now my life is done.

I sought my death and found it in my womb,
I looked for life and saw it was a shade,
I trod the earth and knew it was my tomb,
And now I die, and now I was but made;
My glass is full, and now my glass is run,
And now I live, and now my life is done.

DEREK WALCOTT

ST. LUCIA, WEST INDIES • B. *1930*

The last line of "A Far Cry from Africa" is a wake-up call for all Africans in the Diaspora. I was born and raised in The Gambia (home of Kunta Kinteh, Alex Hailey's ancestor). For a lot of compelling and unfortunate reasons, I had to come to the United States to complete my education. When I read this poem, I hear the voice of my brothers and sisters, I hear the voice of my ancestors, I hear the voice of the dying and the sufferers back home, I hear the voice of the PanAfricanist crying for peace, unity, and prosperity in the continent of Africa. As the line of the poem keeps ringing in my mind, I cannot turn away from Africa and live. This poem reminds me of what my duties and responsibilities are to the people back home. I shall never live if I turn from Africa.

—Abdoulie Jallow, Student, Vermillion, South Dakota

A Far Cry from Africa

A wind is ruffling the tawny pelt
Of Africa, Kikuyu, quick as flies,
Batten upon the bloodstreams of the veldt.
Corpses are scattered through a paradise.
Only the worm, colonel of carrion, cries:
'Waste no compassion on these separate dead!'
Statistics justify and scholars seize
The salients of colonial policy.
What is that to the white child hacked in bed?
To savages, expendable as Jews?

Threshed out by beaters, the long rushes break
In a white dust of ibises whose cries
Have wheeled since civilization's dawn
From the parched river or beast-teeming plain.
The violence of beast on beast is read
As natural law, but upright man
Seeks his divinity by inflicting pain.
Delirious as these worried beasts, his wars
Dance to the tightened careass of a drum,
While he calls courage still that native dread
Of the white peace contracted by the dead.

Again brutish necessity wipes its hands
Upon the napkins of a dirty cause, again

A waste of our compassion, as with Spain,
The gorilla wrestless with the superman.

I who am poisoned with the blood of both,
Where shall I turn, divided to the vein?
I who have cursed
The drunken officer of British rule, how choose
Between this Africa and the English tongue I love?
Betray them both, or give back what they give?
How can I face such slaughter and be cool?
How can I turn from Africa and live?

ROBERT PENN WARREN

UNITED STATES • 1905–1989

I read this poem at the time of my first broken heart. I had no idea that grief could run so deep and leave one speechless. The words identified my reality and helped put it into context. I realized I wasn't the first, nor would I be the last. The human condition requires broken hearts.

—Gay Wayman, 46, Consultant/Organizational Development, Eugene, Oregon

Arizona Midnight

The grief of the coyote seems to make
Stars quiver whiter over the blankness which
Is Arizona at midnight. In sleeping-bag,
Protected by the looped rampart of anti-rattler horsehair rope,
I take a careful twist, grinding sand on sand,
To lie on my back. I stare. Stars quiver, twitch,
In their infinite indigo. I know
Nothing to tell the stars, who go,
Age on age, along tracks they understand, and
The only answer I have for the coyote would be
My own grief, for which I have no
Tongue—indeed, scarcely understand.
Eastward, I see
No indication of dawn, not yet ready for the scream
Of inflamed distance,
Which is the significance of day.
But dimly I do see
Against that darkness, lifting in blunt agony,
The single great cactus. Once more I hear the coyote
Wail. I strain to make out the cactus. It has
Its own necessary beauty.

WALT WHITMAN

UNITED STATES • *1819–1892*

Reading and the public library were integral to our lives, but we owned few books. I still have our copy of the Modern Library edition of Leaves of Grass. *Children read whatever was on the shelves, however best they could. This poem did not make it into the collection; I found it later. My grandmother sang herself through workdays at the Eagle pencil factory and attended public school at night. When she died, her good purse held her wedding contract, fine kid gloves, and the diploma. My mother worked and studied through the Depression—helping her mother run the dress shop and earning a leather bound copy of Mann's* Joseph and His Brothers *for excellence in scholarship. At sixteen, she was accepted at Hunter College, but had to earn her living full-time. I have been educated at public schools from kindergarten through university. My son is a student in the D.C. Public School system. Our children are used shamelessly as photoprops by every passing pol (and occasional poet), but who cares about their schooling? Whitman here may be as bad as the rest in imagining children, yet he finds his way to the heart of the question of education—of knowing and learning—and the importance of public school education.*

—Ann Grossman, 49, Paper Conservator, Silver Spring, Maryland

An Old Man's Thought of School

> *For the Inauguration of a Public School, Camden, New Jersey, 1874.*

An old man's thought of school,
An old man gathering youthful memories and blooms that youth itself cannot.

Now only do I know you,
O fair auroral skies—O morning dew upon the grass!

And these I see, these sparkling eyes,
These stores of mystic meaning, these young lives,
Building, equipping like a fleet of ships, immortal ships,
Soon to sail out over the measureless seas,
On the soul's voyage.

Only a lot of boys and girls?
Only the tiresome spelling, writing, ciphering classes?
Only a public school?

Ah more, infinitely more;
(As George Fox rais'd his warning cry, "Is it this pile of brick and mortar, these

dead floors, windows, rails, you call the church?
Why this is not the church at all—the church is living, ever living souls.")

And you America,
Cast you the real reckoning for your present?
The lights and shadows of your future, good or evil?
To girlhood, boyhood look, the teacher and the school.

Wow! A favorite poem project. I love it. I have hours memorized of so many poets. I go to Russia every year because of their love of poetry. I'm a fifty-three-year-old physician, recently portrayed by Robin Williams in the movie of my name Patch Adams. *If I had to choose one: Walt Whitman, "Song of the Open Road," because it feels like a poetic expression of me— who I am and what I do. It is such a raw celebration of all life and people, without judgments. It writes all to you in the celebration; no nonmembers. I like the suggestion of the revolutionary nature of this love of all life and people and how it might, in its wake, end the suffering parts.*

—Patch Adams, 53, Physician, Arlington, Virginia

This has to be the quintessential American poem. I fell out of a tree ten years ago and landed in a wheelchair, and this section of his incredible life's work is one of the main reasons I even have a life ten years later.

—John Arndt, 42, Educational Services, Singer Island, Florida

from Song of the Open Road (1, 4, & 8)

I

Afoot and light-hearted I take to the open road,
Healthy, free, the world before me,
The long brown path before me leading wherever I choose.

Henceforth I ask not good-fortune, I myself am good-fortune,
Henceforth I whimper no more, postpone no more, need nothing,
Done with indoor complaints, libraries, querulous criticisms,
Strong and content I travel the open road.

The earth, that is sufficient,
I do not want the constellations any nearer,
I know they are very well where they are,
I know they suffice for those who belong to them.

(Still here I carry my old delicious burdens,
I carry them, men and women, I carry them with me wherever I go,
I swear it is impossible for me to get rid of them,
I am fill'd with them, and I will fill them in return.)

4

The earth expanding right hand and left hand,
The picture alive, every part in its best light,
The music falling in where it is wanted, and stopping where it is not wanted,
The cheerful voice of the public road, the gay fresh sentiment of the road.

O highway I travel, do you say to me *Do not leave me?*
Do you say *Venture not—if you leave me you are lost?*
Do you say *I am already prepared, I am well-beaten and undenied, adhere to me?*

O public road, I say back I am not afraid to leave you, yet I love you,
You express me better than I can express myself,
You shall be more to me than my poem.

I think heroic deeds were all conceiv'd in the open air, and all free poems also,
I think I could stop here myself and do miracles,
I think whatever I shall meet on the road I shall like, and whoever beholds me shall
    like me,
I think whoever I see must be happy.

8

The efflux of the soul is happiness, here is happiness,
I think it pervades the open air, waiting at all times,
Now it flows unto us, we are rightly charged.

Here rises the fluid and attaching character,
The fluid and attaching character is the freshness and sweetness of man and
    woman,
(The herbs of the morning sprout no fresher and sweeter every day out of the roots
    of themselves, than it sprouts fresh and sweet continually out of itself.)

Toward the fluid and attaching character exudes the sweat of the love of young and
    old,
From it falls distill'd the charm that mocks beauty and attainments,
Toward it heaves the shuddering longing ache of contact.

I am not someone who has a great knowledge of, or, to be honest, a great love for poetry in general. My chief motivation in picking up Whitman was to investigate a poet that had so much influence on American social history in general and on Kerouac (one of my favorites) in particular. Upon beginning Leaves of Grass *(which is still the only book of poetry I have ever read), however, I was completely enthralled by the joy that Whitman has, and causes the reader to have, for people and events that might otherwise be considered mundane. For me the poem that expresses this idea the most effectively is one entitled "To a Certain Cantatrice." Whitman seems to have a genuine respect for all people that seems all too lacking in today's America.*

—Mike O'Connor, Professor of Philosophy, San Francisco, California

To a Certain Cantatrice

Here, take this gift,
I was reserving it for some hero, speaker, or general,
One who should serve the good old cause, the great idea, the progress and
    freedom of the race,
Some brave confronter of despots, some daring rebel;
But I see that what I was reserving belongs to you just as much as to any.

"Song of Myself" is my favorite poem. I work for the Boston Gas Company. In recent years I have discovered that poetry offers insight and inspiration that I was unable to find on my own. In 1994 I began attending the University of Massachusetts as an English major. This was looked upon by many of my coworkers as nothing less than ridiculous. I guess a ditchdigger who reads Shakespeare is still just a ditchdigger. But the invaluable lesson that I have learned is that poetry is a universal celebration that exists in everything and everybody. It has fueled my own self-esteem, and helped me to take nothing for granted.

—John Doherty, 33, Construction Worker, Braintree, Massachusetts

from Song of Myself (46 & 52)

    46

I know I have the best of time and space—and that I was never measured,
    and never will be measured.

I tramp a perpetual journey,
My signs are a rain-proof coat and good shoes and a staff cut from the woods;
No friend of mine takes his ease in my chair,
I have no chair, nor church nor philosophy;

I lead no man to a dinner-table or library or exchange,
But each man and each woman of you I lead upon a knoll,
My left hand hooks you round the waist,
My right hand points to landscapes of continents, and a plain public road.

Not I, not any one else can travel that road for you,
You must travel it for yourself.

It is not far . . . . it is within reach,
Perhaps you have been on it since you were born; and did not know,
Perhaps it is every where on water and on land.

Shoulder your duds, and I will mine, and let us hasten forth;
Wonderful cities and free nations we shall fetch as we go.
If you tire, give me both burdens, and rest the chuff of your hand on my hip,
And in due time you shall repay the same service to me;
For after we start we never lie by again.

This day before dawn I ascended a hill and looked at the crowded heaven,
And I said to my spirit, When we become the enfolders of those orbs and the
    pleasure and knowledge of every thing in them, shall we be filled and satis-
    fied then?
And my spirit said No, we level that lift to pass and continue beyond.

You are also asking me questions, and I hear you;
I answer that I cannot answer . . . . you must find out for yourself.

Sit awhile wayfarer.
Here are biscuits to eat and here is milk to drink,
But as soon as you sleep and renew yourself in sweet clothes I will certainly
    kiss you with my goodbye kiss and open the gate for your egress hence.

Long enough have you dreamed contemplible dreams,
Now I wash the gum from your eyes,
You must habit yourself to the dazzle of the light and of every moment of your
    life.

Long have you timidly waded, holding a plank by the shore,
Now I will you to be a bold swimmer,
To jump off in the midst of the sea, and rise again and nod to me and shout,
    and laughingly dash with your hair.

52

The spotted hawk swoops by and accuses me . . . . he complains of my gab and my
   loitering.

I too am not a bit tamed . . . . I too am untranslatable,
I sound my barbaric yawp over the roofs of the world.

The last scud of day holds back for me,
It flings my likeness after the rest and true as any on the shadowed wilds.
It coaxes me to the vapor and the dusk.

I depart as air . . . . I shake my white locks at the runaway sun,
I effuse my flesh in eddies and drift it in lacy jags.

I bequeath myself to the dirt to grow from the grass I love,
If you want me again look for me under your bootsoles.

You will hardly know who I am or what I mean,
But I shall be good health to you nevertheless,
And filter and fibre your blood.

Failing to fetch me at first keep encouraged,
Missing me one place scarch another,
I stop some where waiting for you.

RICHARD WILBUR

UNITED STATES • B. 1921

Other poets have awakened me to a new day, reluctant and dreading what lies ahead, but only Wilbur's unique imagination has made the mundane so charming and humorous, and so surprisingly different.

—Alex Moffett, 93, Retired Physician, Grinnell, Iowa

Love Calls Us to the Things of This World

The eyes open to a cry of pulleys,
And spirited from sleep, the astounded soul
Hangs for a moment bodiless and simple
As false dawn.
                  Outside the open window
The morning air is all awash with angels.

Some are in bed-sheets, some are in blouses,
Some are in smocks: but truly there they are.
Now they are rising together in calm swells
Of halcyon feeling, filling whatever they wear
With the deep joy of their impersonal breathing;

Now they are flying in place, conveying
The terrible speed of their omnipresence, moving
And staying like white water; and now of a sudden
They swoon down into so rapt a quiet
That nobody seems to be there.
                        The soul shrinks

From all that it is about to remember,
From the punctual rape of every blessèd day,
And cries,
           "Oh, let there be nothing on earth but laundry,
Nothing but rosy hands in the rising steam
And clear dances done in the sight of heaven."

Yet, as the sun acknowledges
With a warm look the world's hunks and colors,
The soul descends once more in bitter love

To accept the waking body, saying now
In a changed voice as the man yawns and rises,

   "Bring them down from their ruddy gallows;
Let there be clean linen for the backs of thieves;
Let lovers go fresh and sweet to be undone,
And the heaviest nuns walk in a pure floating
Of dark habits,
                keeping their difficult balance."

C. K. WILLIAMS

UNITED STATES • B. 1936

I am an "average" and "ordinary" American. I've worked as a secretary for over thirty years, mostly in New York City. I've read this poem twenty times aloud. To me, he's got it just right—the experience with a buzzing fly and the uncanny sense that more is going on than just a fly buzzing. It's all there: from the low and coarse, to the just-how-it-is, to the higher ground of different dimensions, of missing the being of a friend and pondering his existence in and outside time. It all leads to the moment where the observer is both aware of himself and aware of a "brilliant ardent atom swerving through" the very moment.

—Kathleen Gallagher, Secretary, New York, New York

My Fly

for Erving Goffman, 1922–1982

One of those great, garishly emerald flies that always look freshly generated
   from fresh excrement
and who maneuver through our airspace with a deft intentionality that makes
   them seem to think,
materializes just above my desk, then vanishes, his dense, abrasive buzz
   sucked in after him.

I wait, imagine him, hidden somewhere, waiting, too, then think, who knows
   why, of you—
don't laugh—that he's a messenger from you, or that you yourself (you'd howl
   at this),
ten years afterwards have let yourself be incarnated as this pestering
   anti-angel.

Now he, or you, abruptly reappears, with a weightless pounce alighting near
   my hand.
I lean down close, and though he has to sense my looming presence, he
   patiently attends,
as though my study of him had become an element of his own observations—
   maybe it is you!

Joy! To be together, even for a time! Yes, tilt your fuselage, turn it towards the
   light,
aim the thousand lenses of your eyes back up at me: how I've missed the
   layers of your attention,

how often been bereft without your gift for sniffing out pretentiousness and
    moral sham.

Why would you come back, though? Was that other radiance not intricate
    enough to parse?
Did you find yourself in some monotonous century hovering down the tidy
    queue of creatures
waiting to experience again the eternally unlikely bliss of being matter and
    extension?

You lift, you land—you're rushed, I know; the interval in all our terminals is
    much too short.
Now you hurl against the window, skid and jiiter on the pane: I open it and
    step aside
and follow for one final moment of felicity your brilliant ardent atom swerving
    through.

WILLIAM CARLOS WILLIAMS

UNITED STATES • 1883–1963

"To Elsie" is one of the great poems of post–World War II America. The last lines, a little more than two dozen words, capture the atomized, alienated, disenfranchised, rudderless tail end of the American Century. And yet, even here, there's beauty, or at least the promise of beauty. I come back to this poem again and again. I used it in teaching freshman English to Vietnam Vets in a community college night school in the mid-'70s, and they got it right away. I used it as a call for political engagement in the first editorial I wrote for the Texas journal that I edited in the mid-'80s. I recited the last lines when I was sworn in as an Austin school board member. As an urban public school district, we have to witness and adjust, to try to help our children connect the isolate flecks of meaning and beauty—or this may be our last chance to drive this car.

—Geoff Rips, 48, Journalist, Austin, Texas

To Elsie

The pure products of America
go crazy—
mountain folk from Kentucky

or the ribbed north end of
Jersey
with its isolate lakes and

valleys, its deaf-mutes, thieves
old names
and promiscuity between

devil-may-care men who have taken
to railroading
out of sheer lust of adventure—

and young slatterns, bathed
in filth
from Monday to Saturday

to be tricked out that night
with gauds
from imaginations which have no

peasant traditions to give them
character
but flutter and flaunt

sheer rags—succumbing without
emotion
save numbed terror

under some hedge of choke-cherry
or viburnum—
which they cannot express—

Unless it be that marriage
perhaps
with a dash of Indian blood

will throw up a girl so desolate
so hemmed round
with disease or murder

that she'll be rescued by an
agent—
reared by the state and

sent out at fifteen to work in
some hard-pressed
house in the suburbs—

some doctor's family, some Elsie—
voluptuous water
expressing with broken

brain the truth about us—
her great
ungainly hips and flopping breasts

addressed to cheap
jewelry
and rich young men with fine eyes

as if the earth under our feet
were
an excrement of some sky

and we degraded prisoners
destined
to hunger until we eat filth

while the imagination strains
after deer
going by fields of goldenrod in

the stifling heat of September
Somehow
it seems to destroy us

It is only in isolate flecks that
something
is given off

No one
to witness
and adjust, no one to drive the car

There are many things I love about Williams. I love his ability to combine a career in medicine with an avocation for writing, really a calling to write. I love his very American, and still very modern, voice. His poetry exudes both great joy at the wonders of everyday life, and melancholy that our lives are so short and we are so often imperfect. I see both of those aspects of his writing in this poem. I am married to a wonderful woman and quite happy with my life here in the Midwest. Perhaps my contentment with a fairly ordinary life is why I find Williams so appealing.

—Stuart Allison, 40, Assistant Professor of Biology, Galesburg, Illinois

Danse Russe

If when my wife is sleeping
and the baby and Kathleen
are sleeping
and the sun is a flame-white disc
in silken mists
above shining trees,—

if I in my north room
dance naked, grotesquely
before my mirror
waving my shirt round my head
and singing softly to myself:
"I am lonely, lonely.
I was born to be lonely,
I am best so!"
If I admire my arms, my face,
my shoulders, flanks, buttocks
against the yellow drawn shades,—

Who shall say I am not
the happy genius of my household?

WILLIAM WORDSWORTH

ENGLAND • 1770–1850

I'm a petty officer in the U.S. Navy stationed in Japan. My duties in Japan require me to be constantly deployed. Last spring, I was deployed to the Persian Gulf during the problems with Iraq and the UN Inspectors. There were moments when I was sure that we were going to attack, due to the high tensions. While all of this was going on I was finding myself on edge. You see, on a navy ship you work twelve hours on, and twelve hours off. I was finding it difficult to have moments to myself to relax—until one morning after I had gotten off my usual twelve-hour shift and I decided to make a trip to the ship library. I was in search of a book to read and I found a book of poems. As I sat in the library reading through the poems I found this one poem in particular that stood out. These lines struck me: "When from our better selves we have too long / Been parted by the hurrying world, and droop, / Sick of its business, of its pleasure tired, / How gracious, how benign is Solitude."

—Paul Feltes, Petty Officer, U.S. Navy

from The Prelude (*Book IV, lines 354–70*)

When from our better selves we have too long
Been parted by the hurrying world, and droop,
Sick of its business, of its pleasures tired,
How gracious, how benign is Solitude!
How potent a mere image of her sway!
Most potent when impressed upon the mind
With an appropriate human centre—Hermit
Deep in the bosom of the Wilderness;
Votary (in vast Cathedral, where no foot
Is treading and no other face is seen)
Kneeling at prayer; or Watchman on the top
Of Lighthouse beaten by Atlantic Waves;
Or as the soul of that great Power is met
Sometimes embodied on a public road,
When, for the night deserted, it assumes
A character of quiet more profound
Than pathless Wastes.

When I was in eleventh grade, a world opened for me when a teacher read the poetry of Wordsworth and Keats to us. Here, my own feelings about my connectedness to the earth and to all other life were expressed so simply. This poem still gives me that feeling of whole-

ness I felt in nature as a child, in that classroom as an adolescent, and as an adult, expanding my "philosophical mind."

—Rosemary Wilvert, 56, Homemaker, San Luis Obispo, California

Lines

Composed a Few Miles above Tintern Abbey, on Revisiting the Banks of the Wye during a Tour, July 13, 1798

Five years have passed; five summers, with the length
Of five long winters! and again I hear
These waters, rolling from their mountain-springs
With a soft inland murmur.—Once again
Do I behold these steep and lofty cliffs,
That on a wild secluded scene impress
Thoughts of more deep seclusion; and connect
The landscape with the quiet of the sky.
The day is come when I again repose
Here, under this dark sycamore, and view
These plots of cottage-ground, these orchard-tufts,
Which at this season, with their unripe fruits,
Are clad in one green hue, and lose themselves
'Mid groves and copses. Once again I see
These hedge-rows, hardly hedge-rows, little lines
Of sportive wood run wild: these pastoral farms,
Green to the very door; and wreaths of smoke
Sent up, in silence, from among the trees!
With some uncertain notice, as might seem
Of vagrant dwellers in the houseless woods,
Or of some Hermit's cave, where by his fire
The Hermit sits alone.

            These beauteous forms,
Through a long absence, have not been to me
As is a landscape to a blind man's eye:
But oft, in lonely rooms, and 'mid the din
Of towns and cities, I have owed to them
In hours of weariness, sensations sweet,
Felt in the blood, and felt along the heart;
And passing even into my purer mind,
With tranquil restoration:—feelings too

Of unremembered pleasure: such, perhaps,
As have no slight or trivial influence
On that best portion of a good man's life,
His little, nameless, unremembered, acts
Of kindness and of love. Nor less, I trust,
To them I may have owed another gift,
Of aspect more sublime; that blessed mood,
In which the burthen of the mystery,
In which the heavy and the weary weight
Of all this unintelligible world,
Is lightened:—that serene and blessed mood,
In which the affections gently lead us on,—
Until, the breath of this corporeal frame
And even the motion of our human blood
Almost suspended, we are laid asleep
In body, and become a living soul:
While with an eye made quiet by the power
Of harmony, and the deep power of joy,
We see into the life of things.

                    If this
Be but a vain belief, yet, oh! how oft—
in darkness and amid the many shapes
Of joyless daylight; when the fretful stir
Unprofitable, and the fever of the world,
Have hung upon the beatings of my heart—
How oft, in spirit, have I turned to thee,
O sylvan Wye! thou wanderer thro' the woods,
How often has my spirit turned to thee!

   And now, with gleams of half-extinguished thought,
With many recognitions dim and faint,
And somewhat of a sad perplexity,
The picture of the mind revives again:
While here I stand, not only with the sense
Of present pleasure, but with pleasing thoughts
That in this moment there is life and food
For future years. And so I dare to hope,
Though changed, no doubt, from what I was when first
I came among these hills; when like a roe
I bounded o'er the mountains, by the sides
Of the deep rivers, and the lonely streams,

Wherever nature led: more like a man
Flying from something that he dreads, than one
Who sought the thing he loved. For nature then
(The coarser pleasures of my boyish days,
And their glad animal movements all gone by)
To me was all in all—I cannot paint
What then I was. The sounding cataract
Haunted me like a passion: the tall rock,
The mountain, and the deep and gloomy wood,
Their colours and their forms, were then to me
An appetite; a feeling and a love,
That had no need of a remoter charm,
By thought supplied, nor any interest
Unborrowed from the eye.—That time is past,
And all its aching joys are now no more,
And all its dizzy raptures. Not for this
Faint I, nor mourn nor murmur; other gifts
Have followed; for such loss, I would believe,
Abundant recompense. For I have learned
To look on nature, not as in the hour
Of thoughtless youth; but hearing oftentimes
The still, sad music of humanity,
Nor harsh nor grating, though of ample power
To chasten and subdue. And I have felt
A presence that disturbs me with the joy
Of elevated thoughts; a sense sublime
Of something far more deeply interfused,
Whose dwelling is the light of setting suns,
And the round ocean and the living air,
And the blue sky, and in the mind of man:
A motion and a spirit, that impels
All thinking things, all objects of all thought,
And rolls through all things. Therefore am I still
A lover of the meadows and the woods,
And mountains; and of all that we behold
From this green earth; of all the mighty world
Of eye, and ear,—both what they half create,
And what perceive; well pleased to recognise
In nature and the language of the sense,
The anchor of my purest thoughts, the nurse,
The guide, the guardian of my heart, and soul
Of all my moral being.

                    Nor perchance,
If I were not thus taught, should I the more
Suffer my genial spirits to decay:
For thou art with me here upon the banks
Of this fair river; thou my dearest Friend,
My dear, dear Friend; and in thy voice I catch
The language of my former heart, and read
My former pleasures in the shooting lights
Of thy wild eyes. Oh! yet a little while
May I behold in thee what I was once,
My dear, dear Sister! and this prayer I make,
Knowing that Nature never did betray
The heart that loved her; 'tis her privilege.
Through all the years of this our life, to lead
From joy to joy: for she can so inform
The mind that is within us, so impress
With quietness and beauty, and so feed
With lofty thoughts, that neither evil tongues,
Rash judgments, nor the sneers of selfish men,
Nor greetings where no kindness is, nor all
The dreary intercourse of daily life,
Shall e'er prevail against us, or disturb
Our cheerful faith, that all which we behold
Is full of blessings. Therefore let the moon
Shine on thee in thy solitary walk;
And let the misty mountain-winds be free
To blow against thee: and, in after years,
When these wild ecstasies shall be matured
Into a sober pleasure; when thy mind
Shall be a mansion for all lovely forms,
Thy memory be as a dwelling-place
For all sweet sounds and harmonies; oh! then,
If solitude, or fear, or pain, or grief,
Should be thy portion, with what healing thoughts
Of tender joy wilt thou remember me,
And these my exhortations! Nor, perchance—
If I should be where I no more can hear
Thy voice, nor catch from thy wild eyes these gleams
Of past existence—wilt thou then forget
That on the banks of this delightful stream
We stood together; and that I, so long

A worshipper of Nature, hither came
Unwearied in that service; rather say
With warmer love—oh! with far deeper zeal
Of holier love. Nor wilt thou then forget,
That after many wanderings, many years
Of absence, these steep woods and lofty cliffs,
And this green pastoral landscape, were to me
More dear, both for themselves and for thy sake!

SIR HENRY WOTTON

ENGLAND • *1568–1639*

I have always loved to be outside, exploring. It seems so peaceful, but by lifting a rock, I can find a whole new world, full of lizards and bugs. It's neat to watch them and see how they live, because most of the time all I see are people, and after a while, they seem so ordinary. I think it would be neat if when I grow up and have a job, it would allow me to be outdoors and caring for the environment. It has given me so much, and I only hope that I can return some of the debt I feel someday. I like this poem because it seems so happy and it brings back a lot of good memories of different days throughout the year when I would be outside performing some task and would look around at nature and the world, and I would feel happy and blessed to be alive.

—Elizabeth Kendall, 13, Student, Conyers, Georgia

On a Bank As I Sat Fishing

And now all Nature seemed in love;
The lusty sap began to move;
New juice did stir the embracing vines;
And birds had drawn their Valentines:
The jealous trout, that low did lie,
Rose at a well-dissembled fly:
There stood my friend, with patient skill
Attending of his trembling quill.
Already were the eaves possessed
With the swift Pilgrim's daubéd nest.
The groves already did rejoice
In Philomel's triumphing voice.
   The showers were short, the weather mild,
The morning fresh, the evening smiled.
   Joan takes her neat-rubbed pail, and now
She trips to milk the sand-red cow;
Where for some sturdy foot-ball swain,
Joan strokes a sillabub or twain.
   The fields and gardens were beset
With Tulips, Crocus, Violet:
And now, though late, the modest Rose
Did more than half a blush disclose.
Thus all looked gay, all full of cheer,
To welcome the new-livery'd year.

JAMES WRIGHT

UNITED STATES • 1927–1980

The poem leaps at you, and something moves inside—metamorphosis. It's not just a poem.

—Iris Moon, 18, Student, Williamstown, Massachusetts

This is the poem that changed my life forever. Nothing compares to the excruciating beauty of this poem.

—Sander Zulauf, 52, Professor of English/Editor, Andover, New Jersey

This poem transports; it reminds me of those deeply moving, surprising moments in life when the sheer joy of existence envelops me and I know that even I can evolve.

—Anne Morin, 57, Teacher, Portland, Oregon

A Blessing

Just off the highway to Rochester, Minnesota,
Twilight bounds softly forth on the grass.
And the eyes of those two Indian ponies
Darken with kindness.
They have come gladly out of the willows
To welcome my friend and me.
We step over the barbed wire into the pasture
Where they have been grazing all day, alone.
They ripple tensely, they can hardly contain their happiness
That we have come.
They bow shyly as wet swans. They love each other.
There is no loneliness like theirs.
At home once more,
They begin munching the young tufts of spring in the darkness.
I would like to hold the slenderer one in my arms.
For she has walked over to me
And nuzzled my left hand.
She is black and white,
Her mane falls wild on her forehead,
And the light breeze moves me to caress her long ear
That is delicate as the skin over a girl's wrist.
Suddenly I realize
That if I stepped out of my body I would break
Into blossom.

THOMAS WYATT

ENGLAND • 1503–1542

I came across this poem in college. I loved it then; I love it still. For me, there is, in this deceptively straightforward poem, purified passion, pain, anguish, an acceptance of reality, an acknowledgment of the necessity for continuing effort without hope of success, an earnest vow of fidelity, a resignation to fate. There is in it, however, no regret and, in the last verse, there is a commitment to enduring love and faith. Across close to five hundred years, Wyatt exhorts us to remember him and gives us reasons why. It is a very personal poem.

—Margaret Whitfield, 65, Farm Manager, Great Barrington, Massachusetts

Forget Not Yet

Forget not yet the tried intent
Of such a truth as I have meant;
My great travail so gladly spent
                Forget not yet.

Forget not yet when first began
The weary life ye know, since when
The suit, the service none tell can;
                Forget not yet.

Forget not yet the great assays,
The cruel wrong, the scornful ways,
The painful patience in denays,
                Forget not yet.

Forget not yet, forget not this,
How long ago hath been and is
The mind that never meant amiss;
                Forget not yet.

Forget not then thine own approved,
The which so long hath thee so loved,
Whose steadfast faith yet never moved;
                Forget not this.

WILLIAM BUTLER YEATS

IRELAND • 1865–1939

It struck me, in its brevity and style as a finer distillation of a fundamental truth that was already inside me. In my childhood and adolescence, being at my father's side imprinted in me the significance of things political, first as they motivated his work as a voice for exiled Cubans and later as I tried to find my place in his personal history and our own American history. I thought that joining the military out of high school and traveling would discon-nect me from the politics of home, but of course I was wrong. When I returned from my tour as an infantryman in the Gulf War, I was possessed of a clearer notion of my small role in history, and this clarity increased my desire to go back home and join the political debate surrounding my own country's attitude toward my father's country. But this process of polit-ical familiarization and the accompanying feelings would seem like nothing compared to the flood of emotions that came with leaving the people whom I loved and with whom I was in love. When I read Thomas Mann's grandiose assertion shackling our destiny to politics, followed by Yeats' very human and personal response, I felt for a moment as if I knew what Truth really was and how it lay inside of each of us and far away from politics.

—Steve Conte-Agüero, 28, United States Marine, Quantico, Virginia

Politics

'In our time the destiny of man presents its meaning in political terms.'

—THOMAS MANN

How can I, that girl standing there,
My attention fix
On Roman or on Russian
Or on Spanish politics?
Yet here's a travelled man that knows
What he talks about,
And there's a politician
That has read and thought,
And maybe what they say is true
Of war and war's alarms,
But O that I were young again
And held her in my arms!

When I was a teenager, a boyfriend I had sent me this poem, and led me to believe he had written it—for me, of course. Years later, long after the boyfriend was gone, I came across this poem in a book and was stunned. The boyfriend was a jerk—but the poem is a beauty, poignant and lovely.

—Robin Hackman, 44, Homemaker/Aspiring Fiber Artist, Middleton, Wisconsin

When You Are Old

When you are old and gray and full of sleep,
And nodding by the fire, take down this book,
And slowly read, and dream of the soft look
Your eyes had once, and of their shadows deep;

How many loved your moments of glad grace,
And loved your beauty with love false or true;
But one man loved the pilgrim soul in you,
And loved the sorrows of your changing face.

And bending down beside the glowing bars
Murmur, a little sadly, how love fled
And paced upon the mountains overhead
And hid his face amid a crowd of stars.

Sailing to Byzantium

I

That is no country for old men. The young
In one another's arms, birds in the trees
—Those dying generations—at their song,
The salmon-falls, the mackerel-crowded seas,
Fish, flesh, or fowl, commend all summer long
Whatever is begotten, born, and dies.

Caught in that sensual music all neglect
Monuments of unageing intellect.

2

An aged man is but a paltry thing,
A tattered coat upon a stick, unless
Soul clap its hands and sing, and louder sing
For every tatter in its mortal dress,
Nor is there singing school but studying
Monuments of its own magnificence;
And therefore I have sailed the seas and come
To the holy city of Byzantium.

3

O sages standing in God's holy fire
As in the gold mosaic of a wall,
Come from the holy fire, perne in a gyre,
And be the singing-masters of my soul.
Consume my heart away; sick with desire
And fastened to a dying animal
It knows not what it is; and gather me
Into the artifice of eternity.

4

Once out of nature I shall never take
My bodily form from any natural thing,
But such a form as Grecian goldsmiths make
Of hammered gold and gold enamelling
To keep a drowsy Emperor awake;
Or set upon a golden bough to sing
To lords and ladies of Byzantium
Of what is past, or passing, or to come.

SONE NO YOSHITADA

JAPAN • *Late Tenth Century*

I like the images of nature in this poem, especially how they are blended with magical thoughts, such as a feeling of awe spreading in the twilight as if it were a fine powder or spirit dust. I also love the image of the trees—perhaps hanging low to the ground, their bottom leaves "tangling" with the sunlight as it disappears into dusk. Thinking about leaves and light moving together almost in a dancelike way is relaxing. The poem is almost a meditation for me.

—Kiyoshi Houston, 12, Student Los Angeles, California

The lower leaves of the trees

The lower leaves of the trees
Tangle the sunset in dusk.
Awe spreads with
The summer twilight.

Translated from the Japanese by Kenneth Rexroth

ADAM ZAGAJEWSKI

POLAND * B. 1945

. . . rings with a plurality of voices as truly democratic as it might be European.

—Kevin Brown, 22, Student, Evanston, Illinois

To Go to Lvov

To go to Lvov. Which station
for Lvov, if not in a dream, at dawn, when dew
gleams on a suitcase, when express
trains and bullet trains are being born. To leave
in haste for Lvov, night or day, in September
or in March. But only if Lvov exists,
if it is to be found within the frontiers and not just
in my new passport, if lances of trees
—of poplar and ash—still breathe aloud
like Indians, and if streams mumble
their dark Esperanto, and grass snakes like soft signs
in the Russian language disappear
into thickets. To pack and set off, to leave
without a trace, at noon, to vanish
like fainting maidens. And burdocks, green
armies of burdocks, and below, under the canvas
of a Venetian café, the snails converse
about eternity. But the cathedral rises,
you remember, so straight, as straight
as Sunday and white napkins and a bucket
full of raspberries standing on the floor, and
my desire which wasn't born yet,
only gardens and weeds and the amber
of Queen Anne cherries, and indecent Fredro.
There was always too much of Lvov, no one could
comprehend its boroughs, hear
the murmur of each stone scorched
by the sun, at night the Orthodox church's silence was unlike
that of the cathedral, the Jesuits
baptized plants, leaf by leaf, but they grew,
grew so mindlessly, and joy hovered
everywhere, in hallways and in coffee mills

revolving by themselves, in blue
teapots, in starch, which was the first
formalist, in drops of rain and in the thorns
of roses. Frozen forsythia yellowed by the window.
The bells pealed and the air vibrated, the cornets
of nuns sailed like schooners near
the theater, there was so much of the world that
it had to do encores over and over,
the audience was in frenzy and didn't want
to leave the house. My aunts couldn't have known
yet that I'd resurrect them,
and lived so trustfully, so singly;
servants, clean and ironed, ran for
fresh cream, inside the houses
a bit of anger and great expectation, Brzozowski
came as a visiting lecturer, one of my
uncles kept writing a poem entitled *Why*,
dedicated to the Almighty, and there was too much
of Lvov, it brimmed the container,
it burst glasses, overflowed
each pond, lake, smoked through every
chimney, turned into fire, storm,
laughed with lightning, grew meek,
returned home, read the New Testament,
slept on a sofa beside the Carpathian rug,
there was too much of Lvov, and now
there isn't any, it grew relentlessly
and the scissors out it, chilly gardeners
as always in May, without mercy,
without love, ah, wait till warm June
comes with soft ferns, boundless
fields of summer, i.e., the reality.
But scissors cut it, along the line and through
the fiber, tailors, gardeners, censors
cut the body and the wreaths, pruning shears worked
diligently, as in a child's cutout
along the dotted line of a roe deer or a swan.
Scissors, penknives, and razor blades scratched,
cut, and shortened the voluptuous dresses
of prelates, of squares and houses, and trees
fell soundlessly, as in a jungle,
and the cathedral trembled, people bade goodbye

without handkerchiefs, no tears, such a dry
mouth, I won't see you anymore, so much death
awaits you, why must every city
become Jerusalem and every man a Jew,
and now in a hurry just
pack, always, each day,
and go breathless, go to Lvov, after all
it exists, quiet and pure as
a peach. It is everywhere.

Translated from the Polish by Renata Gorczynski

ZAWGEE

BURMA • *1907–1990*

Because of its bent, its bite. Because it's Burmese, because it's Buddhist, because it's beautiful.

—Lyn Aye, 52, Anesthesiologist, San Jose, California

The Way of the Water-Hyacinth

Bobbing on the breeze blown waves
Bowing to the tide
Hyacinth rises and falls

Falling but not felled
By flotsam, twigs, leaves
She ducks, bobs and weaves.

Ducks, ducks by the score
Jolting, quacking and more
She spins through—

Spinning, swamped, slimed, sunk
She rises, resolute
Still crowned by petals.

Translated from the Burmese by Lyn Aye

PERMISSIONS

Constantin Cavafy, "The City," translated by Edmund Keeley and Phillip Sherrard, from *C. P. Cavafy: Selected Poems, Revised Edition,* edited by George Savidis. English translation copyright © 1975 by Edmund Keeley and Philip Sherrard, revised edition copyright © 1992 by Princeton University Press. Reprinted with the permission of the publisher.

Paul Celan, excerpt from "Not Until" from *Zeitgehoft,* translated by Michael Hamburger, from *Poems of Paul Celan.* Copyright © 1980 by Paul Celan. Reprinted with the permission of Persea Books.

Geoffrey Chaucer, excerpt from The General Prologue from *The Canterbury Tales: Nine Tales and the General Prologue, A Norton Critical Edition,* edited by V. A. Kolve and Glending Olson. Copyright © 1989 by W. W. Norton & Company, Inc. Reprinted with the permission of the publishers.

Sandra Cisneros, "You Called Me Corazon" from *Loose Woman* (New York: Alfred A. Knopf, 1994). Copyright © 1994 by Sandra Cisneros. Reprinted with the permission of Susan Bergholz Literary Services.

Lucille Clifton, "The Lost Baby Poem" from *good woman: poems and a memoir 1969–1980.* Copyright © 1987 by Lucille Clifton. Reprinted with the permission of BOA Editions, Ltd., 92 Park Avenue, Brockport, New York 14420.

Robert Creeley, "The Rain" and "I Know a Man" from *Collected Poems of Robert Creeley 1945–1975.* Copyright © 1983 by The Regents of the University of California. Reprinted with the permission of the author and University of California Press.

Countee Cullen, "Yet Do I Marvel" from *Color.* Copyright © 1925 by Harper & Brothers; renewed © 1953 by Ida M. Cullen. Reprinted with the permission, and copyrights administered by, Thompson and Thompson, New York, New York.

E. E. Cummings, ["i sing of Olaf glad and big"] from *Complete Poems 1904–1962,* edited by George J. Firmage. Copyright © 1931, 1959, 1991 by the Trustees for the E. E. Cummings Trust. Copyright © 1979 by George James Firmage. Reprinted with the permission of Liveright Publishing Corporation.

Robert Desnos, "Last Poem," translated by X. J. Kennedy, from Willis Barnstone et al., *Modern European Poetry* (New York: Bantam Books, 1966). Reprinted with the permission of the translator.

James Dickey, "The Bee" from *James Dickey: The Selected Poems,* edited by Robert Kirschten (Middletown, Connecticut: Wesleyan University Press, 1998). Copyright © 1967 by James Dickey. Copyright © 1998 by Mathew J. Bruccoli, Literary Executor of the Estate of James Dickey. Reprinted with the permission of the University Press of New England.

Emily Dickinson, 288 ["I'm Nobody! Who are you?"], 1052 ["I never saw a Moor—"], 1333 ["A little Madness in the Spring"], 254 [" 'Hope' is the thing with Feathers"], and 328 ["A Bird came down the Walk—"] from *The Complete Poems of Emily Dickinson,* edited by Thomas H. Johnson. Copyright © 1929 by Martha Dickinson, renewed © 1957 Mary L. Hampson. Copyright © 1951, 1955, 1979, 1983 by the President and Fellows of Harvard College. Reprinted with the permission of The Belknap Press of Harvard University Press.

Mark Doty, "The Embrace" from *Sweet Machine.* Copyright © 1998 by Mark Doty. Reprinted with the permission of HarperCollins Publishers, Inc.

Rita Dove, "Daystar" from *Selected Poems.* Copyright © 1980, 1983, 1986, 1993 by Rita Dove. Reprinted with the permission of the author.

Alan Dugan, "Love Song: I and Thou" from *New and Collected Poems 1961–1983.* Copyright © 1983 by Alan Dugan. Reprinted with the permission of The Ecco Press.

Hussein Elhami, "A Lyric in Exile," translated by Shmuel Shoshani. Reprinted with the permission of the translator.

T. S. Eliot, "The Love Song of J. Alfred Prufrock" and "Dry Salvages (II)" from *Collected Poems 1909–1962.* Copyright © 1936 by Harcourt, Inc., renewed © 1964 by T. S. Eliot. Reprinted with the permission of Harcourt, Inc. and Faber & Faber Ltd.

Robert Frost, "The Road Not Taken," "Acqainted with the Night," "Immigrants," "Birches," "A Hillside Thaw," and "Out, Out—" from *The Poetry of Robert Frost,* edited by Edward Connery Lathem.

INDEX

A Bird came down the Walk— 72
Acquainted with the Night 93
Address to a Haggis 38
A dream tree, Polly's tree: 217
Afoot and light-hearted I take to the open road 282
Akhmatova, Anna 5
A little Madness in the Spring 71
All day I think about it, then at night I say it 243
All night the sound had 61
All the new thinking is about loss 107
All things within this fading world hath end 28
All winter your brute shoulders strained against collars, padding 103
Although it is a cold evening 20
Ammons, A. R. 6
And God stepped out on space 142
And now all Nature seemed in love 301
And the stone word fell 5
And yet we should consider how we go forward 247
An old man's thought of school 281
Apple of islands, Sirmio, & bright peninsulas, set 48
Archilochos 8
Arizona Midnight 280
Arnold, Matthew 9
Art 185
Ashbery, John 11
As I sd to my 62
A smile fell in the grass 213
A snake came to my water trough 160
As virtuous men pass mildly away 75
At the Fishhouses 20
Atwood, Margaret 12
Auden, W. H. 14, 16
A wind is ruffling the tawny pelt 278
Ay, Ay, Ay of the Kinky-Haired Negress 36

Ay, ay, ay, that am kinky-haired and pure black 36

Baby Song 102
Baraka, Amiri (LeRoi Jones) 18
Bean Eaters, The 32
Because my mouth 131
Bee, The 67
Before the Birth of one of her Children 28
Bent double, like old beggars under sacks 208
Big Momma 181
Birches 94
Bird came down the Walk—, A (328) 72
Bishop, Elizabeth 19
Black Elk 23
Blake, William 24
Blessing, A 302
Block City 259
Bobbing on the breeze blown waves 311
Boland, Eavan 27
Bradstreet, Anne 28
Brooke, Rupert 30
Brooks, Gwendolyn 31
Browning, Elizabeth Barrett 33
Browning, Robert 34
Brutal to love 101
Burgos, Julia de 36
Burns, Robert 38
Byron, George Gordon, Lord 40

Cancer and Nova 219
Canterbury Tales, The 51
Carroll, Lewis 44
Casey at the Bat 270
Cather, Willa 46
Catullus 48
Cavafy, C. P. 49
Celan, Paul 50

Chaucer, Geoffrey 51
Chicago 244
Church-musick 116
Cisneros, Sandra 52
City, The 49
Clifton, Lucille 53
Coleridge, Samuel Taylor 54
Come into Animal Presence 164
Crane, Hart 58
Creation, The 142
Creeley, Robert 61
Cullen, Countee 63
Cummings, E. E. 64

Danse Russe 293
Darkling Thrush, The 105
Daystar 78
De Quevedo, Francisco 225
Desnos, Robert 66
Dickey, James 67
Diffugere Nives 129
Dirge Without Music 188
Donne, John 74
Do Not Go Gentle into That Good Night 273
Doty, Mark 77
Dove, Rita 78
Dover Beach 9
Do you see the town, how it rests over there 123
Do you see the town? 123
Drayton, Michael 80
Drink to me only with thine eyes 146
Driving Montana 134
Dry Salvages (II) 88
Dugan, Alan 81
Dulce Et Decorum Est 208
Dunbar, Paul Lawrence 82

Ecce Puer 148
Ecchoing Green, The 24
Either you will 230
Elhami, Hussein 83
Eliot, T. S. 84
Embrace, The 77
Emerson, Ralph Waldo 91
Emigrant Irish, The 27
Entrance 231
Epistle to Dr. Arbuthnot 220
Equal to the gods 246
Eros Turannos 235
Eternity 24
Everything the Power of the World does is done in a circle 23

Facing It 156
Fair fa' your honest, sonsie face 38
Far Cry From Africa, A 278
Farewell, thou child of my right hand, and joy 146
Fern Hill 275
finally retired pensionless 181
First Snow-Fall, The 177
Five years have past; five summers, with the length 296
Flea, The 74
Forget Not Yet 303
Forget not yet the tried intent 303
From the private ease of Mother's womb 102
From you I want more than I've ever asked 229
Frost, Robert 92

General Prologue 51
Gift 265
Ginsberg, Allen 99
Girl in a Nightgown 257
Glory be to God for dappled things— 127
Glück, Louise 101
God's Grandeur 126
Grandmither, Think Not I Forget 46
Grandmither, think not I forget, when I come back to town 46
Gunn, Thom 102

Had we but world enough, and time 183
Hall, Donald 103
Happiness 189
Hardy, Thomas 105
Harmonics 196
Hass, Robert 107
Hayden, Robert 109
Heaney, Seamus 112
He disappeared in the dead of winter: 14
Henley, William Ernest 114
Herbert, George 116
Herbert, Zbigniew 118
Here, take this gift 284
Her name tells of how 203
He who bends to himself a joy 24
Hikmet, Nazim 119
Hillside Thaw, A 96
Hofmannsthal, Hugo Von 123
Hog Butcher for the World 244
Home No More Home to Me, Whither Must I Wander? 260
Homer 124
"Hope" is the thing with Feathers—(254) 72

Hopkins, Gerard Manley   126
Hornworm: Autumn Lamentation   157
Housman, A. E.   129
How can I, that girl standing there   304
How do I love thee? Let me count the ways   33
How many dawns, chill from his rippling rest   58
Hughes, Langston   131
Hugo, Richard   134

I am not resigned to the shutting away of loving hearts in the hard ground   188
I caught this morning morning's minion, kingdom   128
Idea of Order at Key West, The   254
I doubt not God is good, well-meaning, kind   63
If all the world and love were young   226
If ever two were one, then surely we   29
If I should die, think only this of me   30
If my feet will arrive again, at my home   83
If when my wife is sleeping   293
If you will tell me why the fen   198
I gaze upon the roast   261
I got out of bed   153
I have been one acquainted with the night   93
I have done it again   214
I have so fiercely dreamed of you   66
I Know a Man   62
I know I have the best of time and space—and that I was never measured   284
I leant upon a coppice gate   105
Iliad   124
I loved you   224
I loved you, and perhaps I love you still   224
I May, I Might, I Must   198
Immigrants   94
I'm Nobody! Who are you? (288)   70
Improvement, The   11
I never saw a Moor—(1052)   70
Infinite consanguinity it bears—   59
In May, when sea-winds pierced our solitudes   91
In Memory of W. B. Yeats   14
In My Craft or Sullen Art   274
In placid hours well-pleased we dream   185
Invictus   114
I sat all morning in the college sick bay   112
i sing of Olaf glad and big   64
Is that where it happens?   11
It is an ancient Mariner   54
It little profits that an idle king   267

I, too, dislike it: there are things that are important beyond all this fiddle   197
it's 1962 March 28th   119
It was not dying: everybody died   138
I wake to sleep, and take my waking slow   241
I walk down the garden paths   173
I want to return to the first urges, those urges that seemed so unconscious of their beginnings   210
I would like to watch you sleeping   12

Jabberwocky   44
Jarrell, Randall   136
Jeffers, Robinson   140
John had   189
Johnson, James Weldon   142
Jonson, Ben   146
Joyce, James   148
Just off the highway to Rochester, Minnesota   302

Keats, John   149
Kenyon, Jane   153
Kinnell, Galway   154
Komunyakaa, Yusef   156
Kunitz, Stanley   157

Lady Lazarus   214
Lao Tzu   159
Last Poem   66
Lately, I've become accustomed to the way   18
Lawrence, D. H.   160
Lazarus, Emma   163
Let us go then, you and I   84
Levertov, Denise   164
Levine, Philip   166
Lights out. Shades up   257
Like oil lamps, we put them out the back   27
Lines, (above Tintern Abbey)   296
Little Black Boy, The   25
little Madness in the Spring, A (1333)   71
Longfellow, Henry Wadsworth   168
Lorca, Federico Garcia   171
Losses   138
Lost Baby Poem, The   53
Love Calls Us to the Things of This World   287
Love Constant Beyond Death   225
Love Song: I and Thou   81
Love Song of J. Alfred Prufrock, The   84
Lowell, Amy   173

Lowell, James Russell   177
Lowell, Robert   179
lower leaves of the trees, The   307
Luncheon on the Grass   211
Lycidas   191
Lyric in Exile, A   83

Madhubuti, Haki R.   181
Manfred   41
Mansion   6
Mark but this flea, and mark in this   74
Maru Mori brought me   200
Marvell, Andrew   183
May the smell of thyme and lavender
   accompany us on our journey   190
Meditation at Lagunitas   107
Melville, Herman   185
Merry-Go-Round   132
Merwin, W. S.   186
Mid-Term Break   112
Millay, Edna St. Vincent   187
Milne, A. A.   189
Milosz, Czeslaw   190
Milton, John   191
Minstrel Man   131
Monet's "Waterlilies"   110
Moody, William Vaughn   196
Moon Sails Out, The   171
Moore, Marianne   197
Moore, Thomas   199
Mother to Son   133
Moving from Cheer to Joy, from Joy to All
   136
Mr. Flood's Party   237
My black face fades   156
My brother comes home from work   166
My Fly   289
My heart aches, and a drowsy numbness
   pains   149
My Last Duchess   34
My mother bore me in the southern wild   25
My Papa's Waltz   239
My prime of youth is but a frost of cares
   277

Names of Horses   103
Naming of Parts   227
Neruda, Pablo   200
New Colossus, The   163
Next Day   136
Nibenegenasábe, Jacob   203
Night Dances, The   213
Night Journey   240
Nobody heard him, the dead man   252

Nobody's serious when they're seventeen
   232
No ship of all that under sail or steam   94
*Notes from a Nonexistent Himalayan
   Expedition*   263
Nothing is plumb, level, or square: 81
Not less because in purple I descended   257
Not like the brazen giant of Greek fame   163
Not until   50
Not Waving But Drowning   252
Now as I was young and easy under the
   apple boughs   275
Now as the train bears west   240
Nymph's Reply to the Shepherd, The   226

Ode to a Nightingale   149
Ode to My Socks   200
Of the dark past   148
O'Hara, Frank   204
Old Eben Flood, climbing alone one night
   237
Old Man on the River Bank, An   247
Old Man's Thought of School, An   281
Oliver, Mary   207
O my love, what gift of mine   265
On a Bank as I Sat Fishing   301
One Art   19
One dot   67
One must have a mind of winter   256
One of those great, garishly emerald flies that
   always look freshly generated from fresh
   excrement   289
On My First Son   146
On Pilgrimage   190
O Solitude! if I must with thee dwell   152
Otherwise   153
Our Land   234
Our sardine fishermen work at night in the
   dark of the moon   140
Out of the night that covers me   114
"Out, Out—"   97
Owen, Wilfred   208

Patterns   173
pebble, The   118
Pham Tien Duat   210
Phillips, Carl   211
Pied Beauty   127
Plath, Sylvia   213
Plutzik, Hyam   219
Poetry   197
Politics   304
Polly's Tree   217
Pope, Alexander   220

Pot Roast   261
Pound, Ezra   222
Preface to a Twenty Volume Suicide Note   18
Prelude, The   295
Proem: To Brooklyn Bridge   58
Prospective Immigrants Please Note   230
Psalm of Life, A   168
Purse-Seine, The   140
Pushkin, Alexander   224

Queen of Carthage, The   101
Quiet Until the Thaw   203

Rain, The   61
Raleigh, Sir Walter   226
Reality is a question   99
Reed, Henry   227
Refugee Blues   16
Rhodora, The   91
Rich, Adrienne   229
Rilke, Rainer Maria   231
Rimbaud, Arthur   232
Rime of the Ancient Mariner, The   54
Ritsos, Yannis   234
River-Merchant's Wife: A Letter, The   222
Road Not Taken, The   92
Robinson, Edwin Arlington   235
Roethke, Theodore   239
Romance   232
Rumi, Jalal al-Din   243

Sailing to Byzantium   305
Sandburg, Carl   244
Sappho   246
Say this city has ten million souls   16
Scars   253
Seferis, George   247
Sentence, The   5
Shakespeare, William   249
Shall I compare thee to a summer's day?   249
She fears him, and will always ask   235
She sang beyond the genius of the sea   254
She Walks in Beauty   40
She walks in beauty, like the night   40
She wanted a little room for thinking: 78
Shut, shut the door, good John! (fatigued, I said)   220
Since that first morning when I crawled   157
Since ther's no helpe, Come let us kisse and part   80
Smith, Stevie   252
Snake   160

Snow Man, The   256
So it came time   6
Soldier, The   30
Song of Myself   284
Song of the Barren Orange Tree   172
Song of the Open Road   282
Song to Celia   146
Sonnet 18 (Shall I compare thee to a summer's day?) (Shakespeare)   249
Sonnet 43 (How do I love thee: Let me count the ways) (Browning, Elizabeth Barrett)   33
Sonnet 138 (When My Love Swears that She is Made of Truth) (Shakespeare)   250
Sonnet VII (O Solitude! If I must with thee dwell) (Jonson)   152
Sonnet XXIV (When you, that at this moment are to me) (Millay)   187
Sonnet 29 (When, in disgrace with fortune and men's eyes) (Shakespeare)   250
So these are the Himalayas   263
Stafford, William   253
Stevens, Wallace   254
Stevenson, Robert Louis   259
St. Francis and the Sow   154
Strand, Mark   261
Strawberries   186
Summer Day, The   207
Sundays too my father got up early   109
Sweetest of sweets, I thank you: when displeasure   116
Szymborska, Wislawa   263

Tagore, Rabindranath   265
Tao te Ching   159
Tea at the Palaz of Hoon   257
Tell me not, in mournful numbers   168
Tennyson, Alfred, Lord   267
Terms in Which I Think of Reality, The   99
That is no country for old men. The young   305
That's my last duchess painted on the wall   34
That was enough   52
Thayer, Ernest Lawrence   270
The art of losing isn't hard to master   19
The bud   154
The buzz saw snarled and rattled in the yard   97
The day is a woman who loves you. Open   134
The eyes open to a cry of pulleys   287
The final shadow that will close my eyes   225

The grief of the coyote seems to make
280
The lower leaves of the trees   307
The night attendant, a B. U. sophomore
179
Then tall Hektor of the shining helm
answered her: 'All these   124
The outlook wasn't brilliant for the Mudville
nine that day: 270
The pebble   118
The pure products of America   291
The sea is calm tonight   9
The snow had begun in the gloaming   177
The snows are fled away, leaves on the shaws
129
The star exploding in the body   219
The Sun does arise   24
The Sun woke me this morning loud   204
the time i dropped your almost body down
53
The time I've lost in wooing   199
The whiskey on your breath   239
The world is charged with the grandeur of
God   126
They eat beans mostly, this old yellow pair
32
They're a curious lot, Manet's scandalous
211
They tell how it was, and how time   253
Things I Didn't Know I Loved   119
31   48
This Living Hand   152
This living hand, now warm and capable
152
This string upon my harp was best beloved:
196
Thomas, Dylan   273
Those Winter Sundays   109
Tichborne, Chidiock   277
Tichborne's Elegy   277
Time I've Lost in Wooing, The   199
To a Certain Cantatrice   284
Today as the news from Selma and Saigon
110
Today we have naming of parts. Yesterday
227
To Elsie   291
To Go to Lvov   308
To go to Lvov. Which station   308
To His Coy Mistress   183
To my Dear and Loving Husband   29
To Return to the Urges Unconscious of Their
Beginnings   210
To the Days   229

To think to know the country and not know
96
To understand others is to be knowledgeable
159
True Account of Talking to the Sun at Fire
Island, A   204
'Twas brillig, and the slithy toves   44
Two roads diverged in a yellow wood   92

Ulysses   267

Valediction: Forbidding Mourning, A   75
Variation on the Word Sleep   12
Vertue   117
Voyages (III)   59

Waking in the Blue   179
Waking, The   241
Walcott, Derek   278
Warren, Robert Penn   280
Way of the Water-Hyacinth, The   311
We are the fools of time and terror: Days
41
We climbed the hill to look over our land:
234
Well, son, I'll tell you: 133
We Real Cool   31
We real cool. We   31
We Wear the Mask   82
We wear the mask that grins and lies   82
Whan that Aprill with his shoures sole
51
What are you able to build with your blocks?
259
When from our better selves we have too
long   295
When, in disgrace with fortune and men's
eyes   250
When I see birches bend to left and right
94
When my father died I saw   a narrow valley
186
When my love swears that she is made of
truth   250
When the moon sails out   171
When You Are Old   305
When you are old and gray and full of sleep
305
When you, that at this moment are to me
187
Where is the Jim Crow section   132
While my hair was still cut straight across my
forehead   222
Whitman, Walt   281

Whoever you are: in the evening step out
  231
Who made the world? 207
Who Says Words with My Mouth 243
Wilbur, Richard 287
Williams, C. K. 289
Williams, William Carlos 291
Will, lost in a sea of trouble 8
Windhover, The 128
Woodcutter 172
Wordsworth, William 295
Wotton, Sir Henry 301
Wright, James 302
Wyatt, Thomas 303

Yeats, William Butler 304
Yet Do I Marvel 63
Yet once more, O ye laurels and once more
  191
Yoshitada, Sone No 307
You Can Have It 166
You said: "I'll go to another country, go to
  another shore 49
You weren't well or really ill yet either
  77

Zagajewski, Adam 308
Zawgee 311
Zeitgehoft 50